D1571300

THE POLICE OFFICER IN
THE COURTROOM

About the Author

Don Lewis has been a trial lawyer for over thirty years, most of them as a prosecutor.

Upon his graduation from Duquesne Law School in Pittsburgh in 1970, he became employed as an Assistant District Attorney for Allegheny County, Pennsylvania. In 1974, he accepted a similar position in Crawford County, Pennsylvania, where six years later he became the elected District Attorney. After a distinguished career in the state courts, Mr. Lewis accepted a position as Managing Assistant United States Attorney for the Western District of Pennsylvania. After two years there, he applied for, and was accepted into a position of Assistant United States Attorney in Tampa, Florida, where he remained as a trial lawyer for four years. In 1988, he returned home to Pennsylvania and began traveling all over the United States presenting seminars on the topics he has written about in this book.

He is the recipient of numerous awards and much recognition from both state and federal law enforcement organizations for his accomplishments as a trial lawyer in Pennsylvania and Florida.

Mr. Lewis currently lives with his wife in Meadville, Pennsylvania, where he is in private practice.

His pride in this work stems from the satisfaction of having, through this book, given something back to the profession around which he has built his life.

THE POLICE OFFICER IN THE COURTROOM

How to Avoid the Pitfalls of Cross-Examination Through
the Proper Preparation and Presentation of Investigative
Reports, In-Court Testimony, and Evidence

By

DON LEWIS

Charles C Thomas
PUBLISHER • LTD.
SPRINGFIELD • ILLINOIS • U.S.A

Published and Distributed Throughout the World by

CHARLES C THOMAS • PUBLISHER, LTD.
2600 South First Street
Springfield, Illinois 62704

This book is protected by copyright. No part of
it may be reproduced in any manner without
written permission from the publisher.

© 2001 by CHARLES C THOMAS • PUBLISHER, LTD.

ISBN 0-398-07212-4 (hard)
ISBN 0-398-07213-2 (paper)

Library of Congress Catalog Card Number: 2001035251

With THOMAS BOOKS *careful attention is given to all details of manufacturing
and design. It is the Publisher's desire to present books that are satisfactory as to their
physical qualities and artistic possibilities and appropriate for their particular use.*
THOMAS BOOKS *will be true to those laws of quality that assure a good name
and good will.*

Printed in the United States of America
MM-R-3

Library of Congress Cataloging-in-Publication Data

Lewis, Don (Donald E.), 1940-
   The police officer in the courtroom : how to avoid the pitfalls of cross-examination
through the proper preparation and presentation of investigative reports, in-court
testimony, and evidence / by Don Lewis.
      p. cm.
   ISBN 0-398-07212-4 (hard) -- ISBN 0-398-07213-2 (paper)
   1. Evidence, Expert--United States. 2. Police--United States. 3. Examination of
witnesses--United States. I. Title.

KF9674 .L486 2001
347.73'67--dc21   2001035251

For my father
and
To all the police officers who, over all the years
of my practice as a prosecuting attorney, have
by their professionalism and dedication to duty,
helped me become a better trial lawyer.
I hope this work can in a small way repay all
of you for what you do to keep America safe.

PREFACE

Effective law enforcement has always been the product of diligent investigation conducted by efficiently trained police officers. From the beginning of their training, law enforcement officers are taught the skills necessary to protect themselves and others, they learn to investigate and detect criminal conduct, and to some degree, they receive instruction on the laws pertaining to arrest, the collection of evidence, and the suspect's rights.

While during my thirty years of practice in criminal courtrooms I have gained a great deal of respect for the efficient manner in which police officers conduct their investigations and for the tenacity and courage they show in the pursuit of criminals, I have also come to realize that, in most instances, they receive almost no training in those matters concerning their responsibilities as witnesses in court. The tendency is to rely solely on the prosecutor to win the case in court. The perceived attitude of the officer is that once the case reaches the courtroom, his job is completed, and the responsibility of obtaining a conviction falls squarely on the shoulders of the prosecutor. This seems natural because of the obvious correlation between lawyer and courtroom. The courtroom is seen as the lawyer's arena, and the officer's understandable assumption is that they are playing on someone else's field and that their only obligation to the courtroom presentation is to remember the facts and testify truthfully. *Nothing could be further from the truth!*

A courtroom is a theater, a stage on which, in every case large or small, a drama is played out for the audience. The only difference between the courtroom and Broadway is that the audience sits in the jury box, and decides how the play is going to end. One important way they do that is by evaluating the performance of the players. Usually, the prime player in each presentation is the police officer. He is observed closely by the audience, and his performance often determines the outcome of the case. The fundamental role of the prosecutor is to orchestrate the presentation of the evidence. Indeed, he has the responsibility of using his closing argument to persuade the jury of the prosecution's position, but even an outstanding closing won't normally save a poor presentation by the witnesses. This is the reason why criminal cases are very often won or lost on the testimony of the police officer. In the performance of his assignment, the prosecutor will try to paint the officer-witness as the hero, riding into court on a white stallion, guns blazing, in pursuit of justice. In order for that image to take with the jury, it is necessary that the officer knows how to ride the horse and how to shoot the guns without misfiring. You may rest assured that any weaknesses detected in the officer's presentation of testimony and evidence will be exhaustively exploited by the defense lawyer. Often, the only defense available to the accused is to attack the credibility of the officer by showing his "guns" are loaded with blanks. When successful, the defense will often create a reasonable doubt in the minds of the jury. If the resulting acquittal is unjust, the officer's efforts have been for naught.

The purpose of this text is to authenticate the importance of the information contained within its covers by guiding and instructing the reader in those areas crucial to the presentation of the evidence in a criminal courtroom case and to emphasize the importance of the part played by the proper preparation of reports and evidence prior to getting into the courtroom. For, once the officer is in the courtroom, it's too late to fix mistakes.

The material will illustrate how closely the officer's credibility is tied to his or her investigative report. In court, the officer's report will serve as his partner. If it is weak, inaccurate, or incomplete when written, it cannot be saved in court. The importance of care taken in its preparation cannot be overstated. Cases can be won or lost solely on the quality of the written report. Weaknesses in the report create opportunities for effective cross-examination, the consequences of which can be devastating to the prosecution's case.

The reader will learn the importance of proper care taken in the handling of evidence, and the consequences in court when it is not. The book examines the various problems which often arise during that time between the arrest and trial, and the steps which can be taken to insure a smooth flowing presentation during the trial.

The text will instruct on the many facets of direct-examination and will take the reader into that world which the officer-witness dreads most, that of cross-examination. Through illustrations offered by way of sample testimony, the officer is instructed in how to recognize and understand the defense strategies employed in each of many different situations, and will learn how to turn attacks by the defense attorney to the officer's own benefit.

It is my sincere wish that this effort will be of service to each of you who hope to benefit by it. Remember, when you, the officer, enter the courtroom, you will generally enjoy the respect of the jurors, and a cloak of credibility. It is up to you to maintain that respect, and that can be done only by offering a well-prepared presentation of your testimony and evidence. Good Luck!

ACKNOWLEDGMENTS

This text began seven years ago and is the result of the assistance of a number of friends and associates. I would like to recognize the contributions of the following people: Warren Zimmerman, Mac Cauley, Jeff Downing, Gary Montilla, and Dennis Moore, all Assistant U.S. Attorneys in Tampa, Florida. These men spent hours with me helping to develop the concept and organization of the text. Without them, this work could not have been possible. Others who had a hand in the development of the text include: John Dawson, former District Attorney, Crawford County, Pennsylvania. He is a close friend whose advice I respect highly; Gerard R. Bey, a retired Pennsylvania State Trooper, good friend, and a top investigator with thirty-six years of active service as a member of that organization and; Al Paleaz, Professor of Law at Duquesne University School of Law. His review of the materials and advice on making it better were invaluable to me during the final preparation of this material.

Last, but certainly not least, my thanks to my wife, Sheryl, for her patience and assistance during the endless hours of work that interfered with many things I'm sure she'd rather have been doing.

I am certain that I am forgetting others who provided assistance along the way. To them, my deepest apologies.

CONTENTS

THE POLICE OFFICER IN
THE COURTROOM

Chapter 1

THE TRIAL PROCESS

1.01 Introduction

The trial of a criminal case is the procedure at which the ultimate factual determination of the charges against the defendant is made. Of course, every person convicted of a crime is entitled to exercise his appellate rights, but in this work, we are concerned only with the process that terminates with the trial.

The trial is where we first see the use of the phrase *Beyond a Reasonable Doubt*. The trial of any criminal charge in the United States requires proof beyond a reasonable doubt before the defendant may be convicted. The term reasonable doubt is defined by the court, and though the actual words used in the definition may vary from jurisdiction to jurisdiction, the meaning conveyed is always the same. The typical definition is that a reasonable doubt is such a doubt as would cause a reasonably prudent person to pause or hesitate before making a decision on a matter of importance in his or her own life. That does not mean that the charges must be proven beyond all doubt, for as the court may instruct the jury, nothing in life is beyond all doubt. Nor must the evidence preclude the possibility of innocence.

In order to convict, the evidence must be sufficient to overcome reasonable doubt. A reasonable doubt may arise from the evidence, *or from a lack of evidence*. It is the lack of evidence which is most vehemently argued by the defense attorney, and which usually creates a reasonable doubt in the minds of the jury.

Each juror is responsible for his or her own verdict, and he or she must be prepared to declare to the court that the verdict reached by the entire jury is their verdict as well. If they are not, and if the entire jury is unable to reach a unanimous verdict, the result is a mistrial, or what is commonly known as a "hung jury." In such a situation, the court will declare a mistrial, and, in most cases, the district attorney must make the decision whether or not to re-try the case.

If the jury reaches a unanimous verdict on all of the charges, the defendant is either convicted or acquitted. Obviously, the jury could, and often does, return to the courtroom with a verdict of guilty on some of the charges, and not guilty on the others. If the jury reaches a unanimous verdict on some of the charges and is "hung" on the others, the court may, after reasonable assurance from the jury foreman that the jury is hopelessly deadlocked on a number of the charges, accept the verdict on the charges upon which the jury has reached a unanimous verdict and declare a mistrial on the others, leaving the option of a re-trial on those charges to the prosecuting attorney.

A defendant may never again be tried upon the facts of a charge upon which a jury has reached a unanimous verdict. This rule of law is called "Double Jeopardy" and works to prevent the defendant from being twice put in jeopardy for the same crime. This rule would also apply in some situations where a defendant is convicted of one charge, but the jury is unable to reach a verdict on another charge. For example, if the second charge is a lesser included offense of the first, and if the second charge is based on the same facts, then the rule against double jeopardy will apply. To illustrate: If a defendant is charged with aggravated assault and simple assault upon the same facts and upon the same person and the jury returns a verdict of guilty on the first count of aggravated assault, but is deadlocked on the second charge of simple assault, the court will accept the guilty verdict on the first charge and discharge the defendant on the second. The same rule would apply if the court accepts a verdict where a defendant is convicted on the second count of simple assault and the jury was deadlocked on the first count; the defendant would be discharged on the count upon which the jury was deadlocked.

In most jurisdictions, the court will instruct the jury that if they convict on one count of a charge which includes lesser or greater included offenses, they should not deliberate on the other, explaining to them that the defendant can be convicted on only one of such charges.

There are certain situations which allow a defendant who was tried before a state jury to be re-tried before a federal jury on the same or similar charges, no matter whether he or she was convicted or acquitted at the state level.

1.02 Types of Trial Proceedings

A. Jury Trials

The trial may be held before a judge and a petit jury, which in most jurisdictions, con-

sists of twelve citizens. Some jurisdictions require as few as six jurors in a criminal trial. In either case, the verdict must be unanimous. Under normal circumstances, the jurors will come from the county where the crime is committed, and where the trial is being conducted. There are exceptions to this rule. If, for example, a judge from the jurisdiction where the crime was committed determines that, for one reason or another, the defendant cannot be assured a fair trial before a jury selected from that county, he will change either *venire* or *venue*. The most frequent causes for such action has to do with pre-trial publicity or the identity of the parties.

When the court rules that a change of venire is required, the judge will go with the attorneys to another county to select a jury, then bring that jury back to the trial jurisdiction, and try the case; this is called a *change of venire*.

In the alternative, a less desirable procedure, called *change of venue*, will occur. In such a situation, the case will be sent to another county where the jury selection and trial will both be conducted with jurors selected from among the citizens from the guest jurisdiction.

In a jury trial, the jury is responsible for determining what the facts are and how they apply to the legal definition of the charges and other matters of law as instructed by the court in its charge to the jury.

Throughout the trial, the judge will make decisions on matters of law which may from time to time arise through objections from one side or another to certain testimony or other evidence. The jury is bound by the court's rulings on these matters, and must view the evidence in light of those rulings.

Simply stated, in jury trials, the judge decides issues of law, and the jury decides issues of fact.

After all of the relevant and competent

evidence has been admitted and the testimony is closed, the attorneys argue their case, after which the judge will instruct the jury on the applicable law, and the jury is sent out to a private room to deliberate upon their verdict.

B. Non-Jury Trials

The second alternative is for a case to be tried before a judge without a jury. These are called *non-jury*, or *bench trials*. In a non-jury trial, the judge decides both the issues of law and fact.

Q. *Who decides which kind of trial will be had?*

In all states and in the federal courts, the defendant is absolutely entitled to a jury trial. Some jurisdictions hold that the prosecution is also entitled to a jury trial, so that even if the defendant chooses to be tried before a judge without a jury, the prosecution may choose to have the case tried before a jury. In other jurisdictions, the decision is solely that of the defendant.

Q. *What about a situation where there are multiple defendants and one of them wants a non-jury trial, while the others want a jury trial?*

In such cases where one or more, but not all of the defendants, opt for a non-jury trial, the court has several options. The judge may try all of the defendants together in one trial, while sending to the jury only those defendants who wish a jury trial and deciding himself the verdict on those who chose a non-jury trial. Another option allows the court to sever the defendants for separate trials. Which option to choose falls within the sound discretion of the trial judge, and may depend upon the evidence and the charges.

Q. *Are there other situations which cause defendants involved in the same indictment or information to be severed for trial?*

Yes. A number of other situations may arise or exist which would cause a judge to order the defendants severed for trial. Each defendant severed will receive a trial separate from the others. Some jurisdictions provide that two juries may be seated to hear the same testimony at the same time, but usually a severance means separate trials for each of the severed defendants. In most, but not all, cases, a request for severance is made by the attorney for the defendant. Conversely, the prosecutor most often wants the defendants to be joined for trial.

The defendant may request a severance on the grounds that, for one reason or another, being tried with the other defendants will somehow prejudice the requesting defendant.

If the prosecution and defense cannot agree on whether the cases should be tried together or separately, the judge may allow argument on the matter, then decide which option to choose.

1.03 Jury Selection

Jury selection is the process of selecting from a panel of jurors, the statutory number of jurors required to sit on the *petit*, or *trial*, jury. While in most state jurisdictions, as well as the federal courts, that number is twelve, some require as few as six.

The manner in which the jury is selected varies from state to state and from county to county. Your local prosecutor will be able to acquaint you with the procedure in your jurisdiction. There are, however, two basic systems employed in the selection of juries:

A. The List System

During the employment of the list system, the judge, or the attorneys, or both, ask questions of the jurors in the panel. Again, this procedure varies from jurisdiction to jurisdiction. Usually, the judge will ask preliminary questions of the entire panel, then will invite each of the attorneys to ask his or her questions. This process is called *voir dire*, a Latin phrase meaning to speak the truth. The questions are asked of the entire panel at once (e.g., Is there anyone on the panel who, because of the nature of the crime charged, believes he or she could not be a fair and impartial juror?) and are usually limited to matters that go to the qualifications of the panel member to sit on the jury (e.g., whether or not they know any of the parties involved in the case; if they would be inclined to automatically accept the word of a police officer as true simply because he is a police officer; or questions regarding whether or not they could follow the courts instructions on the law).

Once the voir dire has been completed, each attorney will begin to strike jurors from the panel until there are only the statutory number of jurors, and perhaps one or two alternates left on the panel. This will be the jury.

B. Individual Voir Dire System

During jury selection conducted by employing the individual voir dire system, each juror is brought into the courtroom separately and placed on the witness stand to be asked questions outside the hearing of the other prospective jurors. This is obviously the more time-consuming method because each question must be repeated to each panel member separately. In most jurisdictions, this system is usually employed only in the most serious cases. For example, in murder cases, the court will almost always honor a request for individual voir dire. In other cases, where a significant amount of attention has been drawn to the case by the media, but not enough to cause a change of

venue, the court will allow each juror to be questioned separately and out of the hearing of the other potential jurors.

After each juror is questioned, the attorneys will alternately exercise their challenges if they have any of that juror. Once twelve jurors are seated along with the number of alternates directed by the court, the jury selection process will be complete.

C. Types of Challenges

In either system of selection, there are two types of challenges which may be made to strike a juror from the panel:

1. Challenges for Cause

Challenges for cause are made when one side or the other alleges that a particular panel member is not qualified to sit as a juror on the case. The number of such challenges available to the attorneys is limitless, as long as they are able to show sufficient cause for the court to believe that the panel member is not qualified. Any showing that the prospective juror is unable to be fair and impartial is sufficient cause for dismissal.

2. Preemptory Challenges

Preemptory challenges do not require that sufficient cause be shown for the prospective juror to be dismissed. Each attorney is entitled to a certain number of preemptory challenges. The number of challenges varies among jurisdictions. For example, in Pennsylvania, the number of preemptory challenges allowed is 20 for a capital murder case, seven for other felonies, and five for misdemeanors. The number is determined by the highest grade of crime. No matter how many felonies or misdemeanors are charged in one case, if a felony, other than murder, is charged, the total number of preemptory challenges available to each side is seven.

In other jurisdictions, the number of preemptory challenges allowed to the defendant and the prosecutor will not be equal and is at the discretion of the court. For example, in a case where there are multiple defendants, the court may allow the attorney for each defendant a certain number of preemptory challenges equal to less than the statutory number allowed an individual defendant, even where the total number of challenges for all the defendants may exceed that number. At the same time, the prosecution may be limited to the statutory number of challenges. For example, in a felony case involving five defendants, the court may allow two challenges for each defendant, while allowing only seven to the prosecutor.

And finally, in some jurisdictions, as in the federal courts, even in a case where there is only one defendant, that defendant is entitled to a greater number of preemptory challenges than is the prosecution.

Reasons for preemptory challenges vary greatly and often depend upon the type of charge being tried. In a case involving a bank robbery, for example, the prosecutor may wish to keep jurors who are involved in occupations where the threat of being robbed is real, or jurors who, themselves, have been robbed. Obviously, the defense will not want such jurors and will exercise preemptory challenges, or possibly argue challenges for cause, to exclude such potential jurors from sitting on the jury.

Though there are no special reasons needed to exercise a preemptory challenge, there are limitations upon who may be stricken. These limitations are most often placed on the prosecution. For example, the prosecution may not categorically strike minority members from the panel if the defendant is a member of that minority. If such a strike is made, the defendant may challenge it, and the prosecutor will be required to justify the strike by showing some reason, other than that person's minority status, for exercising a preemptory strike on that panel member (see *Batson vs. Kentucky*, 106 S.Ct. 1712 (1986)).

Once the jury has been selected, seated and sworn, the trial is ready to begin.

1.04 Opening Statements

Prior to the commencement of the presentation of evidence, both the prosecutor and the attorney for each of the defendants are offered an opportunity to address the jury for the purpose of outlining to them what their side expects the evidence to show.

In a jury trial, the prosecution will always make an opening statement. In some jurisdictions, it is mandatory. In those jurisdictions, if the prosecutor's opening statement does not state facts sufficient to send the case to the jury, the judge may, upon motion of the defendant, dismiss the case.

In non-jury cases where an opening statement is not mandatory and where the issues are simple and the presentation of evidence brief, both sides will often forego the opportunity to make an opening statement.

The prosecutor will be the first to outline for the jury some of the evidence and testimony that he expects to present and will explain to them that his purpose in doing so is to give them a "bird's eye" view of the case so that, as each witness testifies, the jury will have a better understanding of where that testimony, or the evidence offered by that witness, fits into the overall picture being painted by the prosecution.

The defense attorney, on the other hand, has a decision to make. Should he make his opening statement immediately after that of the prosecutor or wait until after the presentation of the prosecution's evidence? If he waits, he will have heard all of the evidence against his client and can tailor his opening accordingly.

While this, at first glance, seems the thing to do, studies have shown that juries often form a lasting opinion of the guilt or innocence of the defendant solely on the basis of the opening statements. For that reason, most defense attorneys will open immediately, hoping to win the jury then, or at least blunt the effect of the prosecutor's opening. There are other reasons why the defense attorney will make his opening statement prior to the presentation of any evidence. If the defendant is intending to present evidence in support of a specific defense, the defense attorney will almost always make his opening statement immediately following that of the prosecutor. For example, where the defense is mental infirmity, alibi, or self-defense, the attorney will usually want to let the jury know that through his statements. Again, the idea is to blunt the impact of the prosecutor's opening statement and to give the jury a preview of where the defense will be going on its cross-examination.

1.05 The Prosecution's Case in Chief

Following the opening statements, the presentation of evidence begins with the prosecution presenting its **case in chief**. In most instances, this is the meat of the trial. It is that time during the trial when all of the evidence sufficient to satisfy each element of the crime or crimes charged against the defendant must be presented. If the court finds, at the end of the case in chief, that the prosecutor has failed to satisfy any one element of the offense, the judge, upon motion of the defense attorney, will dismiss that offense against the defendant. If all of the charges are dismissed, the trial ends and the

defendant is released.

In order to meet his responsibility, the prosecutor will present through direct examination, direct and/or circumstantial evidence by way of exhibits and testimony which tend to show the guilt of the defendant *beyond a reasonable doubt.* At the conclusion of the direct examination of each witness, the defendant, through his attorney, has an opportunity to cross-examine the witness to test his credibility or the relevance or accuracy of his testimony. Obviously, if the defendant chooses to act as his own attorney, he will be allowed to conduct the cross-examination himself.

Once the prosecutor has presented all of his evidence, he will announce to the court that the **prosecution rests**.

1.06 Demurrer or Judgment of Acquittal

At the close of the prosecution's case, the defense has the opportunity to present a motion to the court asking it to stop the case and declare that the charges against the defendant be dismissed. This motion will be made on the defendant's theory that the prosecution has failed to offer sufficient evidence upon which any jury could reasonably find the defendant guilty beyond a reasonable doubt. This may be done at side-bar, or it may require extensive argument, during which time the jury is sent out of the courtroom while the attorneys argue their points to the judge.

If the judge rules that one or more of the elements of a particular charge have not been satisfied by the prosecution, those charges will be dismissed and, in most cases, the rule of *double jeopardy* will apply. If the court rules that the prosecution has satisfactorily met its burden of proof on all of the elements of each charge, the trial will continue and, if he is convicted, the defendant is free to raise the matter again on appeal.

1.07 The Defense Case

At the conclusion of the prosecution's case, and after the court has ruled on any dismissal motions raised by the defense, the defendant has the opportunity to present evidence on his own behalf. Depending upon the charges and the amount of evidence against him, the defendant may choose to testify himself and/or present other witnesses to support the defense, or he may choose to exercise his right not to testify or present any testimony or evidence through any other witnesses.

The defendant is never under the obligation to testify, and in cases where he chooses not to do so, the court must, upon request by the defense, instruct the jury that they may draw no inference against the defendant because of his failure to testify.

Occasionally, the defendant will present no testimony, or fact witnesses, or exhibits to meet the allegations against him, but will present the testimony of character witnesses. The rules regulating the testimony of character witnesses vary from state to state, but basically the purpose for presenting character witnesses is to show that the defendant's character is such that he would be unlikely to have committed the crimes charged. The presentation of character witnesses may, if believed, by itself, raise a reasonable doubt in the minds of the jury about the defendant's guilt and could work for his acquittal.

At the conclusion of the testimony of the defense witnesses, the prosecutor will have the opportunity to test their credibility by cross-examination of each of them.

The subjects of direct and cross-examination are covered in greater detail in Chapters 5 and 6.

1.08 Witnesses

Except for stipulations (agreements between the prosecutor and the defense attorney as to the admission of facts or physical evidence), all evidence admitted at trial must come through the testimony of witnesses. However, before a witness may testify, he or she must be qualified to offer the testimony required for the admission of the evidence.

A. Competency

Depending upon the nature of the witness's situation, or the matter about which the witness intends to testify, a number of matters must be considered in determining the witness's competence to testify.

1. Age

If the age of a prospective witness is an issue, the court, or one or both of the attorneys, will ask questions of the witness regarding matters which will be determinative of that witness's qualifications. Usually, the test is whether the witness knows the difference between right and wrong, and between the truth and a lie, whether he or she understands the responsibility to tell the truth when testifying and whether or not the witness understands the nature of the matter about which he or she is testifying. This usually arises when the witness is very young and may also be relevant when the question of senility emerges with an older witness.

2. Mental Competency

If there is a question regarding the witnesses mental capacity to testify, as in the case of a witness with serious mental or emotional problems, the court may ask questions relevant to that inquiry, or the court may require an examination of the witness by a physician or psychologist to assist the judge in determining whether or not the witness is competent to testify.

3. Relevance of Testimony

In order for a witness to be called upon to testify regarding a certain matter, it must first be determined that the witness's testimony is relevant to the matter under litigation.

4. Character Witnesses

Though the testimony of character witnesses would seem to be irrelevant to the matter at issue, when a person is charged with a crime, that fact alone puts the defendant's character at issue. Therefore, any individual charged with a criminal offense is permitted to offer character testimony for the purpose of showing that a person of such high character would be unlikely to commit a crime.

B. Sequestration

It is not unusual for either or both of the trial attorneys to request a sequestration order from the court. If it is granted, and it is unusual that it is not, the court will instruct that all of the witness for both sides remove themselves from the courtroom until it is time for them to testify. The two exceptions to this order are the defendant and the case agent or prosecuting officer. All of the witnesses who are sequestered are instructed that once they testify, they are not to discuss their testimony with any of the remaining witnesses. If this order is violated, the court has a number of options available to it. The witnesses who have been told of the content of prior testimony may be disqualified, or the disclosing witness may be found in contempt of court.

Sometimes a witness will be allowed to remain in the courtroom following his or her testimony. This will be the case only when the court is assured that no further testimony will be given by the witness.

There are times when witnesses who are not expected to testify will be sequestered. This is most frequent when the request is made by the defense attorney about witnesses who have an interest in the case, and who the defense believes may prejudice the jury by their mere presence. Such is the case when the parents of a murder victim wish to sit through the trial. The defense attorney may argue that gestures or even eye movement or general demeanor will tend to cause the jury to sympathize with the prosecution or prejudice the defendant. There are times when the defense is considering calling one or more of such witnesses to testify. In such cases, if the court accepts the attorney's representation, the witnesses will be sequestered. If the court suspects that the defense attorney is using the request as a ploy to simply avoid the witness's presence during the trial, the court may make a more complete inquiry, or refuse the request without inquiry. By refusing the request without a hearing or at least a side-bar discussion, the court risks a viable appeal issue.

1.09 Rebuttal

At the conclusion of the defense presentation, the prosecutor has an opportunity to offer testimony or other evidence for the limited purpose of rebutting the defendant's case. Rebuttal evidence must, however, contradict the defendant's testimony or evidence. It will not be permitted for the sole purpose of adding more evidence to the prosecution's case.

On occasion, prosecutors may be tempted to hold back certain evidence in an effort to entice a defendant to rely on a particular defense so that they may offer evidence on rebuttal that will directly negate that defense. The court will be alert for the prosecutor who tries to bolster his case by presenting evidence in such a way and may rule such evidence to be inadmissible.

At times the defense will be permitted to present sur-rebuttal if it is relevant and intended to answer the prosecutor's rebuttal.

1.10 Closing Arguments

Once both sides have finished with their presentations, the court will announce that the evidence and testimony is closed, and will call upon each of the attorneys to present his or her **closing arguments**.

In most jurisdictions, the prosecutor, who always has the burden of proof, will have the right to make the last argument to the jury. Depending upon the jurisdiction, this may mean that the defense must be the first to argue, or that the prosecution argues first, then has the right to a rebuttal argument at the close of the defense argument.

During their closing arguments, the attorneys will attempt to convince the jury of their point of view regarding the evidence, or lack of evidence, and its meaning or relevance to the question of the defendant's guilt or innocence.

Reference will be made to the exhibits presented and the testimony offered in such a light most favorable to the side making the argument.

If the attorneys are able to anticipate the contents of the court's expected instructions to the jury, they will select certain words or phrases from it to be used during their argument to further their own argument by associating their side with statements they will later hear from the judge during his charge, in the best interest of their side.

For example: If the prosecution has presented in its case, the testimony of an accomplice, the defense attorney, knowing that the judge will instruct the jury that the testimony of an accomplice should be accepted only after considerable scrutiny, will make reference to the expected instruction, drawing to the jury's attention the disfavor in which the court looks at such testimony, thereby using it to his best advantage.

The attorneys may argue the inferences which can be drawn from the facts and even from the demeanor or responsiveness of the witnesses. Any error made by a witness while testifying will be brought to the attention of the jury in such a way as to magnify the importance of the effect of that error.

The prosecutor will usually go down the list of charges against the defendant and point out to the jury the evidence which supports each allegation. The defense attorney, on the other hand, will highlight the inconsistencies in the prosecution's presentation and will attack the credibility of the state's witnesses.

While the attorneys are expected to point out facts or evidence which would tend to lead the jurors to draw conclusions favorable to their respective positions, they may not, in any jurisdiction, express to the jury their own opinion about the defendant's guilt or innocence or about the credibility of the witnesses or weight of the evidence.

The judge may impose a time limit on the attorneys, or let them take as much time as needed to make all of their points. In making his decision, the judge will consider the number of attorneys in the case, the amount of evidence received, the nature of the charges and the legal arguments available to each side.

1.11 Charging the Jury

At the conclusions of the closing arguments of both attorneys, the judge will instruct the jury on the law applicable to each count charged and on general principles of law that are relevant to the jury's determination of the credibility of the testimony and evidence and the disposition of the charges. In doing so, the judge may or may not review the testimony and evidence for the jury. The more recent policy of the courts is to avoid any review of specific evidence presented during the trial.

1.12 Jury Deliberations

Once the jury has been instructed on the law by the judge, they are taken to a *deliberation room* where they will begin the task of determining the question of whether or not the prosecution has offered enough relevant evidence to convince them of the defendant's guilt beyond a reasonable doubt. The judge will allow the jury to take with them into the deliberation room the exhibits offered into evidence and will provide technical assistance in the operation of any equipment needed to facilitate the operation or understanding of the exhibits.

Once inside the deliberation room, the jury will select a foreperson and organize the deliberation process. While deliberating, the jury is permitted to speak to no one outside the jury room except for courtroom personnel assigned to insure the jury's privacy (usually the tipstaff) and to provide for their needs.

The jury has the right to ask questions of the court during their deliberations. Usually this is done by writing questions on a piece of paper and giving it to the tipstaff. The judge will review the questions, and if necessary review the questions with the attorneys.

The jury will be placed back in the jury box, and the judge will either answer the question or tell the jury, for any number of reasons, that he will not be able to provide an answer to their questions.

1.13 Verdict

Once the jury has reached a verdict on all of the charges, they are brought before the court and, in the presence of the defendant, are asked to announce their verdict. Their verdict must be unanimous.

Following the announcement, the prosecutor or defense attorney may ask for a poll of the jury, at which time each of the jurors is asked to rise individually and confirm that the verdict, as read, was their own.

If the court is convinced, after a reasonable length of time, that the jury will be unable to agree on a verdict, the jury will be declared a **hung jury** and the court will declare a **mistrial**.

In the event of a mistrial, the case will be returned to the prosecutor for a decision on whether or not to retry the case before another jury.

1.14 Conclusions

The entire judicial system is designed to provide a fair opportunity to the prosecutor to present evidence of a defendant's guilt while protecting the defendant's right to a fair trial.

While prosecutors and law enforcement personnel are often quick to criticize the system as leaning to far in favor of the defendant, the rules are made by men and women who sit in the legislative branch of our government, and upon the benches of the courts of our country. While it is understandable that the prosecution sometimes becomes frustrated at what it sees as obstacles to the administration of justice, the fair minded prosecutor and police officer will realize that the laws are there to protect everyone, and that in the eyes of those in whom we have placed this responsibility, there are valid reasons for their rules and decisions.

On the other hand, one will hear just as many criticisms of the system from the defense bar and organizations supporting the rights of the accused. In their view, both the law and the judges tend to favor the prosecution. Evidence of this belief can be found in the fact that while most of the time the prosecution will not object to a non-jury trial, the defense, not trusting the case to the judge's interpretation of the evidence, will request instead a jury trial.

In the end, however, the proper administration of justice requires the cooperation of the prosecutor, defense attorney, and judge, and the fair and ethical application of the rules of evidence which apply to every case.

Chapter 2

REPORT WRITING

2.01 Introduction

The case report is the cornerstone of any investigation. Its importance to the organization, conduct, and ultimate success of an investigation and prosecution of a case cannot be overstated.

Good police work is the result of effective and rapid communication. The success of a criminal investigation depends in large part upon the gathering and preservation of various bits of information and evidence, and the channeling of that information through various segments of the Criminal Justice System, then ultimately to the jury.

The police officer's report is his means of communicating this information to his fellow investigators, the prosecutor, and the court. It is a written record of the direction and progress of an investigation, and to be effective, it must be accurate, concise, and informative.

The quality of the report will reflect directly on the officer's value as an investigator, and therefore will always directly affect his credibility as a courtroom witness. It is, in short, the written record by which the quality of the investigator's work is judged; it can compliment or damage the effect of his testimony.

Too often the importance of the investigation report is underestimated or ignored by the investigator. While it is seen as something necessary in the conduct of their department's records system, investigators seldom appreciate the importance of the report in the courtroom. Consequentially, the report is too often prepared with just enough care and precision to be acceptable to the department but without regard to how its inaccuracies will adversely affect the officer's credibility in the courtroom.

Police officers seldom appreciate the significance of the fact that on many occasions the only opportunity a defense attorney has to cast doubt upon the prosecution's case is to find errors in the investigative report, and exploit them before the jury. It is important to remember that during the attack on the prosecution's case, one of the primary goals of the defense attorney will be to paint the investigation as having been incomplete or poorly conducted, thereby affecting its overall credibility in the eyes of the jury.

Defense tactics employed by lawyers in attacking the testimony of the police officer through his written report are examined and illustrated in the chapter on cross-examination. In this chapter, the reader finds explanations of the functions of the investigative report and guidance to its proper composition.

Some officers are better able to write comprehensive, fluent reports than are others. To them, the preparation of a report presents few problems, while to the others it can be a somewhat difficult and unpleasant task. Every officer has the ability, however, develop proficiency in the drafting of a report through practice and with thought and care in its preparation. It is merely a matter of application and effort.

2.02 Use of the Investigative Report During Testimony

A. The Law

When offered in court by any witness, the investigative report is hearsay, and generally not admissible. Hearsay is a "statement," other than one made by the declarant while testifying at a trial or hearing, which is offered to prove the truth of the matter asserted. There are a number of situations in which statements, appearing on the surface to be hearsay, are not. There are also statements which, although hearsay, are nevertheless admitted as *exceptions* to the hearsay rule. These matters will be covered later in this chapter, and again in other chapters, but for now, it is sufficient to say that police reports are "statements" within the rule and are, therefore, subject to it.

The use of notes or written reports by the investigating officer while on the stand *is* permissible in limited circumstances for the following purposes:

1. Present Recollection Refreshed

As an exception to the hearsay rule, notes or written records or reports concerning matters about which a witness once had knowledge but now has insufficient recollection to enable him to testify fully and accurately are available to him for the purpose of refreshing his recollection while he is on the witness stand. The report or record must have been shown to have been made or adopted by the witness when the matter was fresh in the witness's memory and must

reflect that knowledge correctly.

The witness's access to the material requested for review will be limited to those writings which may be said to have a direct impact on the testimony of that witness, and the court must be satisfied that the witness does not have sufficient present recollection and that the writing will help to refresh his recollection.

It is generally accepted that the investigator cannot be expected to commit to memory all of the details of his investigation, especially if the case is complicated or involves extensive investigative activity. For example, the exact sequence of events which occurred during the investigation, or the names of certain witnesses may not be information that the witness has committed to memory. In such situations the court will almost always permit the witness to use his written notes or report to refresh his memory, even though the document would not itself have been admissible as evidence. It is required that the witness know that the facts stated in the report were correctly stated therein. When it has been determined that the rules have been satisfied, the witness may look at his investigation notes or report, find the information that he needs and then inform the court that seeing it has refreshed his memory concerning the points relevant to the attorney's inquiry. He then must put aside his report and give the answer to the question. The application of the rule is not limited to the officer's memorandum or report. It will apply equally to records, bank ledger sheets, tax records, accounting records, work records, stenographic transcripts, such as transcribed notes of testimony given at a prior hearing, or any other records, papers, letters or reports that can be qualified by the prosecutor as credible. Naturally, proper organization of the material used will facilitate finding the information quickly. Any investigator who has testified knows how embarrassing it can be to have to root through his report on the witness stand, going back and forth through the material searching for the information needed. And doesn't it seem that the bigger the hurry, the more difficult it is to find the information you seek?

The decision as to whether there is a need for refreshing the witness' testimony falls solely within the sound discretion of the trial court, and after the witness's recollection has been refreshed, his testimony must be his present recollection. In such cases where the officer refers to his report during his testimony, the defense attorney will have access to that portion of his report which was reviewed by the witness to use during his cross-examination.

2. Past Recollection Recorded

An entry in a report may be read into the record as a past recollection recorded. However, it may not be received as an exhibit unless offered by the defendant. Even if a witness's recollection is not refreshed by the use of the memorandum or document, he may nevertheless testify from such a document on the theory that the document constitutes a record of a past recollection. It must be shown, however, that the memorandum was made at or about the time of the event recorded, or at least at a time when the event was fresh in the memory of the witness.

As an exception to the rule excluding hearsay evidence, the courts will generally allow such a review on the basis that the guarantee of trustworthiness required for admission is found in the reliability inherent in a record made while events were still fresh in the witness's mind. *The witness need not be totally devoid of recollection for the exception to apply.* The prosecution need only show that the testimony is reasonably reliable and that

reference to it would allow for more complete and accurate testimony from the witness. It is left to the court's discretion to determine to what extent past recollection recorded should be admitted into evidence. The kinds of information which are most often the subject of the exception are: the sequence of events, times and dates, license numbers, birth dates, and other documents, such as those listed in the previous section. If the witness is asked a question relevant to the document, and has a need to refer directly to the document rather than using it to merely refresh his recollection, he should indicate that he has no independent recollection of the event or information, and ask for permission to refer to the document. *If the request is granted, the court will allow opposing counsel to examine the document prior to its use, and to use it on cross-examination.* The prosecutor asking the questions will first ask the witness to identify the document and he may ask several questions to otherwise qualify it. The witness will then be asked to look through his report and find the information he seeks, and read that information as his answer to the question.

3. Elements for Admission

In order for the witness to take advantage of these exceptions, five elements must be met:

a) The officer presently must have no complete and accurate recollection of the matters recorded in the report.

b) The officer either made the report himself or adopted the report of another as correct and accurate at a time close to the time of its making.

c) The information contained in the report is within the firsthand knowledge of the officer, and not information received from a third party.

d) The officer must be able to personally

vouch for the accuracy of the information.

e) The material requested for review must have a direct impact on the officer's testimony. That is, it must be relevant to the inquiry.

4. *Business Records*

It is also possible that entries made into reports or other records pertaining to police business may be introduced as *business records*.

Even though falling within the definition of hearsay, they are admissible when the original entries are made contemporaneously with the event to which they relate in the regular conduct of the investigation.

There are certain elements required for their admission as a business record:

a) The writing must be an original entry made at a time reasonable near the event to which it relates.

b) The writing must have been made in the regular course of business.

c) The circumstances under which the report was made must indicate its accuracy and that it was not falsified. This is generally determined as a matter of judicial discretion.

d) The writer is unavailable to testify as to its contents.

B. Availability to the Defense

1. *Rule of Evidence*

612 of the Federal Rules of Criminal Procedure (all state courts have a similar rule) provides that:

If a witness uses a writing to refresh his memory for the purpose of testifying, either;
a) while testifying, or
b) before testifying, and the Court in its discretion determines it necessary in the interests of justice, an adverse party is entitled to have the writing produced at the hearing, to inspect it, to cross-examine the witness thereon, and to introduce in evidence those portions which relate to the testimony of the witness.

2. *"Jencks" Rule*

In some jurisdictions, opposing counsel will be permitted to examine and use on cross-examination, the entire report of the officer whether or not he uses it while actually testifying. Those jurisdictions follow the Federal Rule as it was set out in the case of, *Jencks v. The United States of America*, 353 U.S. 657 (1957). The "Jencks" Rule, as it has come to be known, requires that upon completion of the witnesses' direct testimony, any reports generated by him must be delivered to the defense for use on cross-examination whether or not they were used to refresh the witness's recollection. In those jurisdictions, the courts generally "encourage" the prosecution to turn over the reports to the defense some time prior to the witness actually taking the stand. This is done so that there is no unnecessary delay between the direct and cross-examination created from the need by the defense to absorb the reports prior to commencing the cross-examination. Some jurisdictions that don't strictly follow Jencks require the prosecution to turn over the police officer's report if it is established that the officer used the report to refresh his recollection about the investigation at a time close to the time when he went on the stand.

Still other jurisdictions require that the officer's report be turned over to the defense by way of discovery prior to the trial.

C. Advisability of Using the Report During Testimony

Whether it is advisable for the witness to

take his report to the stand with him depends on how well the witness knows the facts, and upon the completeness, accuracy, and organization of the report.

1. Knowledge of the Facts

No witness should ever take the witness stand without a comprehensive familiarity with the facts. When it is possible for the officer to testify from his own recollection of the facts rather than relying on his investigative report the rewards are substantial. His ability to cope successfully with cross-examination will increase, as will his credibility with the jury. Juries are more willing to accept the words of a witness who displays a confidence and mastery of his investigation. Often it is difficult for a jury to completely accept the testimony of a witness who must rely on notes to recall what happened during an investigation, especially in a factually uncomplicated case.

2. Complex Cases

If the facts are many or complex, the witness will not be expected to have committed every detail to memory, and if he is asked questions concerning material about which he is unsure, he may have to refer to his notes or to his report. In such a situation, it is good to have the report indexed in a loose leaf notebook. Such preparation reduces the amount of time needed to find the relevant information. Few things undermine the testimony of a witness like taking an inordinate amount of time leafing through a report in an attempt to locate information.

a) The kinds of information upon which the witness chooses to rely on his report should be limited. Exact times, house and license plate numbers, names of minor witnesses, measurements, quotations, scientific terms, and other such specific information are examples of kinds of things that might acceptably require reliance on notes or documents.

b) If the witness anticipates needing only a certain portion of his report to assist his testimony, he should take that portion with him to the stand. This eliminates confusion during the witness's testimony and protects the rest of the report from scrutiny by the defense attorney. Of course, in jurisdictions that follow the Jencks or a similar rule, the defense attorney will get the entire report at the conclusion of the direct-examination.

2.03 Organization and Preparation of the Investigative Report

A. Importance of Proper Preparation

Many officers overlook the importance of a properly prepared written report. This is understandable since police officers are often drawn to the profession by the promise of action. They are the kind of people who want to be doing: investigating, tracking, working in the field. They are among the doers of the world, so it is quite consistent that they dislike the drudgery of having to report about their activities. When one activity is concluded, they want to get on to the next one.

Unfortunately, too much of the ultimate success of an investigation depends on duties other than the type of activity which policemen find interesting and exhilarating, and for which they feel best suited. Report writing is one of those duties. It is one of the least enjoyable but critically important aspects or every police officer's responsibilities. Fortunately, among the traits usually found in the average police officer is a desire to strive for excellence in his work.

Experience shows that once an officer accepts the importance of a properly prepared investigative report, the quality of his efforts to the performance of that duty increase dramatically.

Investigative reports serve and reflect upon the officer and his investigation in a number of ways:
1. They provide a record of the investigation and preserve information for later reference.
2. They provide accurate and pertinent details upon which a clean, strong case can be built. Establishing accurate details enhances further investigation, future reference, and courtroom presentation.
3. They provide assistance to fellow law enforcement officers and agencies in that they:
   a) Facilitate the exchange of information (MO, identification, etc.) and promote teamwork;
   b) Prevent duplication of effort and minimize inconsistencies between reports;
   c) Provide the court and probation departments with information upon which they rely to make sentencing recommendations.
   d) Provide the main source of information used by prosecutors to determine;
      • what evidence exists and where it is located,
      • what crimes were committed,
      • what crimes can be charged,
      • the identity of witnesses,
      • possible defenses, the strength and weaknesses of the case,
      • what kind of a jury to select, and
      • what kind of trial strategy to employ.
4. Reflects on the abilities of the investigator. It is the accuracy and completeness of the

written report by which the quality of the officer's investigation is judged, and it can compliment or damage the officer's testimony on cross-examination.

B. Organizing the Report

1. Elements of the Properly Prepared Report

a) Note taking should begin at the officer's first contact with the case. Often that is at the crime scene. Among other things, notes are a record of the officer's initial observations and reactions to the evidence. That is not to say that the officer should speculate. Indeed, the officer should avoid drawing conclusions in his notes. He should rather characterize his reactions as possibilities or as matters to be considered. If the officer's observations and suspicions turn out to be correct, he looks good for having noted their importance. Those that turn out to be false leads become no more than another of the many matters needing the investigator's consideration.

b) Notes should provide a record of the exact condition and location of the evidence found at the scene. Even though photos can and should be taken, they are sometimes misleading. Therefore, the exact location of the evidence found at a crime scene should be determined by measurements, and those measurements should be recorded in notes or on a sketch of the scene.

c) Notes should be brief but concise with emphasis on accuracy. The officer should take as many notes as needed. They should be made in such a way as to allow them to be expanded upon when preparing the typewritten report. The officer may want to develop a set of signs or abbreviations to use while making notes. Notes should include:

- measurements,
- descriptions,
- names and other personal information,
- conditions,
- events,
- lighting,
- observations,
- any other information which is relevant to the goals of the investigation.

d) Notes should be legible. They should be reviewed for additions or corrections as soon as possible and transferred to a full report at the first opportunity.

2. Destruction of Notes

In most jurisdictions, under normal circumstances, the officer is not required to produce rough notes that were destroyed after the report was transcribed, as long as the notes were not destroyed in an effort to prevent examination by the defendant, and the written or transcribed report is available to the defendant when required.

However, where notes are deliberately destroyed on the eve of trial by the officer for the purpose of preventing its examination by the defense, and the defendant has not been furnished with the information contained in the notes, the officer's testimony may be ruled inadmissible.

3. Reporting Format

Reporting formats vary from one department to another. Some may require strict conformance to a particular departmental form; others do not. Some report forms are very complicated and so detailed that the report is a series of one-word answers to questions provided on the form. Others pro-

vide no guidelines at all and are little more than blank spaces to be filled in by the report writer. The author knew one small town chief of police who required the report to be written in a letter form addressed to him. This is not generally recommended. The form of the report, however, is of importance only to the extent that it provides a guide to the organization of the information. What is of primary importance is the information that goes into the report, no matter what the format. Drug Enforcement Administration (DEA) reports provide a good example of an excellent format. See the sample report found in the appendix at the end of this book, as it points out some of the positive features of this type of format.

4. Environment

When preparing a report, it is important that the writer concentrate on the task at hand. Using his notes and his recollections, he is about to prepare what may well become the most important document at the trial of his case. There should be no distractions. Almost every department has a place where the officers can be alone to work without distraction. It may be an interrogation room or a conference room. If there is such a place, the officer should use it when preparing his report.

C. General Principles and Guidelines

1. Promptness

It is important that the written report be completed as soon as possible after the event to be reported. It may make the difference between being able to refer to the report during testimony, and not. The officer should not wait until the investigation is completed before preparing a report.

Much of the information learned during the earlier stages of the investigation may be forgotten. Given the passage of a significant amount of time, even field notes may not be sufficient to trigger the officer's complete recollection about the events. Supplemental reports can and should be prepared as the investigation progresses.

2. Accuracy

The most important function of an investigative report is to accurately represent the subject matter reported. Care should be taken to insure the accuracy of everything contained in the report. Inaccuracies will almost always come back to haunt the reporter.

- Names should be spelled correctly with middle initials or names and aliases.
- Addresses, VIN numbers, and serial numbers should be checked for accuracy, then checked again.
- Descriptions of persons and places should be examined and checked against other descriptions of the same persons and places that may have been provided by other sources.
- The information must conform to the truth and must be an exact representation of the facts gathered.

Situation 2-1: Mistakes in the report: The following is a transcript of the actual testimony of an experienced and very capable undercover narcotics detective. It is an example of the kinds of trouble and officer can get into by not insuring the accuracy of his report. Names and places referred to have been changed.

Questions by the defense attorney:

Q. Detective Fox, at the time you drew that, . . . can we agree that that's not drawn to scale?

A. We agree.

Q. Okay. And so, therefore, the alley that you've shown isn't wider than, for example, the two streets that you drew; isn't that accurate?

A. No, definitely not. The street is probably wider than the alley, but I'm just drawing.

Q. And, in that regard, the size of the streets, the blocks between the streets, are they pretty uniform in that area?

A. Pretty well, yes, sir.

Q. About how much distance is in a block?

A. In a block?

Q. In a city block?

A. In a city block it's approximately 300 feet.

Q. Okay. And how much, . . . is that 300 feet in length? In other words, . . .

A. Yeah, about 300 feet long. Yes, sir.

Q. Okay. And how do the streets and the avenues run? You have the streets running north and south, is that generally how they run?

A. In the City of Atlanta, the streets run north and south, and the avenues run east and west.

Q. Okay. And you have a . . . have had occasion to dictate a report, did you not?

A. Yes, sir.

Q. Okay. And in your report originally typed was $961\frac{1}{2}$, 8th Avenue South. Is that correct?

A. That's correct.

Q. And what is that address?

A. That's a residence in the area that sits just, you know, in back of the 8th Avenue side of this particular residence. The numbers on the house are for the 8th Avenue address. In other words, I simply copied down the wrong address on that particular house until I went back and saw the correct address. That's when I got it right.

Q. Well, show me on your drawing where $961\frac{1}{2}$, 8th Avenue is.

A. Okay, here we have 7th Place. And the

very next . . . excuse me. The very next building here . . . in other words, you have 8th Avenue right here. 7th Place is really like an alley that runs between this alley and 8th Avenue. So, it has a big building here that has 961 8th Avenue. And normally the half address sits in the rear of the buildings in Atlanta, therefore 961 would be here. And at that time I assumed that the half, . . . the building in the rear was $961\frac{1}{2}$ 8th Avenue. But, naturally, when I found out the correct address, which is on this building, when I got close enough to see it, that's when I made the change in my report, just to make it accurate.

Q. But, that was some time after the report was not only dictated, but typed, is that correct?

A. Yes. It was after the . . . the next day after the report was typed, because it was already typed, therefore, I couldn't type over it. I just had to write it in to make sure it reflects the correct address.

Q. Okay. But, you have changed at the top of the report from $961\frac{1}{2}$, 8th *Street* South, to $961\frac{1}{2}$, 9th Avenue South, but down in the body of the report you change that $961\frac{1}{2}$, 8th *Avenue* South to *$916\frac{1}{2}$*, 9th Avenue South. Why?

A. Well, when you see . . . 961 is 916. If you see a 61, it's just a reverse of the numbers. Because all of them are right there, . . . there are only four buildings involved, and those are the four.

Q. Okay. Could you show me on that building where $961\frac{1}{2}$, 9th Avenue South is?

A. No, that's 9th Street South. You will not find 9th Avenue. Ninth Avenue is nothing compared to this case or this particular drawing. If you see 9th Avenue, naturally it was a misprint.

Q. Okay. So, you are saying that you have a total of three different addresses; the address you say it is, the address that was

originally typed at the top of the report, and the address that got changed in the body of the report. Is that correct?

By the Prosecutor: Excuse me. I think, . . . I'm going to make an objection unless the detective has an opportunity to look at it, because it does not say 9th Avenue South. I would ask the court to . . .

(Counsel conferring)

By the Court: Go ahead, then. I take it that has been resolved. Go ahead.

By the defense attorney:

Q. Let me ask my question. Are you saying then that there is a total of three different addresses involved here? Number one is the address where you say it occurred, number two is the address that you changed at the top of the report, and a third address is the address in the body of the report?

A. As I told you earlier, the City of Atlanta believes in accurate information in the report. When I found out that I put an error in the address in the report, that's when I go make the change. That's why the addresses involved is only one, and that's $916\frac{1}{2}$ 9th Street.

Note: The correction should have been done carefully and in a supplementary report instead of by scratching out a word here and a number there, then adding corrections in pen. Not only was it messy, but it was wrong.

Situation 2-2: Officer led to believe a mistake occurred in writing the report.

Sometimes the officer, when he has not adequately reviewed his report prior to taking the stand, is led by the defense attorney into believing that he has made a mistake in writing the report, when no mistake was made.

Questions by the Defense Attorney:

Q. Officer, you stated on direct-examination

that you heard some voices back along the dirt trail, is that correct?

A. That's correct.

Q. Where were you when you heard the voices?

A. On that dirt trail, approximately fifty, sixty yards from the trucks.

Q. Now, is this after the other officers had come out to brief you about what they had known or thought they knew about what was going on further down the trail?

A. Right. We had gathered at the mouth of the trail.

Q. And, what did you hear the voices say?

A. I couldn't hear what they were saying, just somebody talking. I couldn't make it out; it was unintelligible. You just couldn't make it out, but there was voices coming down.

Q. Well, could you not make it out because it wasn't loud enough, or because they were speaking in a language you couldn't understand, or because there was other noise in the area interfering? What exactly was the reason that you couldn't make out what was being said?

A. Probably the wind and the distance more than anything else. There wasn't any noise being made because at that point we were all gathered right there being totally silent. One guy said we've got trucks up there; there's people up there; everybody get quiet and decide what we're going to do; and, then these sounds are coming down the trail.

Q. How long did you wait there being absolutely silent?

A. This happened no more than five or ten seconds, maximum.

Q. Now, during that five or ten seconds you heard one voice that you say you could– that voice was distinctive as compared to others, but you have no idea what the voice said?

A. Right.

Q. In terms of words?

A. Correct.

Q. And, also in that five or ten seconds, you heard another voice about to respond to that one?

A. No, I heard one person talking to another person. The first person stopped. As the second person started to say something, somebody else interjected. It wasn't within three to five seconds after that that everything got silent. We heard a door shut, and that was it.

Q. But, you have no idea what these three people said, just that you heard three voices?

A. Just noise and voices; we could tell it was human.

Q. Now, you wrote a report subsequent to your participation in this investigation, did you not?

A. Yes, I wrote up a report.

Q. You made a statement to put down on paper, as soon as possible after your participation in the investigation concluded, what you had observed or heard at that time, is that correct?

A. Most of the matters were in the report. I haven't seen it prior to this trial.

Q. Well, let me show you this document and ask whether this refreshes your recollection as to the statement you made subsequent to your participation in the investigation.

A. Okay.

Q. Is that the report you made?

A. Yes.

Q. And the purpose of that report again was what?

A. General statement of facts pertaining to the case, the actions I took, observed, or heard.

Q. The facts being the important ones to your knowledge that you observed or learned during the course of your participation in the investigation, correct?

A. Correct.

Note: Here, the officer, probably unwittingly, answered yes to a question asking him, in fact, if everything in the report is important, and if everything important is in the report. Actually, this is not always the case. Oftentimes, an officer, while investigating will make note of something which later turns out to be irrelevant or relatively unimportant, and there are times when facts which do turn out to be important are not seen as such early in the investigation, and are not reported, although, they should be reported in a supplemental report when its importance is discovered.

Q. Now, in that report you just said that the voices were heard. You didn't say there were two or three voices, or more, did you?

A. No, I didn't. I said voices.

Note: Here, the officer answered the question without first reviewing the report, which he could have done on the stand after the question was asked. He took the defense attorney's word for what was or wasn't in the report. This was a mistake. In his report he actually said that there was more than one voice, but he wasn't sure exactly how many. He never specified a number.

Q. But, now you're sure that it's three voices?

A. Well, I heard more than two people. Yes, so that would make it three, correct.

Q. Well, when did you come to the realization that your report might have been incomplete.

A. I didn't think it was incomplete until now. I made a mistake in my statement or I made an error in not putting the number of voices that I overheard. I didn't think at that particular time that the number of voices made a difference.

Note: There was no mistake made by the officer in the report. He reported that he heard an unspecified number of voices and

when asked on the stand was led into testifying that the number was three. This was the attorney's conclusion, not the officer's, but the officer went with it. The officer should not have testified that he made a mistake when he did not. Had the officer reviewed the report, either prior to giving his testimony, or after he was asked the question by the defense attorney, this mistake could have been avoided. In this case, the defense attorney, after successfully accomplishing his goal, moved on to another area. Fortunately, on re- direct, the prosecutor reviewed the matter with the officer, during which time the officer, while embarrassed, was at least able to clear up the matter.

Situation 2-3:
Questions by the defense attorney

Q. And, would you tell us what this is?

A. It's a statement that I made.

Q. And, is that the report that memorialized what you saw on the morning of the 5th, and the late evening of the 4th?

A. Yes, sir.

Q. In fact, that's the report that you wrote so that you would have a sufficient memory to testify about it's contents later down the line, isn't that correct?

A. Yes.

Q. Did you write any other reports?

A. Not that I recall.

Note: Wrong answer! The officer should have made himself familiar enough about his investigation before going to court to be able to testify as to whether or not there were other reports generated by him in connection with his investigation. It should also be noted here that too often, police officers who have not thoroughly prepared themselves for trial, will use phrases intended to avoid a commitment that could get them in trouble while testifying. Phrases such as "not to my knowledge" are used by many witnesses not only in referring to matters about which they are legitimately not sure, but also about matters which they are simply not prepared to answer because of a failure to review their reports prior to going to court.

Q. Are you saying there may have been others?

A. I don't think so, no.

Q. But, you're not sure, is that right? (The officer doesn't answer)

Q. Okay, so this may be the only report generated by you, correct?

A. Yes.

Q. And you have adopted that as being accurate; isn't that correct?

A. Yes.

Q. Okay, so that's an accurate statement of what you saw occur late on the 4th and early on the 5th of that morning, that's correct, isn't it?

A. Yes, sir.

Note: The officer should have smelled a rat here. Any time a defense attorney tries to get a definite commitment from a witness, especially when he tries to emphasize it by asking essentially the same question twice, the officer should be careful in his answer, and if he is not absolutely sure about a particular matter, he should ask to see the document referred to by the attorney, in this case the officer's report. If no document is referred to, and if the officer isn't absolutely certain of his answer, he should testify that the fact referred to by the attorney is correct to the best of his recollection without the ability to refer to the report. This response is especially effective if the report is voluminous. The officer will appear to the jury to be making every effort to be accurate, and the defense attorney may appear to be trying to trick the witness.

Q. Okay, would you please read to the jury on there where you stated that the voices were panicky?

A. It's not on here.

Q. It's not? Okay, would you then, please tell the jury where you wrote on there twelve months ago, approximately, knowing that you may have to testify in the future that you saw a boat-print mark?

A. I did not.

Q. You didn't?

A. I didn't write it in.

Q. You didn't put in there anywhere that you saw a boat-print?

A. No, sir.

Q. That was an important fact, don't you think, officer?

A. I suppose so, yes.

Q. Okay. You just testified earlier that this was an accurate representation of what you saw on the night of the 4th and the morning of the 5th; isn't that correct?

A. Yes.

Q. On this piece of paper, and let me give it back to you one more time, you did not put on there that you heard any doors slamming, did you, sir?

A. That's correct.

Q. You did not put on there that you saw any footprints, did you, sir?

A. That's correct.

Q. You did put on there that when you finally got to the end of the trail by the water, that the trail stopped. Now, I assume that is the truck trail?

A. It's a dirt trail.

Q. A dirt trail? So, then, you didn't put on here that you followed the truck trail, just a dirt trail, isn't that correct, then, sir?

A. I'd like to see it again.

Q. Okay.

(The officer re-examines the report.)

A. Would you ask your question again, sir?

Q. Sure. You never put on here that you specifically were following a truck trail, did you?

A. That's correct.

Q. And, at the end of whatever trail you were following, you didn't put on there that you found a boat imprint, did you?

A. That's correct.

Mr. Newman: I have no further questions.

Note: These were all mistakes that were correctable if the officer had only done a thorough review of his report after completing it, or at least prior to coming to court. As it is, the quality of the officers investigation now becomes a major question in the case.

3. Order of Reporting Facts

Information organized in the sequence in which it occurred will be more easily understood by others reading the report and will allow the officer quicker reference to specific sections of the reported information.

There are times when, for one reason or another, this is not possible. In such situations, a supplemental report should be made placing the information in its proper sequences by reference, and if the information is of a type that an observer would have been included in the earlier report, and explanation for its absence should be noted, if one is available.

It is important to note that if some order other than chronological is also needed, a cross-reference index should be prepared.

4. Language

The officer writing the report should use language that will be easily understood and interpreted by the average layman who may be reading it. Although some "copspeak" is acceptable, it can be overdone.

For example, when referring to a specific, identifiable suspect, the officer should not use the word **perpetrator**. This is a conclusion and represents an opinion which should not appear in the report. The report should either identify the person by name or as the suspect. The word "perpetrator" should be limited to reference to the unknown person

who has committed the crime.

Example: *Incorrect use of the word Perpetrator:*

"The perpetrator has been identified as John Smith. . . ."

In this situation, the word *suspect* should be used. "The suspect has been identified as John Smith. . . ."

Example: *Correct use of the word Perpetrator:*

"The manner of entry used by the perpetrator was. . . ."

In the correct version, the officer is referring to an unknown person who committed the crime, whereas, in the incorrect version, he is improperly concluding that John Smith is the perpetrator. He may turn out to be the perpetrator, but that's not for the police officer to conclude, and a sharp defense attorney will take advantage of the officer's mistake in doing so.

Situation 2-4: There are times when the improper use of the word "perpetrator" can be more than just a small error. The point made here is that pointing out these kinds of misuse of words by the officer in his report is not just nit-picking. In this example, the officer has to answer to the defense attorney on cross-example for this kind of error in his report.

Questions by the defense attorney:

Q. Officer, on direct-examination you referred to your report, is that correct?

A. Yes, that's correct.

Q. And, when was that report prepared?

A. (The officer checks his report.) I prepared this report on November 20th of last year.

Q. And that was two days after this investigation began, is that correct?

A. That's correct.

Q. And, of course, you were careful to be as accurate as possible, correct?

A. That's correct.

Q. At some point in your investigation you identified my client as the perpetrator, is that correct?

A. That's correct.

Q. And, of course, my client wasn't arrested until several months later, is that correct?

A. Your client was arrested on February 16th. That was two days shy of three months after the crime was committed.

Q. You're right, I'm sorry. And, you waited those three months because why?

A. Because the investigation wasn't completed until then.

Q. So, then, you didn't feel you had sufficient evidence to make the arrest until then, is that correct?

A. I'm not sure what you mean.

Q. Well, you wouldn't make an arrest until you felt you had sufficient evidence, would you?

A. No.

Q. So you didn't arrest my client until you felt you had sufficient evidence, correct?

A. That's correct.

Q. And that would be on or about February 15th, the date the warrant was sworn to, correct?

A. That's correct.

Q. OK. Would you agree that the word perpetrator refers to the person who committed the offense?

A. Would you repeat that, please?

Q. Sure. Would you agree that the word perpetrator refers to the person who committed a particular offense?

A. Yes, I would agree with that.

Q. And that the word suspect refers to one of the possible perpetrators?

A. Yes, I would agree.

Q. So, then, the suspect is the person believed to be the perpetrator, and the perpetrator is the person who actually did commit the crime, correct?

A. Ok, I agree with that.

Q. So, then, if you, as you have already testified, strive for accuracy in your investigation, and in your report, and if you didn't have enough evidence to have probable cause to arrest my client until three months after the initiation of the investigation, why would you, on the third day of that investigation, refer to my client as the perpetrator instead of a suspect.

Note: This testimony was taken from an actual case. The officer had an answer for that question, but it wasn't sufficient to overcome the inference drawn by the defense attorney in his closing argument that the officer was so focused on the defendant from the beginning of the investigation that he never considered the possibility of other suspects. The defendant, against whom there existed more than enough evidence to convict, was acquitted.

The words **advise**, **indicate** and **vehicle**, seem to be three favorite report writing words.

Example: *Improper use of the words; advise, indicate and vehicle.*

"The witness **advised** me that he saw the suspect's **vehicle**," or "The witness **indicated** that he saw the suspect's **vehicle**." The use of this language is vague. A **vehicle** can be anything from a bicycle to an airplane. If known, the vehicle should be identified at least as to type. To **advise** someone of something is to counsel them or to recommend something to them. While the word advised has been accepted through constant improper use, it is ambiguous and ambiguity should be avoided.

If the witness told the officer that he saw the suspect's automobile, the report should read as follows; "The witness **told** me that he saw the suspect's **automobile**" (describe the automobile if the information is available).

To **indicate** is to demonstrate or to give a sign, and is more properly used when referring to the possibility or probability of a fact based upon the evidence.

Example: *Correct use of the word indicate:*

"The evidence **indicates** that the intruder was admitted to the residence."

Slang and **profanity** should only be used in reporting the words of another during the investigation and should be reported as a quote. It goes without saying that the officer should never use slang or profanity in his own descriptions or statements.

Abbreviations: When preparing the final report, only common abbreviations should be used and only where necessary or otherwise appropriate.

Sources of information should always be noted in the report unless the source is confidential, in which case a number or some other designation should be given to the informant so that there is at least a coded reference to the source.

Generally, **opinions** and **conclusions** should be excluded from the report. Like many other rules, however, this one has its exceptions. As the following examples illustrate, opinions are sometimes acceptable:

a) Where the officer is quoting or restating the words of another.
   Example: The witness further stated to me that everything happened so quickly that he wasn't sure how many men he saw going into the building, but he was of the opinion that it was five or six.
   Example: The witness said to me, "I saw him come out of the building at approximately 10:30 p.m."

b) When the officer is providing possible alternative conclusions without pointing to one as more credible than the others.
   Example: "From the evidence found at the scene it would appear that one of the following alternatives describes the circumstances of the perpetrator's entry into the building.
   • The manner of entry may have been made by using a key.
   • The intruder or intruders may have entered the building earlier, before

the employees left and secreted themselves inside until the building was empty.

c) When the officer is giving his best recollection of something he himself witnessed.
   Example: "As the car sped away I was able to get only a fleeting glance at it, but my belief is that it was a green sedan."

5. Hearsay

Hearsay is generally defined as evidence offered in court by a witness concerning information given in an out-of-court statement which is offered for the truth of the matter asserted, and is not within the witness's own knowledge but rather which has been received from another. Hearsay is generally not admissible at a trial. The reason is that it denies the opposing party the right of confrontation, or the right to cross-examine the author of the statement.

Reporting as fact information that came to the attention of the reporter by way of hearsay should never occur. It is not objectionable to include hearsay information in a report, but it must be reported as such and with reference to the source of the information.

Situation 2-5: The officer talked to a number of witnesses and, as a result, draws conclusions about what happened. Such conclusions are proper if they are sound and have been fully investigated. Such conclusions are made in virtually every case in which an arrest is made, for it is upon these conclusions that charges are brought. But, in the courtroom, the officer often fails to separate fact from hearsay or conclusion. This gets him into trouble on cross.

Questions by the defense attorney:

Q. Officer Smith, you state in your report

that my client arrived at the apartment with Mr. Molano in Mr. Molano's car. Did you see them arrive?

A. No.

Q. Were you at the apartment prior to my client's arrival?

A. No.

Q. Was Mr. Molano in the room when you arrived?

A. No.

Q. Did you see Mr. Molano at any time that day?

A. No.

Q. Did you see Mr. Molano's car there at any time that day.

A. No.

Q. Did the defendant tell you that he came to the apartment in Mr. Molano's car?

A. No.

Q. Did the defendant mention Mr. Molano at all during the time that you were with him on April 5th?

A. No.

Q. You testified that the defendant arrived at the apartment in Mr. Molano's car. But, in fact you don't know that of your own knowledge, do you?

A. No.

Note: the defense attorney has inflicted damage on the officer's entire testimony. He has shown that the officer testified about hearsay as though it was fact. Not only was the attorney able to have that portion of the officer's testimony stricken, but the conclusion offered to the jury by the defense attorney on closing argument will be that there must be other portions of the officer's testimony that were presented as fact which were not actually established. More on the subject of hearsay is discussed in the chapter on direct-examination.

6. Included Information

A report should answer the questions: who, what, when, where, how, and why. The first five define the elements of the crime and the last, the motive. You have noticed that motive has been separated from the elements. *Motive is never an element of a crime.* Criminal *intent* is often one of the elements, but should not be confused with motive. *Criminal intent* goes to the question of what the actor intended to do and *motive* goes to the question of why he did it.

a) *Who?*

Once a person relevant to the investigation is identified, the report should identify him specifically so that there can be no mistake about who that person is. He should be referred to by name, and if he is a suspect, identified as such. All other relevant information about this person that would distinguish him from every other person should also be included (e.g., approximate height and weight, scars, tattoos, physical handicaps, color and length of hair, social security number, etc.). The *who* should also include anyone who is a witness or potential witness in the case under investigation and all of the relevant information about that potential witness.

b) *What happened?*

The report should clearly state all of the known facts that would allow the reader to form a mental picture of the details of what happened and what the case is about, including as many details as are available. The manner in which these details should be reported is covered under another heading in this chapter.

c) *When did the event occur?*

The exact time of the event reported, if known, should be noted. If that is not known, an attempt should be made to approximate the time. Such references as "yesterday" or "Monday afternoon" should not be used, except as a quote from a witness. The report should clearly state a date and time. "April 5, 1997 at 5:30 p.m." or

"April 5, 1997 between the hours of 5:00 p.m. and 6:00 p.m." or whichever other times or time periods are appropriate. If the officer is unable to report even a specific time period, he should so state, and later in his report, adding any information that might allow him to be more specific.

Example:

"At some unknown time between April 5, 1997 and April 9, 1997."

d) *Where?*

All portions of the report which make reference to where an event occurred should be specific.

Example:

The body of the deceased was found in the kitchen of his home at 440 Maple Lane, Centerville, Kansas and was positioned as shown in the crime scene sketch. The suspect was apprehended at the northwest corner of the intersection of Park Ave. and Federal St., Centerville, Kansas in front of the Station Restaurant.

e) *How was the crime committed?*

This question seems to be the most problematic since police officers tend to be conclusion oriented and feel that the solution can be found in the answers to the first four questions. The fact is the officer usually has to answer the "how" question before he can fully answer the others. Because this information, when contained in the report, is the heart of the investigation, it will draw the closest scrutiny during cross-examination. In law enforcement, the *how* is often referred to as the **modus operendi**. Modus operendi, or as it is more commonly referred to, MO, is the manner in which the crime was committed and includes the following:

- the weapon used,
- the manner of entry into a building, including types of tools used.
- the time and place of the occurrence,
- the type of items stolen,
- the type of wounds inflicted,

- the manner of escape,
- any other peculiarity which tends to categorize the manner in which the crime was committed.

The reporting of how a crime was committed requires great care and should be done with the utmost concentration. Never commit to an answer to that question until you are certain that you are correct, or unless it is made clear that the report is only estimating or offering an opinion.

f) *Motive*

Answer the question "Why was the crime committed?" and you've determined the motive for the crime. Since the desire to identify the motive for a crime invites speculation and even guessing, reporting on the question of motive requires extraordinary care. At most times during the investigation, the motive is almost always speculation. Motive is **never** an element of the crime. Therefore, legally it is not necessary to prove a motive in order to gain a conviction. It is important, however, to attempt to answer the question of motive since juries are always looking for the reason why a crime was committed, and the failure of the prosecution to provide an answer will often be seen as a weakness in the investigation and may lead to an acquittal.

Motive is personal to the offender and can rarely be known for certain unless he himself reveals it. It is recommended that the investigator include in his report facts uncovered which tend to point to a specific motive. Except in unusual circumstances, the report should not include the officer's opinion or conclusions as to motive. Any references to a specific motive should only be reported as possibilities. This point illustrates the importance of an effective post-arrest interrogation of the suspect.

Until the person who committed the crime actually tells you why he did it, the motive is going to remain an unanswered question. That does not, however, mean that the officer should not address the matter of motive in his report.

Example: Information included in the report:

"It is admitted that the suspect believed his wife was having an affair with one of the suspect's fellow workers, the deceased victim, Sam Bass. It is also known through statements given by witnesses (a list of whom should be included somewhere in the report referring to this point) who were present at the time, that the suspect had threatened the victim with physical violence if the affair wasn't terminated. The suspect is known to have told Arthur Murphy, another coworker of both the suspect and the victim, that the affair was "driving him crazy," and that he knows that if it doesn't stop, he'll do something extreme. It therefore follows that the motive for this crime may have been jealousy.

Note: Here, the officer lists all of the reasons from which a conclusion that jealousy was the motive for the killing, and suggests is as the motive without committing to it absolutely.

7. Specifics of Included Information

Every investigative report should include as much of the following information as comes to the attention of the investigator during the investigation:

a) *File title and file number.*

Every file title should refer specifically to the case reported and should be titled under the name of the victim or victimized property and the number usually reflects the year and number of the investigation (e.g., 98017, representing the 17th investigation by the section or department in 1998).

b) *Date prepared.*

Each report and each supplement to that report should include the date it was prepared and that date should be clearly distinguishable from the date on which the event reported occurred.

c) *Name of the reporting officer.*

d) *Other officers referred to in the report.* Their names should be listed together in a conspicuous place near the beginning of the report.

e) *Subject of the report.* Not the same as the file title, the subject of the report has to do with the specific matter or matters referred to in each report. Obviously, reports will differ in their subject matter and, therefore, the subject of each report should be identified by a brief descriptive word or phrase at the beginning of the report. You will notice on the sample report in the Appendix to this chapter that under item 10 there is a brief description of the subject of the report. Other examples:

- initiation of the investigation;
- debriefing of CI #47; acquisition of exhibits N-7, N-8, and N-9;
- post arrest statement of John Doe;
- identification of subscribers to telephone contact numbers;
- serving of subpoena.

f) *Each report should be written under a paragraph number.* This approach is easier than the narrative approach because the writer need not worry about connecting sentences or the flow of the sentences. It is clear, concise and specifically identifies each thought or phrase contained in the report. It leaves a lot less open for attack by the defense. Details should include headings for grouped, numbered paragraphs relating to such headings as: *Basis of Investigation, Targets,* and *Objectives.* This section should also include the known details of the activities of other officers.

g) *List of gathered evidence.*

Each report should include a list of evi-

dence collected, clearly setting out:
- When it was found;
- a complete description of the evidence
- where it was found (be as specific as possible and use a sketch when it is helpful to do so);
- how was it found (e.g., on view; on information received; as the result of subpoena; through the execution of a search warrant or during a search incident to an arrest)
- by whom it was found?

h) *Custody of evidence.*

Every report which refers to the acquisition of a piece of evidence should state clearly;
- the dates and times that each piece of evidence was found and by whom;
- where exactly it was found;
- when it changed custody;
- the names of the persons giving and taking possession of the evidence;
- the reasons for the exchange;
- the location of the evidence after the exchange.

This is distinguished from a Chain of Custody Report which should be a separate accounting sheet for each piece of evidence which traces the chain of that piece of evidence from acquisition to the courtroom.

i) *Indexing.*

The indexing section should include information about suspects or other subjects, other than law enforcement personnel, mentioned in the report.

Examples:

1) David Smith–NADDIS negative, 516 NW 34th Ave., Miami, FL, mobile telephone number (305) 555-2731.
2) Telephone number (305) 555-7179–NADDIS negative, telephone issued to Juan Manuel.
3) Clifford LNU–NADDIS pending, w/m, Colombian, approximately 25 yoa, 5'7", 130 lbs., medium complexion, black hair, brown eyes, works as stevedore on docks in Turbo, Colombia.

j) *Copies of exhibits.*

Where possible, photocopies of the exhibits referred to in the report should be attached to the report.

k) *Personal information and descriptions.*

When investigating a suspect, efforts should be made to obtain and report as much information about that person as possible. Below is a suggested list of matters that should be covered. It is not intended to be a complete list, as each case or subject may suggest other items to be reported.

Name: In full, using initials only where full name is not known. All aliases and the various spelling of those names along with nicknames should be included.

Addresses: Include all known addresses, past and present, indicating primary residences, offices or other addresses relevant to the subject's activity. Use applicable dates when known. All addresses should be descriptive enough to exclude all other addresses.

Color: Skin color and complexion.

Age: Give exact age and date of birth when known. When not known, estimate age noting that it is an estimate.

Marital status: Include maiden name or aliases of spouse or ex-spouse. List all other members of immediate family by name, sex, age, and present location.

Occupation: List all known occupations (including criminal occupations), names and addresses of employers and dates of employment.

Military service: Include branch, dates of entry and separation, rank at discharge, military occupation, units, dates and locations of overseas duty, and reference to disciplinary record or decorations. All of this information is available from the Military Records Department in St. Louis, MO.

Physical description: Include as much detailed information as is known, such as information regarding scars or tattoos, birthmarks, physical disabilities and aids (e.g., limp, missing fingers, glasses, hearing aid, etc.), and anything that sets this person apart from others (bites fingernails, large ears, unusual jewelry, distinctive dress, nervous habits, personality, etc.).

Photographs and sketches: Note approximate date taken or made and how present appearance may differ. And, if known, what caused the difference in appearance.

Locations: The report should identify all buildings or property relevant to the investigation by including all of the following information;

1) addresses: number and street, town or city.

2) description: number of floors, color, style, outbuildings, fences, distance from known landmarks (especially important in rural areas), and any other unusual or identifiable details.

Example:

The residence of the witness, John Doe, in on the north side of Hunter Road. It is a two story, wooden frame house, white in color. There is a porch on the front of the house that stretches the entire width of the house. Green awnings extend the length of the porch. The driveway is on the south side of the house and extends approximately fifty yards to a separate two car garage in the rear. It is the third house form the intersection of County Road 516, and 1/4 mile west of that intersection.

l) *Vehicles*

To the extent possible, provide all of the following information:

- year,
- make,
- model,
- color,
- license plate number,
- VIN number,
- identifying characteristics, such as customized chasis, tinted windows, wire wheels, phone antenna, damaged areas, ornaments, and any other information that will help to identify this vehicle from all others,
- registered owner.

m) *Property*
- description of the article (TV set, toaster, etc.),
- brand names,
- form,
- size, measurements, color,
- composition (steel, aluminum, plastic, paper, wood, etc.),
- design,
- value.

n) *Identifying marks or characteristics or serial numbers.*

o) *Memorandum of witness interviews.*

Typically, the officer will take notes of his interview with witnesses and later will reduce his notes to a formal memorandum of each interview. Far too often the investigator fails to show the notes or a draft of the memorandum to the witness. As a result of this failure, a problem often arises at trial when the memorandum is characterized as a prior statement of the witness, when more often than not, it would more properly be described as the interviewing officer's understanding of what the witness has said. The problem caused by the officer's failure to go over the statement with the witness is that the witness is unable to make corrections as to attributions which are inaccurate or to correct areas of misinterpretation by the investigator. The investigator who takes the statement should prepare a draft of the memorandum, then show it to the witness to determine whether there are any inaccuracies or misrepresentations in the report before it is finalized. Then, the investigator should have the witness initial each page and sign his name to the last page. If the statement was taken with the use of a tape or video recorder, the report should reflect that, and the location of the tape. This should be done as soon as possible after the taking of the statement.

2.04 Conclusions

When a report is poorly prepared, the effect upon the ultimate disposition of the investigation can be devastating. It can, and often does, result in a guilty defendant going free. This point is discussed and illustrated thoroughly in the chapter on cross-examination. The inconsistencies or inaccuracies of what is in a report and available information which was left out can make an officer's report his worst enemy when he is on the witness stand. In other ways, poorly written reports burden the progress of the investigation.

Avoiding costly mistakes is very easy, but can be somewhat time consuming. It is, however, time well spent. To achieve success as a report writer, care must be taken in the areas of:

1. Organization.
2. Accuracy. No mistakes or speculations. Completeness. All the facts.
3. Fairness. Eliminate bias, be completely objective.
4. Form. Arrangement of the material reported.

A properly prepared report can reap great rewards. Both short- and long-term success will be realized by the officer who takes sufficient time and makes the effort to do this job well. The officer will earn the respect of the prosecutor, the defense attorney, the judge, and most importantly, the jury.

Finally, any time that the officer makes a thorough and accurate effort in the preparation of the report, justice, for all parties, is better served.

Chapter 3

PRE-TRIAL

3.01 Introduction

Many investigators group case division into two main categories: the **investigation** and the **trial**. The thinking is that the investigator has done his job when the arrest is made and the evidence is secured. From that point on, the case belongs to the prosecutor and the officer moves on to another case without much thought to the investigation just handed to the DA. The prosecutor's job is to put the case together for trial and call the officer when he's needed to testify. Nothing could be further from the truth! The prosecution of a criminal case requires a joint effort from the beginning of the investigation to the trial verdict. Both the prosecutor and the investigator must work hand in hand, communicating frequently during the time lapse between the arrest and the trial.

This need for cooperation creates a third major category that is often overlooked and yet may be the most important of all. That category includes all of the matters referred to as **pre-trial matters**. This category is essentially the bridge between the investigation and the trial; the glue that binds the two into one flowing effort. Except that it might mislead one into excluding the importance and effect of pre-trial hearings, **preparation** would be a good word to describe the pre-trial function.

In this chapter, we will explore and examine the purpose and importance of preparing exhibits, witnesses and testimony, and anticipating defenses and other trial issues, and we will provide insight into the function of pre-trial hearings.

3.02 Pre-Trial Hearings

Every arrest triggers a process intended to shield an accused from an unjustified allegation, and to protect the defendant's constitutional rights. Tests and standards vary at each level of the proceedings, requiring more proof from the prosecution at every step. There are four types of proceedings which fall into this category: **grand jury**; **preliminary hearings**, or **probable cause hearings**; **pre-trial motions**; and **trial**.

A. Grand Jury Presentation

The Grand Jury system, as we know it, developed under English Common Law, and are juries of inquiry, employed exclusively in criminal cases and called upon to hear evidence and accusations gathered by investigative agencies or through subpoenas issued upon their own motion or that of the prosecuting attorney.

They are called **grand juries** because at common law they were comprised of a larger number of jurors than the **petit** or trial juries. At common law, the grand jury consisted of not less than twelve, nor more than twenty-three jurors. That is still the rule in many states. In others, the number is set by statute and varies from state to state. The Federal Rules of Criminal Procedure require, for Federal Grand Juries, a minimum of 16 jurors and a maximum of 23.

A jury acting on the presentation of evidence will return a **true bill** or **indictment** upon the agreement by a statutorily set number of jurors (usually two thirds) that the prosecution has satisfied its burden of proof. At the grand jury level, that burden is **probable cause**.

An increasing number of states are eliminating the need for grand jury indictments. Those states are proceeding with formal charging documents, sometimes called **criminal informations**, which are filed by the prosecutor. Most of those states, however, have retained the grand jury for use by prosecutors during certain investigations. These are called **investigative grand juries**, and are used prior to the filing of formal charges in cases where the prosecutor recognizes the need for more information than the police are able to provide without the ability to compel testimony of witnesses or have no other way to obtain evidence.

In some states, investigative grand juries can, and do, return indictments. In other jurisdictions, they are only advisory and act only to gather information upon which the prosecutor may decide to approve or reject the seeking of a complaint. If the DA approves, the information gathered by the grand jury may be used to convince the issuing authority, usually a judge or magistrate, that there is sufficient probable cause to issue a criminal complaint and warrant for arrest. Whether for the purpose of conducting investigations or obtaining indictments, the proceedings before a grand jury are secret and the disclosure of matters occurring there is greatly restricted. Unauthorized disclosure of matters occurring before a grand jury may

result in the filing of a Contempt of Court citation against the person making the disclosure and that person could find himself in jail. Unless authorized by statute or rule of court, even a police officer may not disclose that which he heard, saw, or said in the grand jury room to anyone (even a fellow officer), without leave of the court. When dealing with this matter, the officer should consult with the prosecutor in the jurisdiction served by the grand jury. Present at grand jury proceedings, in addition to the jury members, are the prosecutor, the case agent or officer, a court reporter, and the witness. The witness is not permitted to have counsel present in the jury room, although he may ask, at any time, that the proceedings be interrupted in order to allow him time to leave the room to consult with his attorney. Unless immunity has been granted to the witness, he has the right before, or at any time during his testimony, to invoke his Fifth Amendment privilege and refuse to testify. A grant of immunity, however, can be granted, and in such a case, the witness will be compelled to testify, or face a Contempt of Court citation, which can, and often does, result in the witness being confined to jail until he either purges himself of the contempt by testifying, or until the life of the grand jury expires (which often can be as long as 18 months).

B. Probable Cause Hearings

Although hearing procedures and sequences vary somewhat between jurisdictions, a great majority of jurisdictions provide a hearing, before a judicial officer, usually a magistrate or district justice. These hearings are used to determine if there is sufficient evidence to allow the case to proceed to a trial. At such a hearing, the prosecution must present a **prima facie** case.

According to case law, the test of prima

facie is met when the evidence against the defendant *will suffice until contradicted and overcome by other evidence.* Several states (Ohio is an example) commence an allegation by filing a criminal complaint, followed within thirty days by a presentation of the facts to a grand jury. Presentation of the case to the grand jury eliminates the need for a preliminary hearing. If, however, the 30-day time limit expires without the case being presented to the grand jury, the defendant is entitled to a preliminary, or probable cause, hearing. The reason for this either-or requirement is to satisfy the defendant's right for the facts to be heard by an impartial body of citizens or judicial officer within a reasonable time before being subjected to a trial. For the purposes of this text, we will call such hearings **preliminary hearings**. They are the first inquiry into the facts at which the defendant is present and may be represented by counsel.

1. Procedure

State law requires that a preliminary hearing be held within a specified time following the arrest of the defendant. Depending upon the jurisdiction, this period may be from as soon as 12 hours after the arrest to as many as 30 days or longer if continued on the motion of either side. At the hearing, the prosecution has the burden of presenting sufficient evidence to prove a prima facie case.

The prosecutor, or in the absence of a prosecuting attorney, the prosecuting officer may do this by presenting sufficient evidence and testimony to satisfy this burden. There is no obligation to present all of the evidence. Generally, the prosecutor prefers to offer as little evidence as is needed. To do otherwise is to give the defense more notice about the facts of the prosecution's case than may be desirable at that early stage of the proceedings.

The defendant, either by himself or through his attorney, is permitted to cross-examine the prosecution's witnesses and present witnesses and evidence of his own. In most jurisdictions, however, the defendant's presentation of evidence at a preliminary hearing is limited to evidence which tends to refute evidence presented by the prosecution.

Since, at preliminary hearings, the presiding judicial officer listens to the evidence in the light most favorable to the prosecution, the defendant is generally not entitled to present a defense. Whether or not the defendant is permitted to offer evidence for the purpose of attacking the credibility of specific witnesses by offering the conflicting testimony of his own witnesses is a matter that varies among jurisdictions, with most holding that since the evidence is to be examined in the light most favorable to the prosecution, the credibility of the witnesses is a matter to be attacked only at the trial level or at the time of hearings on matters brought up by way of a pre-trial motion.

Upon the completion of the testimony, the attorneys are generally permitted to argue the merits and significance of the evidence, after which the judicial officer (generally a magistrate) determines whether or not the evidence meets the burden of prima facia. If the evidence is not sufficient, the charges are dismissed and the defendant is released from further jurisdiction on that charge. If the evidence is sufficient, the case is bound over to the trial court.

2. Defense Options and Goals

When facing a preliminary hearing, the defendant has several options to consider. The manner in which the defendant exercises his options depends upon what he wishes to accomplish through the proceeding.

a) *Waiving the hearing.*

The defendant may waive the hearing, thereby saving the prosecution the responsibility of having to present prima facie evidence. If the defendant chooses to waive his hearing, he forgoes certain advantages which the hearing provides, including:

1) *At least partial disclosure of the prosecution's case.*

As already mentioned, the prosecution need not present all of its evidence at the preliminary hearing; only enough to satisfy the burden of prima facia. However, any information at this early stage of the proceedings will be beneficial to the defense. At the very least, the defense case. This will enable the defendant's attorney to find the weaknesses in the prosecution's case and to formulate a defense against the allegations. This alone is usually sufficient to encourage the defendant to proceed to a hearing rather than to waive it.

2) *A transcript of the testimony presented at the hearing*

If a court reporter is employed to take down the testimony at the preliminary hearing, a transcript of that testimony can be made. Such a transcript benefits the defense in that such a transcript serves to lock the witnesses into their testimony at the preliminary hearing, and if they give inconsistent testimony at the trial, the preliminary hearing transcript may be used against them for the purpose of either impeaching their credibility or as evidence of the true facts.

Example: At the preliminary hearing, the witness testified that the defendant's car was blue, and that the first three letters of the defendant's license number were TZR. At the trial, however, the same witness testified that the color of the defendant's car was brown and that the first three letters of the license plate were CZR. The prior testimony may be used either to attack the witness's credibility, or to show the truthfulness of one statement over the other (i.e., the defendant's car was actually brown and the first three letters of his license plate were CZR. The defendant may argue to the jury that the prosecution learned the color and license plate number of his car after the preliminary hearing. Therefore, the testimony at the preliminary hearing was incorrect, leading the jury to consider the question of reasonable doubt regarding whether or not it was the defendant's car that was leaving the crime scene).

3) *The possibility of the failure of the prosecution to meet its burden, thereby causing dismissal of the charges.*

When the prosecution fails to meet it's burden of proof at the preliminary hearing, the case will be dismissed, and the defendant will be released from further responsibilities under the charges. If, however, the charges are dismissed without prejudice, as is most often the case, the prosecution may apply to refile the charges. Most jurisdictions allow this even when the prosecution fails to show new or additional evidence. In such situations, the prosecution will probably offer more evidence at the hearing than they did at the first hearing.

Why the defendant would ever waive his hearing? There are circumstances under which waiving the hearing is in the defendant's best interests in spite of the benefits of having such a hearing. These benefits include:

• *The possibility of a plea-agreement.*

If the defendant and the prosecutor have agreed to a specific disposition of the case, a plea may be made before the magistrate, or, if the charges are such that they are beyond the jurisdiction of the magistrate, the defendant will agree to waive the hearing and the plea will be taken before a judge at the trial court level.

- In other instances where the defendant intends to plead guilty or request acceptance to a special program allowing for a disposition of the case without a trial or plea of guilty, *he may wish to avoid the added publicity which may accompany a preliminary hearing.*
- *The defendant may want to appear cooperative with the officer or the prosecutor by relieving the prosecution of the burden of a preliminary hearing.* Usually, in return for the waiver, the defendant will make some agreement to obtain a proffer of the evidence or expanded discovery. If the prosecutor is hoping to work out a plea agreement later and doesn't want to expose the weaknesses in the case that might come out during a preliminary hearing, he may be willing to supply the defendant with copies of the police reports, lab reports, the identity of one or more of the witnesses along with the witnesses' statements, or other evidence that would probably be presented at the hearing. Also, by doing this, the prosecutor will not be required to present the testimony of his witnesses, thereby denying the defense of any "prior testimony" that such a hearing would provide to the defense for use in confronting the witnesses during the trial. Absent such motivations, a defendant will rarely waive a preliminary hearing.

b) *Passive attendance.*

Most often, the defendant will force a preliminary hearing but not present evidence himself. The defendant will use the proceeding merely as a means of discovering as much as possible about the prosecution's evidence, and to lock the witnesses into their testimony. For that reason, the presence of a court reporter is important to the defense attorney.

Seldom does the police officer have the opportunity to prepare as well for a preliminary hearing as he does for trial. If there is time to discuss the case with the prosecuting attorney prior to the hearing, it will probably be brief unless the case involves a charge of homicide or some other complicated or serious offense. The defense attorney knows this and will take advantage of it if he is able. He will meticulously probe each witness for facts which will form the basis for a pre-trial motion or a defense at trial. The aggressive defense attorney considers this opportunity crucial to his client's chances for a successful defense.

With discovery as his goal, the defendant will almost never present evidence at the preliminary hearing. To do so would allow the prosecution an opportunity to uncover at least something of the defense strategy, and to lock the defense witnesses into their testimony. Obviously, the defendant wants to avoid that, preferring instead to spring the defense at trial, thereby depriving the prosecution of the ability to properly prepare for the defense.

c) *Presentation of defense witnesses.*

Though the defendant has a limited right to do so, he will rarely present evidence on his own behalf at a preliminary hearing unless he feels that offering such evidence will provide a realistic opportunity for the case to be dismissed or the charges to be reduced. If the defendant has a legitimate defense, such as an alibi, he may have offered it to the investigator or prosecutor prior to the hearing in the hope that the proceeding might be avoided and the charges withdrawn. The presiding magistrate or justice is not, in most jurisdictions, empowered to rule on matters of a constitutional nature, such as a defense allegation that the evidence was illegally seized, or that a confession was improperly extracted from the defendant. Those matters, as we shall see, are most often handled by the trial court judge pursuant to pre-trial motions.

3. The Officer as the Prosecutor

From time to time, in almost every state jurisdiction, the police investigator is faced with having to handle a preliminary hearing without the assistance of a prosecuting attorney. These usually involve minor offenses, but occasionally the officer will be forced to handle a hearing on a major felony on his own. In such instances, the officer would do well to keep the following in mind:

a) *Meet with the prosecutor and discuss with him what evidence and witnesses are needed.* In difficult cases, even though the prosecutor may not be available for the hearing, he will usually be eager to provide guidance as to how the hearing should be handled.

b) *Collect the evidence and contact the witnesses.* It is also wise to interview the witnesses again before the hearing. Make sure you and the witnesses are on the same page. Witnesses tend to forget, or even change their minds about wanting to become involved in the prosecution of the case. They don't mind providing the officer with information at the time of the investigation, but when it comes time to go to court, they sometimes become less willing to cooperate.

c) *Prepare the presentation.* When doing so, *make a list of the elements of the crime* and anticipate presenting the minimum of evidence required to satisfy those elements, thereby presenting a prima facie case. Keep in mind that you must present prima facia evidence on each of the elements. The idea is to avoid massive discovery by the defense but still get your case bound over for a trial. If it is possible to present evidence sufficient to have the case bound over to the trial court without using your strongest evidence, you will avoid having to expose that evidence.

Example: Burglary–The defendant was seen leaving the victim's residence by a neighbor who heard the alarm go off just before the defendant came out. The defendant's fingerprints were found in the house. The defendant was identified by a pawn broker as the person who pawned one of the stolen items, and the defendant, in his statement after arrest, offered an alibi that the investigator is able to disprove.

As in every case, the officer must first prove that a crime was committed (corpus delecti). In a burglary case, that can be accomplished by offering the testimony of the owner of the property to prove that his house or business was entered by a person who had no authority to enter; that certain items were taken, and that the defendant was not authorized to enter the building or to remove anything from it. The officer might then call to the stand the witness who can identify the defendant as the person leaving the building. If his identification is strong, there may not be a need to present any other evidence, especially if he is also able to identify items which the defendant had in his possession when he left the building. If the identification needs corroboration, the officer might wish to produce the fingerprint evidence. Save the testimony of the pawn broker and the person who can destroy the alibi for the trial. If the defendant gave a self-incriminating statement, prove the corpus delecti, offer the defendant's confession, and rest.

d) *The use of a court reporter is a consideration in some cases.* Usually the prosecution will not request that the testimony be recorded, but there are some circumstances that may present such a need. If there is a reason to believe that an important witness may, due to illness, age, or other circumstances, die or be otherwise unavailable to appear at the trial, it is recommended that his or her testimony be transcribed. If the defendant has the opportunity to cross examine the witness, even if that witness is unavailable for trial, the testimony will be received at trial by reading the transcript of the witness's preliminary hearing testimony. The defendant need not have exercised his right to cross examine, it is only necessary that he was afforded the opportunity to do so. If you are aware of any circumstances that would raise the advisability of having the preliminary hearing transcribed, you should inform your prosecuting attorney of those circumstances as soon as those circumstances arise so as to allow him the time to consider the matter and secure the services of a court stenographer.

4. Hearsay at Preliminary Hearings

In most jurisdictions, the use of hearsay is permitted at preliminary hearings as long as the prosecutor is able to assure the magistrate that the witness will be available for trial, and the officer should take advantage of that. By testifying himself about statements made to him by witnesses, the defense is deprived of the opportunity to attack that witness on cross-examination. Nor can that witness effectively be cross-examined at trial about the officer's preliminary hearing testimony. Check with the prosecutor in your jurisdiction concerning the rules and case law concerning limitations on the use of hearsay at preliminary hearings.

C. Summary Proceedings

In most jurisdictions, the magistrate's court *is* the trial court in cases involving summary offenses or other offenses which do not go on to a misdemeanor and felony court. Some jurisdictions have separate courts for misdemeanor and felony offenses. Still other jurisdictions allow the magistrate to dispose of minor misdemeanors as well as summary offenses. Most traffic violations are summary offenses as are some cases of disorderly conduct, retail theft, and other minor offenses. In such cases, the rules of evidence apply just as they would at the trial of a felony or misdemeanor offense, and the rules allowing hearsay at a preliminary hearing disallow it when the hearing is a trial within the jurisdiction of the magistrate.

These cases are usually factually simple cases to handle and the officer will often find it his responsibility to present the evidence without the assistance of a prosecuting attorney.

Situations arise from time to time which can complicate matters for the prosecuting officer. Defense arguments regarding a particular point of law through which the defense hopes to have one or more of the charges dismissed are a frequent problem for the officer handling the hearing without the aid of a prosecutor. All but the best of magistrates, the great majority of whom are not attorneys, are sometimes intimidated by the defense attorney's persuasiveness. This may lead to the failure of some or all of your charges. When this or other problems appear to the officer to be insurmountable, a request should be made to delay the proceedings, explaining that the case is too important not to take precautions to protect it from dismissal on the strength of an argument which the officer believes to be incorrect. He should inform the magistrate that he wants the opportunity to contact the prosecutor's office for advice or assistance. Generally, such an argument is made at the conclusion of the hearing, and the court will most often delay his ruling on the matter in order to allow the officer to contact the prosecutor. In matters arising prior to the end of the testimony, the officer should inform the magistrate of his concern over the court's ruling; and if the ruling might have the effect of putting the officer's case out of court, he should ask for a short recess and call the prosecutor's office. Even a rookie officer should never be reluctant to call a prosecutor in such a situation. That's what they get paid for!

D. Suppression Hearings

Suppression hearings are proceedings brought upon motion of an accused before the trial court for the purpose of determining the admissibility of some or all of the evidence in possession of the prosecution. The basis of these motions is found in the **Exclusionary Rule**, first defined in the case of *Weeks v. U.S.*, 232 U.S. 383 (1914), which essentially states that evidence obtained by the police or their agents in violation of a defendant's constitutional rights will be excluded from the trial of the defendant's case. Over the years, the Exclusionary Rule has been redefined and expanded, or limited, in every jurisdiction in the United States. What follows is intended to familiarize you with the types and styles of motions which are being filed by defendants in criminal cases.

Note: The law will not be the same in all jurisdictions, and in matters posing the potential for a suppression motion, the officer should consult with his county prosecutor.

There are basically two types of suppression motions:

1. Motions to Suppress Physical Evidence

Motions of this type are brought by defendants in an effort to cause the trial court to exclude certain evidence from the defendant's trial. These motions usually involve evidence gathered by the police during a search of the defendant's person or property, and allege that the evidence was seized in violation of the defendant's Fourth Amendment right to be free from unreasonable searches and seizures. Such a motion may also allege that the seizure was the result of a bad interrogation. Most often, searches of the defendant's home, or automobile, will be conducted upon the authority of a search warrant. A search warrant will issue upon the showing of probable cause to believe that certain property or contraband held illegally by the defendant is located at the place to be searched. This information is included in an affidavit to the warrant, and must be specific as to the type and description of the items to be seized. It is also required that the property to be searched be described in such a way as to exclude all other properties. Your prosecutor will be willing to help you to compose the warrant and affidavit.

Even when the officer has the right to enter the defendant's property to search, there are times when the defendant will complain that at least some of the evidence should be suppressed. These will usually be based on the complaint that the officer exceeded his right to search.

Situation 3-1: The officer obtains a warrant to search the home of the defendant.

Proper entry is made and the search begins. The warrant asks for the right to search for a television, two stereos, and a motorcycle believed to have been taken in a burglary, and now in the possession of the defendant. All of the items to be seized have been sufficiently described. The officers search for one-half hour and find all of the items listed in the warrant. The search is continued, however, in hopes that other contraband or stolen items will be found.

Questions by the defense attorney at the suppression hearing:

Q. Officer Grant, when you applied for the warrant to search my client's home, you listed all of the items you believed you might find there, is that correct?

A. That's correct.

Q. And, when you went to my client's house, you searched for and found all of the items you were looking for, is that correct?

A. That's correct.

Q. However, when you had found all that was on the warrant, you continued to search, isn't that correct also?

A. Yes, that's correct.

Q. And, it was during this part of the search that you found the cocaine, isn't that correct?

A. Yes.

Note: In this situation, the officer went beyond the limits of his authority to search, and in most jurisdictions, the cocaine would be suppressed, even though the items he found pursuant to the warrant would be admissible.

Situation 3-2: While searching for a stolen television and two stolen stereos, the police search the dresser drawers in the defendant's bedroom.

Questions by the defense attorney at the suppression hearing.

Q. Officer, you went into my client's house and property with a warrant to search for a television, two stereo units, and a motorcycle, is that correct?

A. That's correct.

Q. And nothing else was included in your warrant to search, is that correct?

A. Yes.

Q. And while searching for these things, you looked in my client's dresser drawer, is that correct?

A. That's correct.

Q. May I assume that you did not expect to find the television or the stereos or the motorcycle inside one of the drawers, correct?

A. That's correct.

Note: The case law regarding search and seizure does not allow the police to search in places where they could not reasonably find those items for which they are authorized to search. As the saying goes; "You can't search for an elephant in a match box."

Note: However, if the police had been authorized to search for cocaine and not any other drug, and had found marijuana, or drugs other than cocaine, they could legally have seized those drugs since one could expect to find cocaine in any location, no matter how small. Any contraband, other than that for which the officers are authorized to search, may be seized if the search is conducted in places where they may reasonable expect to find the items targeted by the warrant.

Note: *Always be prepared to testify as to the order of the areas searched and the order of the items found.* If the attorney is able to convince the court that at some point the search went bad (e.g., the search extended into areas not allowed under the warrant), everything that came after that point may be lost, and at times, and under certain circumstances, even that which was found before that may be lost.

2. Motions to Suppress Statements

Any time a defendant provides the police with a statement admitting to all or part of the crime, the defendant's attorney will always scrutinize the situation and the statement for the possibility of errors which may give rise to a motion to suppress that statement.

The first place where the defense will attempt to obtain evidence to support such a motion is likely to come at the preliminary hearing while the attorney is cross-examining the police officer. If the defense is able to get what they want from that hearing, you may be certain that information will form the basis of the defendant's motion.

Assuming that the arrest is lawful and the statement is not the result of illegal police activity, the defendant may move to suppress a statement that he concedes giving, on the basis that it was taken in violation of his right to remain silent under the Fifth Amendment, alleging that:

a) there were no effective warnings given to the defendant;

b) the statement was not given voluntarily, since the police used unfair tactics during the interrogation, or;

c) the statement was given after the defendant asked to speak with an attorney before going any further with the interview.

Note: When testifying before a jury, it is advisable for the testifying officer to refer to the interrogation as an interview rather than an interrogation. The word *interview* carries a far less intimidating connotation than does the word *interrogation.*

This section is not intended to provide instruction in the area of Constitutional Law, but it will suffice here to point out that such motions usually claim that the defendant was not adequately advised of his right to remain silent, that he did not understand that right, or that unfair tactics were used to obtain the statement. If you wish to see a sample of such a motion, your county prosecutor should be more than willing to accommodate you. It is *critically* important that the officer who testifies at a suppression hearing understands the concepts of the controlling law. You should, at a minimum, understand what the defense is trying to accomplish, and why, before you take the stand. *You should always read the motion before the hearing.* Doing this will give you an understanding of the weaknesses in your case and how the facts affect the issues, and it will also help you to avoid being led into pitfalls by the defense attorney's questions. This is not to suggest that the officer should testify untruthfully, but as any courtroom savvy officer knows, a clever defense attorney will have ways of leading an unwitting witness into trouble before the witness realizes his plight. This can result in the facts being changed enough to turn a good seizure, or confession, into a bad one.

3.03 Understanding the Trial Issues

Before an investigator goes into court to testify, he should understand the issues that will be the focus of the trial.

A. Elements of the Offense

It is always important that the investigator understands the elements of the offense. They are the acts or conditions that make up the offense and must be proven beyond a reasonable doubt before a defendant can be convicted. The prosecution must meet this burden on *all* of the elements of *each* charge. *Example:* Burglary, sample statute:

A person is guilty of burglary if he enters

a building or occupied structure, or separately secured or occupied portion thereof, with intent to commit a crime therein, unless the premises are at the time open to the public or the actor is licensed or privileged to enter, Section 3502, Pennsylvania Crimes Code Annotated, Sheldon S. Toll.

Elements:

1. Entry or actual penetration of the building must be made by the actor, or a portion of the actor's body, or by some instrument or tool operated by the actor,
2. The building must be an occupied structure as opposed to an abandoned one. There is no requirement that the occupants of the building be present at any time during the burglary. Some jurisdictions recognize the crime as being more serious when it is occupied by increasing the penalty if any person or persons are present when the burglary is committed.
3. There must be an intent to commit a crime (e.g., theft) inside the building; and,
4. The actor must not have been licensed or privileged to enter.

If the investigator understands these elements, it follows that he should be aware of what evidence will be required to prove them. Understanding the elements gives direction to the investigation, and allows the officer to adequately prepare himself, his witnesses, and his exhibits for trial.

B. Special Issues

In addition to the elements, other issues are important to the investigator preparing to go to court:

1. Motive

Though motive is never an element of an offense, proving it is always valuable to the prosecution of any case. It gives the jury an additional reason to believe that the evidence proves the defendant's guilt. The investigator should always be alert for evidence of a suspect's motive for committing the crime. Discovering motive can, and usually does, lead to the development of a suspect.

The officer on the stand should take special care when testifying about motive. Any conclusions reached by the officer should be based on evidence that reasonably points to the motive, and not on pure speculation. This point is discussed in more detail in the preceding chapter on report writing, and also in the chapter on direct examination.

2. Modus Operandi

In many cases, understanding the manner of operation employed in the commission of the crime avails the investigator of valuable evidence against a defendant. Often the modus operendi, or MO, will provide valuable information about the person who committed the crime. For example, the manner of entry into a building may indicate that the actor was a small person, or an agile person, or that the actor was known to the victim.

This information is important in developing a suspect and provides circumstantial evidence against the defendant at trial. In considering evidence of modus operandi, the investigator should be ever mindful that inconsistent MO evidence can be very damaging in court.

Example: In one particular case, the manner of entry was through a hole cut in the metal wall of a building. The hole was far too small to have accommodated the defendant in the case, against whom other convincing evidence existed, tending to prove his participation in the crime. This evidence therefore suggested the existence of a second burglar who was eventually captured and convicted. Had that inconsistency not been resolved, the defense, in pointing out the impossibility of his client's ability to gain entry in the manner suggested by the prosecution, could have created a reasonable doubt in the jury's mind about the remaining evidence.

3. Evidence Identification and Examination

The jury's understanding and appreciation of exhibits is always important to the credibility, and sometimes the admissibility, of evidence. If there is any question as to whether or not the integrity of the evidence has been preserved, or whether or not the evidence can be preserved after its collection, one should make every effort to effect its preservation or restoration. Often, the manner of collection will determine the ultimate integrity of a piece of evidence.

If the collection has adversely affected the evidence, the officer should immediately bring the problem to the attention to one of his supervisors, or explore the possibility that a certain type of expert in the relevant field may be able to save the evidence for its eventual admission into evidence against the defendant. The prosecutor's office can be of assistance in this type of matter and often will undertake the task itself.

3.04 Understanding and Preparing for Anticipated Defenses

If the defendant chooses to go to trial on his case, his attorney will offer or suggest, and argue, either some defense to the allegations against his client, or some reason why the prosecution's case is not strong enough to convict his client. The defense may accomplish this by effective cross-examination of the prosecution's witnesses, or by the presentation of witnesses and exhibits tending to support the chosen defense.

Each offense suggests possible defenses. For example, the nature of the offense or the relationship between the defendant and the victim may suggest a defense. Here we examine some of those defenses called affirmative defenses, the likely crimes which suggest them, and how to prepare to meet them.

An affirmative defense is one in which the defense offers evidence tending to show that the defendant could not have committed the offense, or that the evidence excuses, justifies, or mitigates the defendant's actions (e.g., alibi, accident, self-defense, insanity).

In most jurisdictions, the defendant has the burden of proving the affirmative defenses by a preponderance of the evidence. In others, the defendant need only allege the defense, either through the cross-examination of prosecution witnesses or by his own witnesses. In those jurisdictions, the prosecution must then assume the burden of disproving the defense. Checking with the prosecutor will insure that the investigator is aware of which rule prevails in his jurisdiction.

A. Insanity Defense

The test required to satisfy the insanity defense varies among jurisdictions, and the investigator should acquaint himself with the test or tests employed in his jurisdiction.

The investigator will usually find that the more serious or heinous the crime, the more likely the chance of the *insanity defense.* Multiple or particularly brutal murders, for example, often suggest the possibility of such a defense. The apparent senselessness of a crime, or evidence of ritual or other strange activity by the perpetrator before, during, or following the commission of the crime, also serves as an indication that the defendant may avail himself of the defense.

Since the insanity defense is an "I did it . . . but" defense, it is seldom seen in cases where the defendant's identification is in question. If this defense is anticipated, the investigator should, in preparing to meet it, take the following investigative steps:

1. Look for evidence of planning, secretiveness, or flight.

   The defenses of "insanity" or other mental infirmity (diminished capacity, irresistible impulse, heat of passion, etc.), are intended to negate the element of specific intent and, depending upon the degree of the defendant's illness, to lower the degree of the crime, or excuse the defendant completely. Such actions by the defendant as planning, secretiveness or flight are evidence of the defendant's awareness of the wrongful nature of his act, and of his ability to form the specific intent required to complete the crime.

2. Inquire of witnesses concerning the defendant's actions, demeanor, and statements made prior to, during, and following the actual commission of the crime. Evidence of cool, calculated actions or words consistent with intent or plan are especially valuable pieces of evidence in combating a defense based on mental infirmity.

3. Check with the defendant's family, fellow employees, classmates, friends, and neighbors regarding the defendant's pattern of behavior prior to the crime. The defense attorney will interview them with the hope of securing statements from them about the defendant's behavior that will support a contention that the defendant's mental illness was pronounced and of some duration. In his attempt to confirm his own beliefs or to otherwise protect his client, the defense attorney may, and often does, sometimes unwittingly, use his powers of persuasion or suggestion to obtain the desired information.

   If the investigator is able to interview these people about the defendant's demeanor and behavior without suggesting the possibility of mental infirmity before the defense has an opportunity to interview them, the truth about what is known of the defendant's mental condition is more likely to be forthcoming. If it is clear to them by the defense attorney that the defendant's mental condition is an issue in determining his guilt or innocence, people who are friends or relatives of the defendant will sometimes make statements tending to support the defense, either out of a desire to help the defendant or because they believe it impossible that the defendant could have committed the crime charged unless he was mentally unstable.

4. Make notes of the defendant's demeanor after his arrest and ask jailers to do the same. If his alleged condition is an act, the defendant will usually do or say things after his arrest, or in the jail, which are inconsistent with his claim.

5. If the nature or manner of commission of a crime is particularly unusual or gruesome, the officer should consider the possibility that a sane perpetrator may be copying the crime, either from a known crime already committed by someone else, or from a novel or movie the defendant may have read or seen.

B. Alibi Defense

The defense of *alibi* is used when the defendant contends that he was somewhere other than the scene of the crime at the time of its commission. The defendant may suggest an alibi at the time of his arrest, or he may develop one at some later time.

Obviously, a legitimate alibi is going to

absolve the defendant. It is not uncommon, however, for the defendant to fabricate an alibi. He may find family members or friends who will lie for him, or he may have set up an alibi in advance of the commission of the crime (e.g., punch a time clock at work, leave, commit the crime, return to work, and punch out at the end of the day). In any case, the investigator must investigate the alibi as soon as he suspects or becomes aware of the intention of the defendant to rely on that defense.

1. If the defendant claims to have been out of town, press him for the name of the hotel or the address of the residence where he stayed, his mode of travel, and the name of the common carrier. If he drove, ask him for gasoline credit card receipts or for information about where he stopped to refuel. Even if his alibi is legitimate, he may have trouble remembering some details, but if he appears vague about most of the information, or refuses to give details, he is probably not being truthful.

2. Ask him what he was doing at the time the crime was being committed, whom he dealt with, or who may have seen him. If the defendant gives the names of some people he expects will support his claim of alibi, interview them separately, probing into contradictions between that person's statement and that of the defendant or other witnesses. A defendant who asks someone to provide a false alibi seldom rehearses the details of the alibi with that person.

3. Inquire about details of his activity. If he had lunch with someone else, where and with whom. If he witnessed an unusual event, what and where; what the weather was like; what topics were discussed in any conversation he had with others.

The more details you are able to gather, the easier it will be to trip up the phony alibi. Be aggressive in your inquiries. Don't accept vague answers. Press for details. Don't count on the strength of your case to rebut the alibi, check it out yourself.

C. Entrapment Defense

A person is entrapped when he is induced or persuaded by law enforcement officers, or their agents, to commit a crime that he was not otherwise predisposed to commit. This defense is most often used by defendants who are charged with making a sale of narcotics to an undercover police officer or informant, but can be used in any case where the defendant had contact with the police officer or an informant prior to or during the commission of the crime.

If the transaction was taped (video or audio), and it should be whenever possible, the defense is obviously much more difficult to assert. The defendant's words will be on tape for the jury to hear in the face of his allegations of persuasion or coercion by the police. The officer should be aware that at times the defendant will, even without knowing that the officer or his agent is wired, make exculpatory statements such as, "you now, if it weren't for you, I wouldn't be involved in this kind of thing." The officer should not let a statement by the defendant, who is trying to cover all the bases, stand uncontested. If he does, the statement will come back to haunt the prosecution at the trial of the case. Instead, he should call him on the statement when it is made. An appropriate response will depend on the defendant's statement, but should have the effect of blunting the statement or exposing the reason for it.

Example:

Statement by the suspect: "You know, I didn't want to do this. I don't know how I let you talk me into stuff like this."

Response by the undercover officer: "What are you talking about, this whole thing was your idea. What's going on? Are you working with the police, or wired or something?"

Note: It should be noted, however, that the entrapment defense does not apply simply because the police, or their agent or informant, initially raises the subject of the illegal activity to the defendant, or even suggests to the defendant that he should commit, or participate in the commission of the crime. The police are permitted to offer or create an opportunity for the defendant to commit the crime. It is only important that he does not provide additional inducements for doing the illegal act.

Proof of other drug dealing activity by the defendant who claims to have been entrapped will severely damage his assertion that he was not predisposed to commit that crime.

If the defendant had contact with an undercover officer on previous occasions when the officer was unable to purchase narcotics from him, the subsequent meetings should be taped because of the likelihood that the defendant will allege that he refused to sell narcotics to the officer on the first occasion or occasions, and that it was only after the officer provided inducements or played on his sympathy that the defendant finally agreed to deliver the drugs.

D. Lack of Guilty Knowledge or Intent

If a defendant claims lack of guilty knowledge, or that the act was a mistake, or that he lacked unlawful intent, he must first admit that he committed the act. At such times, the defendant will usually acknowledge most of the basic facts which show that he committed the act, yet he will deny knowing that it

was wrong or that he intended any wrongdoing.

Depending on the crime, one will usually be able to overcome this defense by finding evidence of:

1. Motive;
2. Planning and preparation;
3. Conspiratorial relationship;
4. Experience and expertise of the defendant in the matter about which he claims ignorance;
5. Flight;
6. Destruction or concealment of evidence;
7. Intimidation of witnesses by the defendant;
8. Evidence of other, similar crimes (MO).

E. Self-Defense

The claim of self-defense is a contention by the defendant that he committed the act alleged, but not the crime charged, for the reason that the victim, by his threatening actions against the defendant or another, left no reasonable alternative for the defendant, but to act as he did.

If the defendant assaulted or killed another person and claims self-defense, the jury will be asking a number of questions in the jury room. The answers at which they arrive will determine the outcome of the case and will depend, to a large extent, on the thought given to them by the investigation in anticipation of the defense being raised. In self-defense cases, you may anticipate jurors to consider the following:

1. Was there a weapon used?
2. What is the nature of the injury?
3. What was the degree of force used?
4. Did the defendant have an obligation to withdraw?
5. Did the defendant have a reasonable opportunity to withdraw?

6. Does the defendant have a prior history of violent behavior?
7. What was the nature of the relationship between the defendant and the victim?
8. Were there any witnesses to the assault, and are they associated with the defendant?
9. Does the physical evidence square with the defendant's version of the facts?
10. Was the defendant acting in a reasonable manner to defend himself or another from the probability of death or serious bodily harm at the hands of the victim?

Note: If the officer is aware of the impact of the answers to these questions, he will be more likely to make an attempt to answer them prior to the trial and to make an effort to repair or explain any damage they may have on the prosecution's case.

F. Factual Defenses

1. Reasonable Doubt

Unlike the defenses listed above, the defense of reasonable doubt is not an affirmative defense: therefore, the defendant has no burden of proof to make the defense. The law requires that the prosecution proves its case beyond a reasonable doubt. Most courts define a reasonable doubt as such a doubt as would cause a reasonably prudent man to pause or hesitate before acting on a matter of great importance in his own life. The court will instruct the jury that if the prosecution does not meet this burden, the defendant must be acquitted.

Defense attorneys will seize upon the slightest inconsistency or flaw in a case and, by expanding or magnifying it, argue that the shortcomings of the prosecution should create a reasonable doubt in the minds of the jury and result in the acquittal of the defendant.

This defense will be used in one way or another, in every jury trial and, knowing this, *the police officer should search for the weaknesses in his case and bolster them where possible.*

For example, the defendant may raise the question of reasonable doubt about the strength of the evidence offered to prove the elements of the offense, or even that proof of one or more of the elements was omitted all together. They may argue reasonable doubt concerning the facts, or the testimony of one or more of the witnesses offered by the prosecution, or the proof regarding the defendant's identity, or of any other matter of importance to the prosecution's case.

Note: The officer should never rely on the prosecutor to find and deal with the weaknesses in the case. As distasteful as it is, the best results are achieved by the officer who reviews his statements and evidence, then reviews them again. Every time the facts of a case are reviewed, something new will appear that the reader hadn't seen on an earlier review. *It's your case to win or lose, not the prosecutor's!*

2. Conflicting Identification

It is not unusual for witnesses to disagree on the identification of suspects in criminal cases, even when all had the same opportunity to observe the person. There are several ways these differences arise:

a) *Descriptions*

It is not unusual for different witnesses to give conflicting descriptions of the same person. If the identity of the actor is a question to be resolved at the trial, conflicting descriptions present a problem for the prosecution and should be reconciled as early as possible, if possible. If the investigator makes reasonable inquiries into the reasons for the description given, he will find that often the differences can be explained and remedied.

Example: In a bank robbery case, one teller described the robber as being five feet seven or eight inches tall; the other said he was about five feet four inches tall, a significant difference. Upon further questioning by the investigator, it was learned that both of the tellers were judging the size of the robber by their own height. When the teller who was about five feet four inches herself and who described the robber as about her own height, realized that she was wearing high heels at the time, she changed her description to five feet six to seven inches tall, still somewhat different from the description given by the other teller, but not significantly. Keep in mind that if the witnesses are judging the height of a suspect on the basis of their own size, they sometimes tend to estimate those who are taller than they as taller than they actually are, and those shorter than themselves less than their actual height.

Most of the time, an investigator who is willing to take his time and make detailed inquiries will be able to find an explanation for discrepancies, especially large ones, in descriptions given by witnesses.

3. Line-ups (Both Live and Photo)

More troublesome than discrepancies in descriptions is the situation where two witnesses view the same line-up or photopack and, either pick two different people, or only one witness is able to make any identification. Here, the officer has to be very careful because if the court is convinced that, in any way, the line-up was suggestive, the identification will probably be excluded from the trial.

It is proper to explore with the witness who does not pick the suspect, areas concerning eyesight, distance, or obstructions

that may have caused confusion in the witness's mind or rendered him uncertain in his identification. Don't carry on such a conversation with the witness while he is in the process of viewing the line-up or photopack. Again, it could be considered suggestive. Obviously, discussions with the witness prior to the viewing concerning these matters will be helpful during the line-up. For example, if there were three eye witnesses and each of them had a different viewing angle, those in the line-up may be required to assume a position which is consistent with the viewpoint of each witness.

Further discussion on this matter is found in the Chapter on Cross Examination.

4. Lack of Physical Evidence

Defense attorneys will always argue that there isn't enough evidence to convict their clients. Making a thorough and timely search for all available evidence will make it difficult, or impossible, for the defense to put them on the defensive by suggesting that their investigation was not complete. Such preventative measures will, at least, minimize the effect of his argument.

5. Prosecution's Reliance on Testimony of Accomplice or Informant

In the eyes of the law, the testimony of accomplices and informants differs somewhat from the testimony of other witnesses, but are viewed pretty much the same by juries.

The law, as charged by the courts in most jurisdictions, is that the testimony of an *accomplice* must be considered with more caution than the testimony of other witnesses because the testimony is said to emanate from a corrupt source, and that in testifying against a partner in crime, the witness may, hoping to get more favorable treatment in his own case, give false testimony against his partner.

Regarding the testimony of the paid informant or the informant who is facing other unrelated problems of his own, the courts caution juries that such testimony must be considered more carefully than that of other witnesses because such a witness may have reason to make a false statement. Naturally, defense attorneys use that charge to their best advantage whenever possible. In such cases, it is important to be able to corroborate the witness's statement with as much evidence as possible.

Any evidence that tends to support the testimony of such a witness is important. Audio and photographic surveillance are recommended ways of gathering supporting evidence. Picking an informant who has a clean background and commendable motives is another.

If the investigator uses his common sense, he will be able to analyze the possible defenses in almost any case. This is an appropriate application of the old saying, "to be forewarned is to be forearmed."

3.05 Gathering Evidence For Trial

Juries are favorably impressed when the prosecution's case is presented in an organized and orderly fashion. This often translates into the jurors taking a more favorable view of the evidence and has on many occasions resulted in a weak case becoming stronger, and a strong case becoming almost impregnable.

Preparation is the key to such a presentation. Much of that preparation is the responsibility of the prosecutor, but other responsibilities fall on the shoulders of the investigator.

A. Witnesses

Witnesses for the prosecution should be interviewed prior to going into court concerning the facts about which they will testify and about what to expect when they get to the courtroom. Often the prosecutor prefers to do this, but if he does not, the investigating officer should. Emphasize for the witnesses that they should use their own words when giving their testimony. Tell then that they should answer only the questions asked. Too many times you will get a witness who, when asked what time it is, wants to tell you how to make a watch. Remember, most of these witnesses have never been in court before. They will be nervous and looking for direction. In order to help them through the process of preparing to go into court, each witness should have been briefed in the following way.

1. Review with the witness, in a general way, all of the important facts to be covered in his testimony. Refresh his recollection if you must, but let him tell you in his own words what it is that he will say. If you tell him what his prior statements were, or tell him too much about how to testify, he will be trying to remember what you said instead of using his energy on his own recollection of the facts. In short, the witness should be encouraged to remember what happened, not what you think happened.

2. Talk with the witness about what to expect when he gets to the courtroom. The witness will be nervous about it and will be looking to you for guidance. Don't sugar-coat it, but don't overdramatize it either. Explain to him that the jurors will be people just like him, and that the prosecutor is there to protect him from unfair questioning and harassment by the defense attorney. Let him know that it is okay if he forgets something, as long as he

is telling the truth as best he can recall it.

3. Explain who the main characters at the trial will be. Take the witness to the courtroom if that is possible; otherwise draw him a diagram so that he will be familiar with the layout of the courtroom before trial. Show him where he will stand to take the oath, and where the witness chair is located. Explain where the jury and the judge will sit, and where the defendant will be with his attorney. Ask the witness if he has any questions, and answer them in terms he will understand.

4. Emphasize that he should not answer questions that he doesn't understand and that he should not guess at an answer. Tell him that if he does not understand a question, he should say so, and ask that the question be repeated another way.

5. Emphasize to the witness that he should tell the truth. When the witness is on the stand and is asked by the defense attorney if he spoke to anyone about his testimony before going to court and what he was told to say, he will say that you told him to tell the truth. You look good and the witness looks good.

6. Explain to the witness the importance of being as accurate as possible about the facts offered in his testimony. Make sure that he realizes that he should take all the time necessary to think about his answer before giving it.

7. Explain to the witness that he may have to wait for awhile after his arrival at the courthouse before he is called to the stand, and explain to him that every effort is being made to minimize his wait. It is very aggravating for a witness to have to wait; he will be nervous to start with and waiting only prolongs this agony. If you forewarn him, at least he will have some idea of what to expect. If you do not, you may infuriate him and run the risk of alienating him as a witness.

B. Subpoenas

Court hearings require witnesses and, from time to time, business or other records, or other physical evidence. The process used to officially summon them to court is the subpoena. Without subpoenas, neither witnesses nor any other evidence can be required to appear in court.

A subpoena can be served by handing the notice to the witness and is usually served by the county sheriff, the case officer, the prosecutor, a constable, or a process server. Federal Marshals often serve federal subpoenas.

The person serving the subpoena should make sure that he keeps the return to prove that service was made. The court gets very unhappy when trials are held up because witnesses don't show up. If it can be shown that service was made, at least the prosecution is off the hook.

The person serving the subpoena should have the proper address at which service is to be made and should be told the time of day that the witness is most likely to be there. The case officer should keep track of his witnesses throughout the investigation and up to the date of their court appearance. Any other information that is peculiar to a particular witness should be kept by the officer. The officer might keep a schedule of witnesses in his report.

The following information is important information for the officer or prosecutor preparing to issue trial subpoenas:

1. Subpoenas **ad testificadum** are subpoenas calling the person named on the subpoena to go to the place of the hearing on the date printed, for the purpose of giving testimony.

2. Subpoenas **duces tecum** are subpoenas commanding the holder of some paper, records, or other pieces of evidence which are relevant to the issues being litigated,

to produce that evidence at the location of the hearing on the date printed. The holder is usually required to qualify the evidence for admission by testifying, so be sure that the subpoena makes it clear that such a person should be the one to being the evidence to court.

3. Whom to subpoena. Prosecutors and officers alike think of witnesses other than those associated with law enforcement when considering whom to subpoena and overlook the need to subpoena other officers or lab technicians.

   The supervisors for these people have schedules to work out, just as your supervisor does. You may not be concerned about the willingness of the officer or technician to testify, but his supervisor needs the information for his schedule planning. This is especially true if your witness is with another department or is a federal agent. The general rule to follow when considering whom to subpoena is *everybody you want to testify.*

4. Exhibits. In preparing for trial, the condi-

tion and exact location of all exhibits should be determined. It is always a good idea, where possible, to get the exhibit into the hands of the prosecutor as soon as possible after collection. Doing so cuts down on chain of custody problems and reduces your workload when preparing for court.

3.06 Conclusions

Most police officers are aware of their responsibilities to their investigations and many are aware of the dangers that await them at trial. Few, however, appreciate the need to properly prepare for trial. Merely reading over the police report prior to going into court, without considering the matters raised in this chapter, will almost certainly provide the defense with opportunities to walk away from an otherwise solid case. *Unfortunately, there are no rest periods between arrest and trial.*

Chapter 4

USE OF EXHIBITS

4.01 Introduction

It has been said that people remember more of what they see than of what they hear. With the possible exception of a confession and some eyewitness identifications, there probably isn't anything that can be said in a courtroom that compares with what can be shown. With many jurors, the prevailing attitude is **don't tell me, show me**. What you tell them is testimony; what you show them are exhibits.

A trial is a struggle for the minds of the jurors. Exhibits are powerful weapons in that struggle.

Before jurors will accept the testimony of a witness, they will first weigh that witness's credibility. If, for any reason, they don't like the witness, they may not accept his testimony, or if they do, may not give it much weight. On the other hand, an exhibit speaks for itself. Its value as evidence may vary, but its credibility is generally unquestioned; *what you see, is what you get.*

Attorneys, for both the prosecution and the defense, love to get exhibits into the hands of jurors. If the jury can see it, they can understand it. They can take exhibits into the jury room with them and every time they look at it they are reminded of the argument of the side that presented it. It's something they can put their hands on, something that they can see, something that is real to them. To the average juror, testimony is testimony, but exhibits are real evidence. The value of an exhibit will vary depending upon its strength and relevance. The relevance of an exhibit, of course, is not something that will change, or if it does, it's not something the investigator can usually do anything about. Its condition, on the other hand, contributes or detracts from the exhibit's strength and value as evidence.

In this chapter, we will discuss the collection, preservation, and use at trial of physical evidence, and the investigator's responsibilities regarding its proper handling.

4.02 Theory of Admission

Black's Law Dictionary defines evidence as: "Any species of proof, or probative matter, legally presented at the trial of an issue."

A. The Law

Any matter of fact, whether exhibit or testimony which is relevant, competent and not prejudicial, is admissible as evidence.

Evidence is relevant if it tends to make any fact that is of consequence to the determination of an issue more probable or less probable than it would be without that evidence (*U.S. v. Stevens*, 595 F.2d 569 (10th Cir. 1979)).

Evidence is competent if it is legally qualified for admission. In addition to how the mechanical or physical condition of an exhibit qualifies it for admission, fairness is often the measure of its competence. Relevancy and competency are not necessarily interchangeable. An exhibit may be relevant but not competent. For example, an out of court statement may be relevant to the issues in the trial, but, if it is hearsay, and is not admissible under one of the exceptions to the rule, it violates the fairness standards observed by the courts, and therefore is not admissible. Proper preservation and chain of custody are other matters considered in the court's determination of the competence of evidence.

To be admissible, evidence must not violate any of the rights of the accused. The court will exclude any evidence which it deems to be an infringement on the right of the defendant to a fair trial. Information which may be relevant, but which tends to be inflammatory, has been excluded on the grounds that it is prejudicial and would, therefore, tend to unfairly influence or prejudice the jury against the defendant.

For example, color photos of a homicide scene which depict graphic or extremely bloody images have been determined to be prejudicial. In the majority of states, in most instances, the court's rationale is that that unless there is some specific relevance to the color, the color tends to inflame a jury and is, therefore, prejudicial (*U.S. v McRae*, 593 F.2d 700 (5th Cir 1979)).

All of the three main determinants; **relevance**, **competence** and **non-prejudicial value**, must be present before an exhibit, or any piece of evidence, is admissible.

B. The Qualification Process

The qualification process is the procedure used by the courts to determine the admissibility of evidence. This is done in one of three ways:

1. Stipulation

If both the prosecution and the defendant agree that the evidence meets the criteria for admission, and if neither side has any other reason for wanting to hear the witness, whose testimony would otherwise be needed to qualify the evidence, a stipulation is announced to the court and the evidence is admitted without the need for the testimony of the qualifying witnesses.

For example, a defense attorney, who is shown a lab report on which is written the results of a chemist's drug analysis, may wish to agree to stipulate to the results, avoiding the need for the appearance of the chemist to testify in court.

Neither side is forced to accept a stipulation, however, and may in spite of the other side's willingness to stipulate, wish to go forward with the witness's testimony.

For example: The prosecution puts an expert on the stand who brings with him an impressive list of qualifications. The defense attorney is willing to stipulate to the expert's qualifications without requiring the prosecution to go through all of the witness's credentials or achievements. The reason for the offer to stipulate is that the defense attorney, realizing the probable effect on the jury of hearing of the witness's many achievements, wants to avoid the jury being so impressed with that witness that the chances of any successful attack on the witness's conclusions would probably be minimal. The prosecutor, on the other hand, refuses the stipulation for the very reason that he wants the jury to hear the witness tell them about his impressive background.

2. Certificate of Authentication

Before certain evidence may be admitted,

there must be a showing that the information is accurate and that the defendant is the person about whom the information is relevant.

For example: A prosecutor wishes to admit records to prove that the defendant was convicted of, and has spent prison time for, certain crimes in the past. If the information is otherwise relevant, the prosecutor has the obligation of proving that the records admitted are accurate and that the person to whom they refer is the defendant. This is accomplished by either personal identification or fingerprint comparison. Such evidence as this requires the prosecutor to obtain certified copies of the record requested, and a witness to identify that the defendant as the person to whom the records refer, either by personal identification, or by fingerprint comparison.

3. *Testimony of Witnesses*

If there is no stipulation as to the admissibility of the evidence, and it is not of the type acceptable by certification, the evidence must be qualified by the testimony of someone legally competent to do so. The determination as to who is competent to qualify an exhibit is based on the ability to testify about such things as the exhibit's relevance, competence, chain of custody, condition at the time of collection, unaltered state, markings, or any other information required by the court for admission of the evidence. This may require the testimony of more than one person.

4.03 Collection of Evidence

The manner in which an exhibit is collected often plays a major role in determining its admissibility.

A. Who Should Collect the Evidence?

The investigator should remember that in many cases, every person who takes possession of a piece of evidence is eventually going to be required to testify in the qualification process determining the admissibility of the evidence. This is in order to satisfy the court's requirement that the prosecutor prove a chain of custody tracing the evidence from the place from where it was collected to the courtroom. In order to minimize the potential courtroom problems, the officer should limit the number of people involved in the collection process. It is helpful if the chief investigator or the person primarily responsible for the collection of the evidence personally oversees the collection process and the crime scene photography. In most cases, that will eliminate the need for an excessive number of witnesses.

B. What Should Be Collected?

Any and all evidence that may bear on the facts of the case, on the identity of the person who committed the crime, on the method of operation (MO), or on motive should be collected.

When it is clear from the crime scene, or from the complaint received, what crime has been committed, and if the investigating officer has a complete familiarity with the elements of that crime, the collection of evidence becomes more organized. The officer has an idea of the kinds of evidence that may be available at or away from the crime scene, and that allows him to put special emphasis on locating evidence which will tend to prove not only identity of the perpetrator but the elements of the crime as well.

C. When Should the Evidence Be Collected?

Even though the value of the evidence may be affected by the timing of its discovery, from the standpoint of admissibility, it often doesn't matter as much when the exhibit was found as does its condition when found.

The condition of evidence, however, is often affected by the passage of time prior to its discovery. Therefore, in all cases, evidence should be collected as soon as possible after its existence and location become known.

D. What to Look for

From the outset, the investigator should always be on the lookout for clues which will lead to evidence which tends to prove how the crime was committed. This type of evidence is often subtle and requires as much deductive reasoning as it does searching out, but it is often important, and sometimes critical to the outcome of a trial. It is important that the investigator employ every means available to him to locate such evidence. The investigator should keep himself current on new techniques and equipment which become available to assist in the discovery and identification of evidence.

E. Use the Victim's Assistance

Victims are almost always able to provide clues during an investigation which go beyond their eyewitness accounts.

For example, one way to develop clues in an investigation involving a crime scene is to go over the scene with the victim, as in a burglary or arson. The location or even presence of items on the property that may not have any meaning to the investigator may take on a special significance with information provided by the victim, or owner of the property.

In a situation involving an unavailable victim (as in a homicide), find someone else who can be eliminated as a suspect and who is familiar with the scene. That person will be able to assist the investigator by bringing to his attention the presence of items that don't belong at the scene or the absence of some item that should be there, the condition or arrangement of items at the scene or anything else about the scene which might provide a clue for the investigator.

F. Equipment

Every occupation necessitates the use of special equipment; for the carpenter, a hammer and saw; for the plumber, a wrench; and, for the surgeon, a scalpel. The police investigator also has need of certain equipment to assist in the gathering of evidence:

1. Pen and Pad

No effective investigator is ever very far from his note pad and pen, and the importance of making frequent use of them cannot be overstated.

2. Measuring Tape

In any case where measurements are taken and are expected to be used as evidence to be presented to the jury, the accuracy of those measurements may be critical.

3. Camera

While the use of the camera may fall within the expertise of the photographer, the use of a camera is essential in most cases. Every crime scene, no matter what the crime, should be photographed prior to being disturbed. Remember, once it is disturbed, a crime scene can never be put back the way it was, and the investigator never knows when the exact location of evidence or its position in relation to other items or evidence may become critical to the case.

If the investigator employs the use of a photographer, he should direct that person's activities so that the needs of the investigation are met. Most large cities have police photographers who are experienced in crime scene photography and will know how to properly photograph the crime scene. Even so, the investigator should point out specific photographic needs.

G. Investigative Resources

Investigators should be aware of, and keep up with, the various and growing number of investigative and scientific resources available to assist police in their investigations. Lazer equipment is being used to lift fingerprints and even to go into computers to recover erased material. DNA classification is a process that, despite the results in one particularly strange and famous case, has gained a great deal of credibility. Petroleum companies are available to analyze oil and gasoline stains. Anthropologists can give you more information about a person from a footprint in the ground than you would believe possible, and a forensic psychiatrist is able to profile a suspect on the basis of available facts about a case. The list goes on and on. Many publications are available that list the names and locations of experts in every imaginable area of science and art.

The aggressive investigator will avail himself of every resource available, and will constantly be talking with other investigators or prosecutors to pick up new information, or information with which he was not familiar.

H. Exhibit List

An exhibit list is always recommended and, in cases involving a large amount of physical evidence, can be very important to the success of the prosecution, especially in cases where the investigator is called upon to provide specific and detailed information concerning an exhibit. The exhibit list should have areas designated for the following information:

1. Number of items in the exhibit.
2. The exhibit identity (e.g., .38 cal. Smith & Wesson revolver).
3. An exhibit identification number, if one has been assigned.
4. The exact location where the exhibit was found. This should be accompanied by a photograph and a sketch or diagram showing the exhibit's location in relation to other items in the area, and measurements documenting distances. The name of the individual who found the exhibit should also be noted.
5. Date on which the exhibit was discovered or confiscated.
6. Whether lab work is required, and the date the item was sent to the lab along with the name of the person who transported it there.
7. Date the exhibit was returned from the lab and who brought it back.
8. The present location of the exhibit. Every time the exhibit is moved (to court, another lab, the DA's office, or wherever) a log should be kept documenting the details of the move.

If these steps are followed, the investigator always knows where the exhibit is located, so that when he needs to recover it, he knows where it can be found. Moreover, it assists the officer-witness on the stand under cross-examination, and documents the chain of custody.

4.04 Preservation of Evidence

If evidence is not properly preserved, its admissibility may be adversely affected, or, at the very least, its value will be diminished.

A. The Law

To be admissible as evidence, an exhibit must be shown to be exactly that which it is represented to be. In other words, it must be shown to be the same item that was collected during the investigation. In order to insure the integrity of each exhibit it should be packaged and marked separately. The investigator collecting the evidence should seal the container with tape, and put his initials or some identifying mark across the tape. The time and date should also appear on the container.

The prosecution must also show that the condition of the exhibit has not been substantially altered between the time of its collection and presentation at trial. This can usually be accomplished by ensuring the integrity of the exhibit's location during storage.

B. Deterioration

If the evidence is of the type that will naturally deteriorate over the time between its collection and the trial, you should notify the prosecutor as soon as possible. If the defendant is already in custody and charges are filed, the prosecutor may be under an obligation to inform the defense of the condition of the evidence and, if the evidence tends to deteriorate over time, the prosecutor will want to offer the defense an opportunity to examine it as soon as possible, thereby avoiding a complaint by the defense to the court that the prosecution allowed the evidence to deteriorate before allowing them to examine it or have it examined by an expert of their choosing. Such a complaint in the form of a motion by the defense to the court could lead to the exclusion of the evidence at trial. More than one case has been lost in such a way.

To avoid this damaging, sometimes fatal situation, the investigator should take the necessary steps to retard the rate of deterioration of the evidence. The courts understand that some substances will deteriorate after the passage of some time. However, if the defense is able to prove to the court that their inability to examine the evidence is prejudicial to the defendant, *and* a result of the failure of the prosecution to take steps that were available to them to prevent or retard the deterioration, the court may rule the evidence or test results from a prior examination of the evidence to be inadmissible.

In a DUI case, for example, once blood is collected from the suspect and submitted to the lab (usually the hospital technician who draws the blood will fill two vials), the officer is sometimes notified by the analyzing lab that if the sample is not claimed within thirty days of their examination, both samples will be destroyed. If the officer withholds filing a complaint until learning the results of the examination, and more than thirty days goes by before the defense has a reasonable opportunity to have the second sample analyzed by a private lab of their choice, some jurisdictions will consider a motion by the defense to suppress the results of the state's testing.

When fragile or easily deteriorated exhibits are evidence in a case, each of those exhibits should be photographed as soon as possible after collection. In such cases, the courts will usually rule that if the failure of the defense to examine the evidence was not the result of negligence on the part of the prosecution team, the photographs are admissible.

C. Security

All exhibits should be handled by as few people as possible and kept in a secure area with limited access. The fewer people who handle the evidence, the less likely the chances are that the evidence will become lost, destroyed, or contaminated. This will naturally decrease or eliminate the problems that will arise in connection with proving the chain of custody.

Moreover, unless the prosecution can prove that the evidence was kept in a secure place with limited access, thereby reducing the chances of contamination, the court may, and has on many occasions, exclude the evidence from the trial.

If such evidence is crucial to the prosecution's case, such exclusion could result in the failure of an otherwise strong case.

D. Identification

The purpose of marking exhibits is to allow for easy, unambiguous identification by everyone involved in the investigation, prosecution, and trial of the case.

Depending upon the size, physical make-up, and specific investigative needs of an item, marking may be relatively simple or very difficult, even impossible.
1. Large items present a fairly simple situation. They may be marked with initials and an identification number almost anywhere on the exhibit that won't interfere with work required of crime scene technicians or laboratory personnel.
2. Small items can present more of a prob-

lem. Some may not provide adequate space to place a mark, or may be of some material not conducive to markings (e.g., liquids or soft materials). In such cases, an identifying sketch or photograph depicting unique features should be made so that the item can be recognized later. The evidence should then be sealed and marked in a container adequate for the purpose of preserving it.

In other cases, there may be available space, but it may be so limited that it is not possible to include more than the investigator's initials and one digit or less. Trace evidence, or other items too small to mark should be placed and sealed in an appropriately marked evidence container.

E. Descriptions

Every evidence container should describe its contents, and if there are markings on the exhibit itself, those markings should be noted on the evidence container. Any special care required of the item should be noted (e.g., contents perishable, keep refrigerated).

F. Transportation

1. Security

Each item should be packaged for transportation with the security of the item in mind (e.g., locks, seals, refrigerated containers) and where care is required, the proper mountings and cushioning should be employed.

2. Fragile Items

Appropriate steps should be taken to insure the safe transportation of fragile items and the packaging should clearly reflect the fragile nature of the contents.

3. Time

Some items such as perishables (e.g., liquids, wet items) should be given priority consideration so that deterioration doesn't cause the loss of evidential value. Distances from the lab and mode of transportation should affect the type of packaging used to transport the item.

G. Chain of Custody

Of all the problems presented to a prosecutor in the course of placing exhibits into evidence, the one most often encountered is the chain of custody problem. Compounding that problem is the fact that the prosecutor is rarely able to cure any problems created by a defective chain.

A defective chain may affect the admissibility of the evidence and will always affect its value. *Chain of custody is defined as successive possessions in a sequence of transfers of possession.* **Example:** Officer A transfers possession of an item to officer B, who then transfers it to officer C, who places the evidence in the evidence locker. All three parties, A, B and C are links in the chain of custody.

H. Importance of a Proper Chain

It is necessary to the admissibility of evidence that the prosecution is able to insure that the item presented in the courtroom is the same item that was collected during the investigation. It is essentially a matter of the materiality of the evidence. For example, in a drug trial, the package containing the controlled substance is material only if it is the same package that the defendant is charged with having possessed or distributed. Chain of custody is part of the process required to prove that it is the same package or, at least, the contents of the package are the same as were originally confiscated.

1. The Law

Some courts have held that chain of custody discrepancies go to the value of the evidence and not to its admissibility (*U.S. v. Vansant*, 423 F.2d 621 (9th Cir. 1970), cert. denied, 400 U.S. 835). Generally, however, if the chain is tainted or interrupted in such a way as to raise serious questions regarding the integrity of the evidence, the court will exclude the evidence. This is largely a matter that falls within the discretion of the court.

2. Procedure

The procedure should be kept simple. For example, when a residence is searched, one officer should be in charge of collecting all items seized. He should mark all items, note the location where they were found and take the items into his custody. He is the officer who should be responsible for the possession and movement of the evidence. He should move the evidence to the evidence room and, as soon as possible, transport it to the lab or other locations where its presence is required. If that can be done, the number of chain witnesses is reduced and less confusion results at trial when the decision is made as to who the required witnesses will be.

4.05 Categories of Evidence

There are many different types of evidence (e.g., scientific test results, photographs of a crime scene, the testimony of a witness). But, there are only two categories of evidence: direct evidence and circumstantial evidence.

A. Direct Evidence

According to *Black's Law Dictionary*, direct

evidence is: "That means of proof which tends to show the existence of a fact in question, without the intervention of proof of any other fact" (Black, Henry Campbell, *Black's Law Dictionary*, 4th ed., St. Paul, West, 1951).
Examples:

1. Admission of Guilt

A police officer interrogates a suspect who admits to the commission of the crime. The officer gives testimony in court that the defendant made the statement and to its content. The content of that testimony is direct evidence because it goes directly to the question in issue: the defendant's guilt.

2. Eyewitness Testimony

A witness testifies in court that he saw the defendant shoot the victim. The testimony of that witness is direct evidence.

3. Line-up Identification

A witness's identification of a person in a line-up or from a photopack is direct evidence.

B. Circumstantial Evidence

Circumstantial evidence is that evidence which tends to prove the existence of facts from which an inference of other facts, such as the guilt of a defendant, can be drawn.
Examples:
1. An eyewitness testifies at trial that he went into a movie theater and at that time the weather was clear and dry. When he came back out some time later, the sidewalks and streets were wet, and that water was dripping from the marquee of the theater. The testimony is circumstantial evidence that it rained while the witness was inside the theater. The witness didn't see it raining, but he could conclude from what he saw when he left the theater that it had rained while he was inside.
2. A fingerprint lifted from the counter top of a bank teller's window is circumstantial evidence that the person belonging to the print was in the bank and put his hand on the counter.

C. Direct vs. Circumstantial Evidence

A distinction is drawn between direct evidence and circumstantial evidence. However, in terms of the admissibility and implementation of either, there is no difference between them. Have you ever heard the expression, "It's only a circumstantial case"? The insinuation, of course, is that a case based only solely on circumstantial evidence is a weak case, and that the stronger case is one based on direct evidence. That is not a correct assumption. I'm not sure where circumstantial evidence got such a bad reputation, but it is not deserved. Many times a case based on circumstantial evidence is much more conclusive than a case based on direct evidence.
Example:
1. Police arrive at the scene of a homicide. Present when they arrive is the deceased, a person by the name of John Jones. Standing near the body is woman named Mrs. Smith, and a man, Mr. Smith, who is her husband. Lying on the floor near the deceased is a .38 caliber revolver. Here is the direct and circumstantial evidence:
Direct evidence
• The husband, Mr. Smith, tells the police that he was the person who shot the deceased. Mrs. Smith agrees.
• According to the testimony of the medical examiner who performed the autopsy, the victim died as a result of a gun-

shot wound.

Circumstantial evidence:

- The bullet removed from the deceased is proven by ballistics tests to have been fired from the .38 caliber revolver found on the floor.
- The fingerprints of Mrs. Smith are found on the weapon, the prints of Mr. Smith are not.
- A paraffin test on the hands of Mrs. Smith prove positive, and on the hands of Mr. Smith, prove negative.

Who shot the deceased? The direct evidence points to the husband, but the inescapable conclusion drawn from the circumstantial evidence is that the wife, Mrs. Smith, shot the deceased.

The fact is that any offense, overt act, or element of any offense may be proven by circumstantial evidence.

4.06 Demonstrative Evidence

Black's Law Dictionary defines demonstrative evidence as: "That evidence addressed directly to the senses without intervention of testimony." It has been referred to as physical evidence or real evidence, and as evidence that the jury can see, touch, feel, or smell (Black, Henry Campbell, *Black's Law Dictionary*, 4th ed., St. Paul, West, 1951).

A. The Law

Any relevant physical evidence which is competent, relevant, and is not unduly prejudicial may be introduced into evidence. The question of what is or is not unduly prejudicial is one for the court's discretion, using a balancing test to determine whether the prejudicial effect of the evidence outweighs its probative value. If the court decides that it does, the evidence will be ruled inadmissible. As the value of the evidence increases, so must its prejudicial seriousness in order for the evidence to be excluded as being unduly prejudicial.

B. Incrimination Factor

Defendants often object to the introduction of evidence such as fingerprints and recorded undercover conversations, complaining that they are violative of the defendant's Fifth Amendment rights against self-incrimination. Such evidence is not inadmissible on constitutional grounds because it is not testimonial in nature (*Gilbert v. California*, 388 U.S. 263 (1967), 87 S.Ct. 1951, 18 L.Ed.2d 1178). The undercover recording comes the closest to fitting the definition of testimonial, but it lacks the requirement of being made while under police custody or interrogation.

C. Advantages of Demonstrative Evidence

1. Corroborates Testimony

Often a piece of physical evidence will corroborate the testimony of a witness and give that testimony more credibility than it would have had without the physical evidence.

Example:

A bank teller testifies that the defendant is the person who robbed the bank. A bank surveillance photo taken at the time of the robbery clearly shows the defendant leaving the bank with a gun and the money bag in his possession. Obviously, the physical evidence (photo) is valuable corroboration of the witness's testimony.

2. Memorializes Testimony

A piece of physical evidence introduced during a witness's testimony can be used by the prosecutor in his closing argument to emphasize the testimony of that witness or strengthen the accusation against the defendant. Moreover, the exhibit will recall that testimony or argument for the jury each time they examine the exhibit in the jury deliberation room. This is especially important in a long case involving the testimony of many witnesses.

4.7 Scientific Evidence

A. Definition

Scientific evidence is evidence relating to, or employing, the methodology of science.

The Law

1. Admissibility

The same test as is used to determine the admissibility of other types of evidence is used in determining the admissibility of scientific evidence. The difference is in the qualifications of the witness.

2. Expert's Qualifications

In order for a witness to qualify as an expert in a given area, the court must be satisfied that the witness has a substantially more complete knowledge of the subject matter to be testified to than does the average person. This is usually, but not always, shown by having the witness testify regarding the extent of his education and practical experience in the area. Sometimes, experience alone will suffice.

Example:

The police officer who has worked for years as an undercover investigator in the field, and has had substantial contact with drugs and drug transactions, may be qualified to testify as to the street value of a particular type of drug even though he has never received formal schooling in the subject.

B. Expert Testimony

Most scientific evidence will require the testimony of an expert. Some evidence, like information from radar speed detection devices and breathalyzer machines can be offered by the officer who operates them if it can be shown that he is certified to operate the equipment, and that the equipment has met the required standards set by the jurisdiction. The most commonly used areas requiring the testimony of an expert are:

1. Controlled Substance Identification

Testimony identifying a particular substance as a controlled substance must be given by one who is qualified to make such an identification, usually a chemist. Once the court recognizes that person as an expert in the field of drug identification, he or she is permitted to render, in open court and under oath, an opinion as to the composition of the substance submitted for identification, which opinion is reached following the administration of scientific tests of the substance. Out of court, and occasionally for limited purposes in court, a police officer experienced in drug investigations may be qualified to render an opinion as to the nature of the substance in question. Such an opinion by an officer may provide probable cause for a search warrant or an on view arrest, but not for admission into evidence of the substance in court.

2. Forensic Pathology

In many cases, the determination that a body is deceased is easily made by the investigator. The determination as to the cause of death, however, must be made by a qualified pathologist. Other conclusions drawn by the pathologist, such as time of death, whether a wound could have been self-inflicted, and whether a body was moved from one place to another after death, are also often critical issues in a homicide case and should be answered by the pathologist. It should be noted here that a coroner who is not a licensed physician may not render an opinion as to the cause of death but can only relay information received from a pathologist. *Never take the word of the non-physician coroner for the cause of death, always wait for the pathologists report!*

3. Comparative Micrography

The most common types of evidence for which comparative micrography is used used ballistics and toolmark comparisons. Conclusions of an expert in these areas result from comparison of marks made by the bore of the weapon on the bullet or by a tool on some surface (e.g., crowbars, screwdrivers, or other tools used for prying). The proper collection of the mark producing instrument and the questioned surface is of the utmost importance. Every investigator should cringe every time he sees a TV cop picking up a gun by sliding his pencil up the barrel. Any impressions or scratches left by the pencil on the bore will cause additional marks on the test bullet that will not be on the questioned bullet and could, and probably will affect the outcome of the comparison tests.

4. Fingerprint Identification

Most jurisdictions require a minimum of twelve identifiable characteristics common to both the questioned and known print. Even though often visible to the naked eye and easily recognizable even by the layman, the in-court identification of fingerprints requires the testimony of an expert. Proper

collection and preservation of the questioned print is critical to a successful comparison examination.

4.08 Examples of Demonstrative and Scientific Exhibits

A. Blood

Blood is usually found in one or more of five forms: fresh blood, clotted blood, blood smears, blood stains or blood flakes. Manner of collection:

1. Fresh Fluid Blood

A clean medicine dropper should be used to siphon the blood from the surface and to place it into a clean vial to be sealed to prevent contamination. The vial should be marked properly, refrigerated, and submitted to the lab as soon as possible after collection.

2. Clotted Blood

A clean metal or plastic instrument (e.g., knife or razor blade) is used to pick up the sample from the surface and place it into a vial. The vial should then be sealed and marked. This same method is used to collect blood flakes.

3. Blood Smears or Stains

If the blood is on a hard surface such as a countertop, linoleum floor, or smooth concrete, and if it is dried, it may be collected by using a dampened cotton swab, applying it to the blood stained area until it becomes reddish-brown in color. The swab should then be placed into a clean vial, sealed, and marked.

4. Blood Soaked Clothing

This type of evidence should be collected and placed into vials or bottles (a separate container for each piece of clothing) and allowed to dry, then removed, placed into plastic bags, and submitted along with the vials or bottles to the lab.

B. Photographs

To lay a proper foundation for the admission of photographs, either the photographer or someone present when the photo was taken should testify that the photo is a fair and accurate representation of the objects, persons, or conditions depicted.

Posed photos, motion pictures, or video reconstructions are admissible if there is accompanying testimony to prove that the exhibits are accurate representations of that which is depicted.

C. Maps, Models and Diagrams

The exhibit need not be to scale to qualify for admission but, depending on its purpose, must present a reasonably accurate representation. Where the exhibit is prepared out of court, it may be qualified by the person who prepared it, or any person who can testify to its accuracy, even if he or she did had no part in its preparation.

1. *The Law:*

Maps, models, diagrams and other such exhibits which represent a place or something which cannot be brought into court are admissible only to illustrate or compliment the testimony of a witness.

2. *Uses:*

a) Maps or aerial photographs can be used to illustrate the relationship of one location to another, to locate a specific site, to show a getaway or chase route. They can be maps of one street or of the whole world, depending upon the need.

b) Models can used to illustrate in three dimensions; the locations of rooms in a house, the comparative sizes of buildings or objects, the manner of entry into a building, the workings of a machine or weapon, or any other situation or condition best illustrated by such an exhibit.

3. *Diagrams* are most often used to illustrate crime scenes, but are also useful to show such things as the chain of command or structure of a criminal organization, or to trace the various locations of a specific person or thing or to illustrate, by outline, a criminal scheme.

4. *In court demonstrations* or reenactments are valuable to illustrate the manner in which a particular physical event occurred, or to illustrate the impossibility of a certain manner of occurrence, such as a self-defense claim.

D. Frequently Used Prosecution Exhibits

Crimes of Violence

1. *Photographs.*

a) Crime scene.

Photos of the crime scene should be taken from every possible angle, showing the relationship to other locations and items of possible evidence in the area of the crime.

b) The victim's injuries.

The defendant at the time of the arrest, including close ups of any marks or injuries he may have received while committing the crime. When possible, both color and black and white photos should be taken, and those taken should be blown up to 8 x 10.

2. *Clothing of the defendant and the victim.*
   a) Match clothing up with the description given by the victim and witnesses.
   b) To be used in court in connection with testimony regarding fiber comparison and other lab tests.
3. *Weapons used.*
   Photos of weapons have a positive impact on the jury, especially if the court doesn't allow the actual weapon to go out with the jury. Photos of the weapons may also be used in connection with the testimony of the ballistics expert.
4. *Comparison photos;* ballistics, finge prints, toolmarks, etc.
   Often crucial, and usually the most valuable evidence in a trial, testimony on this evidence will generally come from an expert witness and should reflect evidence against this defendant to the exclusion of all others.
5. *Maps and aerial photos.*
   Maps and aerial photos add to the "show" you're putting on for the jury. Valuable is visually tracing, for the jury, the location of the crime scene, the path of escape, direction of travel, and in the case of aerial photos, a view of the entire crime scene. This can be especially important where travel time is of significance to the case, in that once jurors can see how far the distance was rather than trying to judge it from measurements in blocks or miles, they will be less likely swayed by defense arguments on that subject.
6. *Diagrams of the scene* with measurements showing the exact location of evidence and, in a homicide case, the body. (see also the text in the chapter on report writing regarding the importance of this practice.)
7. *Molds and models of foot, hand, tire or tool*

impressions.
Often overlooked by investigators, especially in small departments, the importance of this evidence often makes the difference between a conviction and an acquittal. It's acceptable to lose a case because the evidence isn't there, but unacceptable when uncollected evidence was known to exist.

8. *DNA evidence.*
   If a match is made, this evidence will identify your suspect to the exclusion of all others. Notwithstanding a famous case to the contrary, this evidence is usually indisputable, and though expensive to obtain, should be used when necessary. As the old saying goes, "What price justice?"
9. *Line-up or photopack photos.*
   Care must be taken in the selection of the individuals shown in the line-up or photopack. Sometimes in an important case without much other than a witness's identification to present to a jury, the tendency is to allow the suspect to stick out a little bit from the other subjects in the line-up. Remember what you show the witness, you'll eventually have to show the jury, and they do know the difference between fair and unfair.
10. *Any other relevant physical evidence gathered at the scene.*

Burglary and Crimes Against Property

1. *MO Photos.*
   Criminals usually commit the same kinds of crimes in the same way. The manner in which they commit the crime can be the criminal's signature, and often identifies him as the perpetrator without otherwise convincing evidence. Therefore, the motis operen-

di should be thoroughly documented with photographic evidence of the following:
   a) Point of entry
   b) Disturbed areas
   c) Escape vehicle
2. *Comparison photos.*

   As in any other case, where there is evidence found at the crime scene which can be compared to other evidence found in the defendant's possession or in a place which can be identified with the suspect, it should be collected and submitted for comparison. Examples of such evidence are:
   a) Fingerprints
   b) Toolmarks
   c) Footprints
   d) Tiretracks
3. *Recovered stolen property and photos of same.*

   Such evidence should be photographed prior to it's collection since it's location may become important later during the investigation. For example: where stolen property is recovered from the bedroom of the suspect who shares the premises with several other people, but who alone occupies that particular bedroom, photos of the item inside the suspect's room establishes the location of the evidence at the time of it's discovery. It's amazing how many times investigators get confused about where certain items of evidence were discovered during a search.
4. *Diagram of scene showing locations and movements.* In some cases, where heights and depths need to be illustrated, model will serve the witness better than a diagram or photo.

Narcotics

1. *Photos.*

   There are several reasons for taking photos of the seized evidence: Photos can go out with the jury where the actual narcotics will not usually be allowed out of the court's possession; if much of the evidence was used during testing, photos will give the jury an accurate of the amount involved; in the unlikely event that the evidence is lost or stolen while in the possession of the police, photos will establish their existence at the time of their seizure.
2. *Aerial,* showing surveillance routes.
3. *Location of transaction.*

   It's not uncommon for the location of the transaction to become an important piece of evidence in a drug case. If, for example, the transaction takes place inside a home or other building, photographic surveillance may, without the use of sophisticated equipment not available to many departments, be impossible to complete. Photos of the outside of the building during the time of the surveillance will provide for the jury an answer to the defense counsel's question about why surveillance of the transaction was not taken.
4. *Photos of the suspect,* other than the mug shot taken, which show his appearance at the time of the arrest or surveillance should be taken, especially if the suspect has the profiled appearance of a drug dealer. You may be certain that he won't look the same at trial.
5. *Surveillance photos* showing the suspect's meeting with the informant or undercover officer, especially if the transaction is expected to take place in an area

unseen by the surveillance team. (See item 1 under this section.)

6. *Tapes; video and audio* surveillance.

   Even where photographic surveillance is impossible, it may be possible to equip the undercover officer or the informant with a body wire so that conversation between the undercover officer and suspect can be documented.

7. *Contraband after seized.*

   It may become relevant for the jury to see that the evidence placed in police custody is the same evidence, in both identity and quantity, as that recovered at the time of the seizure.

8. *Fingerprints.*

   Fingerprint collection should be attempted on any items received from the suspect, especially in undercover operations where there is no "buy-bust" and the suspect is allowed to leave. Seldom do the police submit the "plastic baggie" containing the contraband for fingerprint analysis. The excuse is either that too many people handled the evidence between it's seizure and placement in the evidence locker, or that once it was submitted to the lab for analysis, it was too late to have it checked for prints, or that fingerprints can't be lifted from that kind of a surface (I've actually heard this excuse used dozens of times, and had the defense bring in an expert to testify that the officer's statement was untrue). In such cases, fingerprints, if available, will connect the suspect with the narcotics container.

9. *Handwriting samples and blow-ups for in-court comparisons.*

   This is especially valuable where such things as an "owe sheet" was confiscated. If the prosecution is able to show that the handwriting on the sheet was

that of the suspect, you've gone a long way in convincing a jury that this was not a one-time thing with the defendant, or that the contraband belonged to another who had equal access to the drugs.

10. *Proof of residence,* rent receipts, etc.

11. *Telephone bills.*

    Obviously, evidence proving phone calls were made between the undercover officer and the suspect, or between the informant and the suspect, will be damaging to the defendant who denied any such contact.

12. *Any other items which are relevant* to the commission of the crime, such as owe slips, etc.

Vehicular Crimes

1. *Photos.*
   a) Aerials, showing all relevant locations surrounding the incident.
   b) Position of vehicles,
   c) Point of impact and debris,
   d) Damage to vehicles.

2. *Diagram of scene* showing direction of travel and impact point.

3. *Trace evidence.* Evidence of paint or material transfers (fiber, skin, etc.).

4. *Breath or blood analysis report.*

5. *Photos or videotape of defendant while driving,* during the field sobriety test, and after arrest. Videotape is especially valuable and departments who use it may expect a much higher percentage of their cases to end in pleas. Regrettably, too many departments refuse to use video equipment, some intentionally abstaining for the practice believing that sometimes video of the suspect doesn't really show how intoxicated the suspect is, and believing that juries usually believe the officer's opinion, anyway, so why take the chance of

taping the suspect. This approach is not as effective as those departments think it is. When the defense attorney questions the officer about the failure to use videotape, especially when it was available to him, the officer tends to lose some of his credibility. The same holds true for the use of audio-taping equipment where the officer is expecting to testify that the defendant's speech was slurred.

Sex Crimes

1. *Photos of the scene and the victim,* especially if she shows evidence of physical assault, and photos of the defendant at the time of the arrest.
2. *Diagram or maps of scene.*
3. *Clothing of victim and defendant.* Collection of this evidence may show that the victim's clothing was torn or soiled during the attack, or the location on the clothing where trace evidence was recovered.
4. *Weapons used* (to show force or threat of force).
5. *Line-up or photopack photos.*
6. *Medical admission and examination records.*

Fraud

The importance of collecting the following kinds of evidence should be obvious to any fraud investigator, and further explanation should not be necessary.

1. *Handwriting exemplars.*
2. *Fingerprints.*
3. *Printouts of bank account data.*
4. *Records and contracts.*
5. *Accounting analysis sheets.*
6. *Blow-ups of handwriting exemplars.*

Arson

1. *Photos of damage outside and inside.*
2. *Photos of origin location.*
3. *Evidence of incendiary or explosive origin.*
4. *Diagram of the scene.*
5. *Items found in possession of the defendant linking him to fire.*
6. *Receipts for materials used.*
7. *Defendant's clothing* along with analysis for matching chemicals.

4.09 Conclusions

The investigator should always be looking for physical evidence to strengthen his case. Even where the defendant has confessed, the evidence should be processed. The process of collecting, preserving, and presenting evidence is difficult and tedious. It requires thought, care, thoroughness, and patience. The investigator who is willing to pay the price will be the one who will reap the benefits.

Chapter 5

DIRECT-EXAMINATION

5.01 Introduction

The purpose of direct-examination is to elicit testimony which will *provide* or *support* direct and circumstantial evidence. It is the heart and soul of the prosecution's case, the vehicle used by the prosecution to place before the jury all of the evidence against the accused. It is the prosecutor's opportunity to take center stage in the production that is a criminal trial. At the same time, it provides the police investigator the opportunity to take control of the case on the witness stand by presenting his evidence and testimony in a competent and professional manner. If the investigator has done his work competently and has prepared himself for his court appearance, he will not only enhance his own image in the view of the jury, but he will be going a long way in boosting the credibility of his evidence and bringing his investigation to a successful conclusion. Obviously, the importance of a competent prosecutor can't be overstated, but any prosecutor will admit that his case is only as good as the police officer's investigation, and the manner in which he presents it during his direct-examination. If the investigator doesn't put forward a strong case from the witness stand, there is little the prosecutor can do to convict a guilty defendant.

5.02 Appearance and Demeanor

A. Proper Attire and Appearance

A professional appearance is important to the testifying officer's credibility. It is always preferable for the police officer to come into court wearing a suit and tie, or a conservative sport jacket and tie along with shined shoes. Pinky rings and gold chains should be left at home. Female officers should wear a conservative dress, skirt, or dress slacks, and blouse. The officer should never wear a weapon in the courtroom and should refrain from wearing anything which may appear to be excessively authoritarian (e.g., handcuff tie clasp). If you are a male undercover detective and have long hair and an earring, arrange (style) the hair as neatly as possible and remove the earring. Testifying is a serious matter and the officer should dress for the occasion.

It is not uncommon for a police officer to come into court on a duty day and expect to be in court for only a short time before getting back out on the street. Most of the time in those situations he will, of necessity, be wearing his uniform. When the situation requires the officer to wear a uniform in court, the prosecutor will let the jury know through your testimony, your reasons for coming into court in uniform. Many officers believe that wearing their uniform in court enhances their image in the eyes of the jury, but studies show that a growing percentage of jurors resent such a blatant showing of authority. They see the courtroom as an even field, not the officer's home field. They see the officer who dresses properly as respecting the court and attempting to be fair in the presentation of their case.

Throughout this chapter the use of the words credible and credibility are repeated over and over. The reason for this is the importance of the police officer's credibility. If there is no credibility, there is no believability. If there is no believability, there can be no conviction.

B. Manner of Speaking

When addressing the jury, the witness should always speak clearly and deliberately, and should never slur his speech or cover his mouth with his hand. He should speak loudly enough to be heard by the jury member farthest from the witness stand. At times, attorneys will move closer to the witness when asking a question. When, for example, the prosecutor hands the witness an exhibit and asks questions about it, he will probably remain close to the witness stand during the officer's testimony about that exhibit. The tendency of the witness will be to speak to the person asking the question and not through him to others in the courtroom. Presumably, the prosecutor already knows what the witness is going to say; it is most important that the jury does also. If they are not able to hear the witness's testimony and do not inform the court, which they are reluctant to do, then what the witness has said will be lost to them and to the prosecution's case.

When speaking to the jury, the witness

should make eye contact with them. If you are a witness, let them see the truth of your testimony in your eyes.

Take your time when responding. Don't blurt our anything without thinking. When you or any witness rushes through testimony, the jury often misses the point. They are hearing the facts for the first time; give them an opportunity to absorb your testimony.

C. Attitude and Approach

Much of the weight given to your testimony by the jury will be determined by the attitude you display on the stand and the manner in which you deliver your testimony. Be polite at all times. "Yes, Sir," "Yes, Ma'am," or "Yes, Your Honor" should be used in your response to the prosecutor, the defense attorney, and the judge, even when you feel that the person addressing you is being unfair. The jury expects it of you and if you remain the calm professional, even in the face of an inexperienced, error prone prosecutor, or an irate defense attorney, the jury will reward your patience and courteous manner. Don't get so polite, however, that you allow the questioner to put words in your mouth.

1. *Appear confident but not cocky.* If you display confidence in the facts about which you are testifying, the effect will be to build the jury's confidence in your credibility. If you seem wishy-washy and unsure of yourself, or display a lackadaisical attitude, you will not generate much enthusiasm with the jury regarding your testimony. Never look or act beaten or embarrassed if something goes wrong. If you don't react negatively, the jury may not either. Never make faces of pain, disappointment, or boredom, or change your manner of speech.

2. *Do not appear to be unfair or biased* in your recitation of the facts. If there are facts

which favor the defendant, bring them out without hesitation. This will accomplish two things: it will make you and your investigation more credible

3. Don't forget that you are basically telling a story to twelve jurors who will probably be hearing it for the first time. *Give your case a sense of realism.* Make it interesting and give it an appropriate degree of drama. Try to give the jury more than "just the facts"; make the case come alive. The idea is not to simply inform, but to re-create with words. It is your opportunity to take center stage, to captivate your audience; *take it.* By doing this in an effective, but not overdramatic or arrogant way, you can strengthen a weak case and put a so-so case over the top.

4. *Don't separate the crime from the criminal.* Bring the defendant into the case by portraying his actions in such a way as to bring home his brutality or cunning. As the defendant sits in the courtroom, he will, by design, probably look more like a choir boy than a killer or robber. By skillfully describing his actions, appearance, and demeanor at the time of the crime, you can strip the facade away so that the jury can see him for what he is.

5. *General Suggestions:*
   a) Don't act like a smart aleck or as though your testimony should never be questioned. A little confident humility can go a long way with a jury.
   b) Do not chew gum in court.
   c) Do not smoke where the jury can see you.
   d) Do not speak to the defense attorney, the defendant, or defense witnesses within sight of the jury, or anywhere for that matter, unless it is necessary. In any case, don't let the jury think you are socializing with the other side; otherwise the seriousness of the case will be diminished in their minds. Be aware

that the defense attorney will probably try to engage you in casual conversation in front of the jury.

e) Do not interject humor into the trial, but don't ignore it either. Almost every case will have its lighter moments, no matter how serious the issues. However, let the attorneys interject the humor. It is acceptable to respond in the appropriate manner, but beware of the defense attorney who attempts to turn the case into a farce.

f) Avoid speaking to the jurors outside the courtroom. The court will probably instruct the jury not to speak with you and not to take it as a snub that the officers and attorneys avoid contact with them.

g) Maintain a good erect posture. Slouching in your seat is very unprofessional and significantly damages your image.

h) Do not interrupt the judge or the attorneys when they are speaking. If one of the attorneys or the judge interrupts you while you are testifying, stop testifying, and wait until the matter which caused the interruption is resolved.

i) Stop your testimony when an objection is made, especially if it is made by the prosecutor. When the defense attorney objects, it will be seen as rude or unfair if you do not stop testifying while the attorney makes his argument. When the district attorney makes an objection, you are probably making a statement that may be detrimental to your case.

j) Avoid police jargon. Speak in language that the jury will understand. This is especially true when referring to times. Jurors don't use military time, and will not be impressed that you do. They will be confused if you say that something occurred at 17:30 rather than

5:30 pm. For more on this subject, see the discussion in the chapter on Report Writing.

D. Preparation

As in any other endeavor, performance in the courtroom is only as good as its preparation. The more thoroughly you prepare for your testimony, the more effectively it will be presented. It takes considerable thought and a concentrated effort to adequately prepare for court, and your performance at trial may well be the difference between a conviction or an acquittal.

Keep in mind that you are not preparing for sake of preparation, but for the jury. All of what follows is necessary before a competent and professional presentation can be offered by the police officer in court.

1. Organize Your Material

Gather all available material which contains information about your case. Too often, investigators feel that they are responsible only for what they, themselves, did. In some ways that is true, but by familiarizing yourself with the work and results of the efforts of your fellow investigators on the case, you will be in a position, while you are on the stand, to better understand the role your work plays in the overall picture being presented to the jury. Familiarizing yourself with the reports and notes of the other investigators will add immeasurably to your effectiveness as a witness.

2. Review Reports

Once all available reports and information have been gathered, make sure you are familiar with everything in them. As the school teachers say: "There will be a quiz on it, later."

Familiarize yourself not only with the contents of the reports, but also with which information is in which report and, in a lengthy report, where the information is located within the report. It is much more impressive to be able to go directly to needed information in the report than to fumble through it page by page, searching for what you want. Any officer who has taken the stand has experienced the embarrassment of having to look for material in his report. And doesn't it seem that the more you try to under those circumstances, the harder it is to find?

During your review of the report, be sure that the information contained therein is correct. The corrections should have been made earlier, but if they haven't, this is your last opportunity to make them.

3. Evaluate the Strengths and Weaknesses of the Case

Ascertain which evidence supports the prosecution's theory and which may damage it. Determine if any of the strengths directly negate any of the weaknesses. Look for the reasons why the deficiencies exist. Can they be corrected? Can they be turned into strengths? Is there any way to diminish their impact? Any weaknesses which are discovered should be discussed with your prosecutor. He's the member of your team who may have solutions for some of your problems. Remember, you and the prosecutor are a team, and without mutual cooperation, the chances of success diminish greatly.

4. Gather and Prepare Evidence

Your case reports should already have the evidence listed. Make a master list of the evidence and try to arrange it in an orderly fashion. This will help you and the prosecutor during your pre-trial interview.

a) Determine if any of the evidence will require charts, maps, diagrams, or other types of demonstrative evidence. You should consult with the prosecutor about this.

b) Check chain of custody reports to be sure that each piece of evidence can be properly qualified for admission. If there is a problem, try to resolve it.

c) Where distance is an issue, be sure you have measured the relevant distances at the scene (e.g., surveillance point to crime scene), and since distances are often determined by reference points in the courtroom, you should familiarize yourself with the measurements of the courtroom and of distances from the witness stand to other locations in the courtroom, especially if that information will help illustrate a distance to which you will be referring during your testimony.

d) Locate the evidence. Make sure the evidence is in your custody or in the prosecutor's custody and not still at the lab or somewhere else where you do not have access to it.

e) Check scientific test results. Be sure that all of the evidence requiring scientific analysis or comparison was submitted and that the work was completed.

f) Make a list of people who will have to be served subpoenas in connection with the qualification or presentation of evidence.

5. Meet with the Prosecutor

The prosecutor will usually request a pretrial meeting with you. If time gets short and the prosecutor hasn't contacted you, it would be prudent for you to contact him and request a meeting. If your request is ignored or refused, contact your superior and tell him of your problem. In most cases, the problem will be solved without creating an unpleasant climate. Discuss the theory of the prosecution and of the defense. It is necessary that you understand what constitutes the elements of the crime and what evidence supports each. The prosecutor will have a theory upon which the case is predicated. Make sure you know and understand that theory, how the prosecutor plans to implement it, and what part you play in its presentation. It is equally important that you understand the defense theory, since that will tell you how the defense attorney will come after you on cross-examination, and what points he will try to bring out of your testimony.

Discuss the facts and the exhibits. Make sure you and the prosecutor have a mutual understanding of the facts and get any contradictions straightened out before trial. Again, time should be spent at your meeting going over the evidence, its location, chain of custody, specific needs, and special witnesses.

6. Other Matters for Discussion with the Prosecutor

a) Physical difficulties or shortcomings of which you are aware that affect you or any of the other witnesses (e.g., hearing, speech, vision, nervous reactions, depth perception, etc.).

b) Problem areas not apparent from the facts or exhibits, such as: hostile witnesses, mistakes in the report, unavailability of witnesses, chain of custody, and changes in the condition of evidence.

c) Prior contacts with the defendant. Prioritize in such discussions anything in your prior contacts with the defendant that would tend to support an allegation by him that you have personal reasons for going after him. Any other information about your knowledge of, or prior contact with, the defendant that might affect the case should also be discussed.

d) Problems in your background. Any information about yourself that might present opportunities for the defendant to attack you or the case should be shared with the prosecutor (e.g., prior disciplinary action or lawsuits, mental health therapy, etc.).

e) Witnesses' background. Any information that might affect the credibility of any of the prosecution or defense witnesses.

f) Any other matters you feel the defense attorney might raise that could cause a problem, such as: distances, lighting, obstacles, distractions, interrupted view of the defendant, etc.

g) It is a good idea to visit the crime scene with the prosecutor and key witnesses. The prosecutor will have a better perspective of the scene and of the positions and movements of the key witnesses. It will also allow the witnesses to refresh their recollection of the events and will provide an opportunity to iron out inconsistencies in the statements of the various witnesses. Most prosecutors will protest that they don't have the time to do that, but be gently insistent, especially in an important or complicated case. Such preparation can pay large dividends.

E. Rules of Evidence

The Rules of Evidence deal with much more than the handling, introduction, and admissibility of exhibits. They are the rules by which the entire trial is conducted. They affect who may testify, the questions asked, the manner in which they may be asked, which testimony is relevant and competent and which may, while passing those tests, still be inadmissible as being unduly prejudicial to the defendant. They control the manner of the authentication of evidence and of qualifying experts. *They are The Rules of the Game.* Some of those which most directly affect the testifying officer are:

1. The Hearsay Rule

The factors to be considered in evaluating the testimony of any witness are perception, memory, and narration. In order to encourage the witness to do his best with respect to each of these factors, and to expose any inaccuracies which may enter in, the Anglo-American tradition has evolved three conditions under which witnesses will ideally be required to testify:

a) He must be present in the courtroom when testifying;

b) His testimony must be made under oath;

c) He must be subject to cross-examination.

From that thinking evolved the Hearsay Rule, which defines Hearsay as: *". . . a statement, other than one made by the declarant while testifying at the trial or hearing, offered in evidence to prove the truth of the matter asserted"* (Federal Rule of Evidence, 801).

The following exercises are presented to illustrate the way in which the Hearsay Rule is applied during trial testimony:

Situation 5-1: Hearsay

Questions by the prosecutor to the investigator:

Q. Officer, where did you find this weapon?

A. In a sewer near the corner of Market and Chestnut Streets.

Q. Do you know how it got there?

A. Yes, the defendant threw it in as he was running away from the P & J Bar.

Q. How do you know that sir?

A. One of the witnesses outside the bar saw him throw it there.

Objection by the defense attorney: Hearsay.

Ruling: Sustained. Reason: The testimony is:

1) Out of court statement;
2) Made by a person not in court to testify;
3) Offered for the truth of the matter asserted.

Under what circumstances would this evidence be admissible?

The witness who actually saw the defendant throw the weapon may testify as to what he saw.

What if the witness is not available?

In that case, the evidence is not admissible unless it can be offered for some other purpose.

Is there any other exception under which this testimony might fall?

If the statement is offered to explain why the officer looked in the sewer, the court may, in its discretion, allow the statement. In such a case, the court would instruct the jury of the limited purpose for which the statement was admitted.

Final ruling: Hearsay. Not admissible

Situation 5-2: Hearsay Exception Statement against interest.

Question by the prosecutor to the investigator:

Q. Officer, where did you find this weapon?

A. In a sewer near the corner of Market and Chestnut Streets.

Q. Do you know how it got there?

A. Yes, the defendant threw it in as he was running away from the P. J. Bar.

Q. How do you know that sir?

A. The defendant told me that he threw it there.

Objection: Hearsay.

Ruling: Overruled. Reason: Statement against interest.

1) Is it hearsay? Yes. It is;
   a) Out of court statement;
   b) Made by another;
   c) For truth of the matter asserted.
2) Why is it admissible?
   a) It is an exception to the Hearsay Rule.
   b) It is a statement by the defendant against his own interest (an admission of guilt).

Final ruling: Hearsay Exception. Admissible

Situation 5-3: Non-Hearsay Statement. Reason to Act.

The prosecutor is questioning the police officer on direct-examination.

Q. Officer, you stopped the defendant's car at the intersection of North Main and Azalea, is that correct?

A. Yes, sir.

Q. What was the reason you stopped the car?

A. It fit the description of the car seen leaving the scene of the crime.

Q. How did you get that description?

A. Over my police radio.

Objection: Hearsay.

Ruling: Overruled. Reason: Reason to act.

Does it fit the test for hearsay?

1) Out of court statement–yes (came over radio).
2) By another–yes (dispatcher or another officer).
3) For the truth of the matter asserted–No, not to show the truth in what was said, but to show why the officer acted the way he did.

What if the information came from an unknown person and not from the police officer?

As long as the statement is offered solely to show the incentive or reason why the officer acted, it is not hearsay.

Final ruling: Non-hearsay statement. Admissible

Situation 5-4: Hearsay Exception. Prior Consistent Statement.

In this situation, a rape victim's testimony was attacked on cross-examination as a recent fabrication. The prosecutor then put the officer on the stand to testify about a prior consistent statement made by the victim.

The prosecutor questioned the officer:

Q. Officer, when did you first talk to the victim, Mary Spaulding.
A. On the evening of April 27 of this year.
Q. Is that the same day on which the rape allegedly occurred?
A. Yes, sir.
Q. At what time did you talk with her?
A. At about 11:30 p.m.
Q. You heard Miss Spaulding testify that the rape occurred at about 10:00 p.m.?
A. Yes, sir.
Q. What did Miss Spaulding tell you about the rape when you talked to her?

Objection: Hearsay.

Ruling: Overruled. Reason: A prior consistent statement of a witness may be offered for the purpose of corroborating the credibility of that witness's testimony when it has been attacked as recent fabrication. Here, we have a fresh complaint made by a rape victim shortly after the crime occurred.

Note: This exception is only available when present testimony has been attacked as a recent fabrication, and when you have a judge who understands the hearsay rule.

Final ruling: Hearsay exception. Admissible

Situation 5-5: Hearsay exception. Present Sense Impression.
The prosecutor questions the officer:

Q. Officer, you were on the desk when the

call came in from a person identifying himself as Officer Michael Gray, is that correct?
A. Yes, sir.
Q. And that was a phone call, not a radio call?
A. Yes, sir.
Q. And did you know Officer Gray?
A. Yes, sir.
Q. Do you recognize Officer Gray's voice when you hear it?
A. Yes, sir.
Q. In your opinion, who's voice were you listening to on the phone?
A. Officer Gray was speaking.
Q. What did he say?

Objection: Hearsay.

There was proffer that the decedent's statement on the phone was that the defendant was yelling through the door that he was coming in and that he was going to kill Officer Gray. Ten minutes later, Officer Gray was found shot to death in his apartment.

Ruling: Overruled. Reason:

A statement describing or explaining an event or condition made while the declarant was perceiving the event or condition, is admissible as an exception to the Hearsay Rule.

Final ruling: Hearsay Exception. Admissible

2. Other Exceptions to the Hearsay Rule

Res Gestae:

Res Gestae is a statement made as a spontaneous response to a startling event made close in time to the event or to the speaker's first knowledge of the event. It is an exception to the Hearsay Rule. The theory of its admissibility is that circumstances may produce a condition of excitement which temporarily stills the capacity of reflection and produces statements free of conscious fabrication. The determination as to when a statement is considered Res Gestae is a factual matter and is discretionary with the judge.

What about the time factor? How much time can pass?

Time doesn't matter, technically, if the response is made at a time close to the time when the speaker learns of the matter about which the statement was made.

Situation 5-6: Res Gestae.

Questions by the prosecutor:

Q. Officer, where was Mr. Wilson when you first contacted him about the murder of Mr. Rose?

A. In Cedar Rapids, Iowa.

Q. And that is how far from this city?

A. About eleven hundred miles.

Q. And, when did you first contact him?

A. In March of this year.

Q. When you contacted him, was Mr. Wilson aware that Mr. Rose had been murdered?

A. No, he was not?

Q. He still hadn't heard of the murder almost eight months after it occurred?

A. He said he had not heard about it until I told him.

Q. What did he say when you told him that?

By the defense attorney: Objection, Your Honor, this is hearsay.

By the prosecutor: Your Honor, this would fall under the Res Gestae exception to the Hearsay Rule.

The judge asked the attorneys to approach the bench for a side-bar conference. At that time, the prosecutor told the judge that the officer would say that Mr. Wilson said, "I knew that damn Robertson (the defendant) would get him sooner or later."

By the court: Overruled on the basis that the statement is an exception to the Hearsay Rule.

The passage of time is, however, circum-

stantial evidence that may show that the response is not spontaneous, but a product of reflection. If it could be shown that the witness, Mr. Wilson, was aware of the killing at a time prior to his being told about it by the officer, and if that time would have been long enough, in the opinion of the court, for the witness's statement to the officer to have been the product of reflection, the statement would probably be disallowed as a violation of the Hearsay Rule.

Must a Res Gestae statement always follow an event?

No!

Example: The statement of a passenger in a car, in which the driver was killed after colliding with the defendant's car, was that the deceased driver said, seconds before the crash, "What is that nut doing?" This is a Res Gestae statement.

Prior inconsistent statements.

When a witness testifies, any prior statements made by that witness, either in court on another occasion, such as a preliminary hearing, or outside of court, which are inconsistent with that witness's present testimony, are admissible as evidence tending to impeach that witness's credibility. Since it is not offered for the truth of the prior statement, but rather as proof of the falsity of the present testimony, it is not hearsay.

These exceptions are the ones most frequently encountered. If you wish to learn more about them or the other exceptions that apply in your jurisdiction, it is recommended that you consult with your prosecutor.

3. Leading Questions

A leading question is one which suggests the answer. Leading questions, with few exceptions, are prohibited on direct-examination. The interpretation of what fits the description of a leading question varies from judge to judge, but if the officer has prepared his testimony, and if the prosecutor understands the correct way to present direct-examination, this should not be much of a problem for the officer on the witness stand.

Example:

Incorrect:

Q. Officer Smith, is it true that when you interviewed the witness, he told you the defendant was wearing a hat and a false mustache?

Correct:

Q. Officer Smith, what, if anything, did the witness tell you about the defendant's appearance?

4. Opinion Evidence

Expert witness: Any witness who, by knowledge, skill, experience, training, or education is qualified as an expert on a certain subject may, when relevant, give an opinion on that subject.

Often, we think of experts as scientists or forensic specialists who have, through education and years of practical experience, gained an almost magical familiarity with their subject. The range of "experts," however, is endless and can include almost anybody who fits the definition. The average adult, for example, may qualify as an expert in certain areas such as observations of sobriety. After years of watching people who drink alcohol to excess, and seeing their reaction when they have too much, most men and women are able to give an acceptable opinion of whether or not a person was intoxicated. Law enforcement officers are "experts" in areas without even realizing it until called upon to give opinions on matters within those areas.

It should be kept in mind that the sole purpose for putting an expert on the stand is to elicit from that person an opinion on a matter within the area of his or her expertise.

For example, the investigator on the case,

or another police officer, may be qualified as experts in areas relevant to their investigations. They may include:

a) Modus operendi. The investigator who has had years of experience investigating in a particular area, such as burglary, will probably qualify as an expert in examining and identifying methods, techniques, and equipment employed by the criminals during the commission of their crimes. On the other hand, officers new to investigation, or to a certain area of investigation may not so qualify.

b) Common investigative techniques. Again, experience educates an investigator as to the best ways to carry on the investigation of certain crimes. Most large cities divide their detective units into groups specializing in a particular crime: the Homicide Division, the Robbery Division, and so forth. These investigators either are, or probably soon will be, able to qualify as experts in their area of investigation, and when the situation calls for it, may be qualified to give an opinion regarding some aspect of those kinds of investigations.

c) The street value of drugs or stolen merchandise. Any investigator who works burglary or theft investigations will come into almost constant contact with people who deal in stolen merchandise. Such officers become knowledgeable about the market for all sorts of merchandise, and become acquainted with the street value of such items.

d) Degree of sobriety. As we have seen from the discussion above, any officer or civilian who has a well-developed degree of familiarity with others who have consumed an excessive amount of alcohol may qualify to render an opinion as to a person's degree of sobriety.

e) In other areas, a non-expert who has no specialized training or education in a particular area may give an opinion if a proper foundation has been laid, showing that the witness has enough information on which to base an opinion, and if the opinion is rationally based on that information. Examples would include observations concerning the physical condition of another whom the witness has observed ("he walked with a limp as if he had a stiff leg") and apparent mental disorder ("he only starred straight ahead when I spoke with him, not answering my questions, and when he did give an answer, it didn't make any sense. He had a twitch, and kept jerking his head in one direction or another. He kept repeating that he father had sent him to save all mankind. In my opinion he has serious mental problems.") and approximate speed of a vehicle.

5. *Relevancy*

Relevant evidence is evidence having a tendency to make the existence of any fact that is of consequence to the determination of the issue more probable or less probable than it would be without the evidence (Federal Rules of Evidence, 401). Usually, relevant evidence will be admissible and evidence which is not relevant is inadmissible. The application of this Rule is subject to the discretion of the judge.

You may find, depending upon the judge, that often the defendant will be given wider latitude with reference to the admissibility of collateral matters on the issue of relevancy.

5.03 Testifying

A. Oath

The jury watches and evaluates each witness from the minute that witness rises to take the oath (and in the case of the case agent or investigator who is sitting at the prosecution table throughout the trial, the jury is evaluating his demeanor and non-verbal behavior during the entire trial). Listen to the oath and take the process seriously. Don't elaborate an answer. A simple "I do" will suffice, but don't look bored while listening, and don't give your response while you're in the process of sitting down. Be the professional that the jury expects you to be.

B. Introductory Questions

Before getting into the facts of the case or the evidence gathering process, you will be asked certain introductory questions. The purpose of these questions is to identify you to the jury and to acquaint them with you. Such questions are intended to set the stage for your testimony about the case. You will be asked questions about some or all of the following matters:
1) Name and rank.
2) Length of time on the force.
3) Credentials–when asked about your credentials, include any specialized training you may have had, especially if that training is relevant to the issues of that trial.
4) Date of first entry into the investigation; may have been on the day of the incident, as in the case of a homicide or robbery, or it may have been when crime was discovered, as in a fraud investigation, or it may

have been on the day you received information about the crime, as in an ongoing conspiracy. In any of those situations, you should be prepared to identify a particular date which represents the beginning of the investigation.

5) Circumstances of entry into the investigation, e.g., "I was operating a patrol car in sector number 6, which is the south side area of the city. At about 11:15 p.m. (avoid using the military time of 2315 hrs. It confuses the jury, and some may think you arrogant or at least inconsiderate). I received a radio call to proceed to 2193 Hartford Way because of a report of a domestic disturbance at that location."

6) You may be asked to identify the other officers involved in the initial investigation, especially if you are the lead investigator on the case. This is information that you should be prepared to provide without hesitation and without reference to notes.

C. Predicate for Qualifying Questions

Any time a police officer gives testimony in the form of an opinion with regard to investigative techniques employed or with regard to the presentation of evidence gathered, the court requires certain procedures to be followed in order to qualify the witness as capable of preserving such evidence or testimony and to establish that piece of evidence preserved as competent and relevant to the case.

For example, any time an exhibit is presented in court by a testifying officer, it must first be marked as an exhibit and shown to the witness, who must then testify that he recognizes, and can identify, the exhibit. From that point, questions may be anticipated as to the manner in which the evidence was gathered, the precautions taken for

preservation of the evidence, the chain of custody from the time of its discovery to its presentation in court, and other matters designed to demonstrate the materiality and admissibility of the exhibit. The following are examples of these predicate or qualifying questions.

1. General

The exhibit will be marked by the Clerk of the Court for identification or will have been pre-marked by the prosecutor.

Situation 5-7:
Questions by the prosecutor:

Q. I show you what has been marked for identification as State's Exhibit #1 and ask you to examine it, please.
Note: The officer should examine the exhibit long enough to be certain that he is able to identify it as one that he has seen before, or to be able to testify as to what it is if he hasn't seen it before. The officer should not labor over the examination of an exhibit just to impress the jury.

Q. Are you able to identify it?
A. Yes.
Q. How are you able to identify it?
Note: At this point, the officer should briefly explain how he recognizes the exhibit. If by markings made by him on the exhibit or on a sealed container containing the evidence, he should respond with the location of the marking on the exhibit, the type of marking it is (e.g., a letter [never an "x"] or initials) and whatever information which may be attached to the exhibit which was written by the officer for purposes of recording the date, the location, or other pertinent information.

Q. When and where did you first see this exhibit? How did it come into your possession?
A. (The witness will briefly, but completely,

describe the circumstances under which the exhibit came into his possession.)

Q. Upon its coming into your possession, what did you do with it?

Note: In a chronological and orderly fashion, the officer should state exactly what he did with the piece of evidence.

Sample response:

A. After I picked the (exhibit) up from the table, I placed upon it the markings I have already described and placed it in this evidence envelope. I sealed the envelope and wrote the information on it that you can see there. I kept it in my possession and took it to the department evidence room in the Public Safety building. There, I turned it over to the evidence room custodian, Sgt. Turner.

Q. When was the next time you saw it?

Note: This probably will have been when he next removed it from the evidence room. If that is so, there should be an exhibit sheet upon which this information is written.

Example:

Q. May I refer to my exhibit sheet? On May 3, 1984, I went to the evidence room and retrieved the (exhibit)."

Depending upon the case and the circumstances of the investigation, there may be some additional questions to establish chain of custody.

You will be asked questions regarding whether or not the exhibit had been kept in a secure place, and who else may have had access to it. It is prudent to insure the integrity of the exhibit, otherwise an issue of possible tampering or contamination will open up for the defense, and the evidence may be lost to your case.

Q. Is the (exhibit) in essentially the same condition now as it was when it was collected?

Note: Always make yourself familiar with what happened to the exhibit between the time it was collected and the time it is presented in court. For example, it may have been taken to the lab for analysis. If the evidence is marijuana or some other drug, the lab will have used some portion of the material for testing. Another kind of exhibit may have black residue remaining from efforts to remove fingerprints from it. These and other changes in the make-up, consistency, or appearance of the exhibit should be explained to the jury.

The prosecutor will then move for admission of the exhibit into evidence.

2. Specific Pieces of Evidence

Situation 5-8: Handgun

A handgun is found by the investigator under the front seat of the defendant's car upon his arrest. Ballistics tests match a bullet from that gun as coming from the same gun as a bullet found in the body of the deceased. Questions by the prosecutor:

Q. Detective Miller, I show you now what has been marked as State's Exhibit #15 for identification and ask you to examine it.

Note: The witness should examine the exhibit briefly to determine if he recognizes it, and its relevance.

Q. Have you examined the exhibit, sir?
A. Yes, I have.
Q. And do you recognize it?
A. Yes sir, I do.
Q. What is it?
A. It is a .38 caliber Smith & Wesson revolver.
Q. Have you seen this revolver prior to today?
A. Yes, I have.
Q. How is it that you recognize this revolver as one that you have seen prior to today?
A. The tag that is on the weapon is one that I put on it. On it I wrote my initials and

the date. I also recognize it because of the section of the grip that is missing and because of the scratches on the barrel. I also recorded the serial number of the weapon and it is the number on this exhibit.

Q. When and where did you first see it?

A. I saw it for the first time on Saturday, February 6, 1988 in an automobile being driven by the Defendant, Mr. Mope, after I had stopped him at the corner of Tack and Ryan Streets in the city.

Q. What became of the weapon after you first saw it?

A. I took it into my custody.

Q. What did you do with it then?

A. I put it in a bag, took it back to the squad room, transferred it to an evidence bag and put it in the safe in our evidence room, after placing this tag on it.

Note: The exhibit has now been properly identified and upon showing of a proper chain of custody, will be ready for admission, subject to a showing of relevance.

Q. When was the next time that you saw this weapon?

A. On Monday, February 8th, when I removed it from the safe to transport it to the crime lab.

Q. And was the weapon transported to the lab on that day?

A. Yes, sir. I took it myself.

Q. Do you remember who, at the lab, you gave it to?

A. No, but I signed the book and noted the time. The person receiving it initialed the book.

Q. When did you next see the weapon?

A. On March 18th, when I picked it up at the lab.

Q. What did you do with it then?

A. I returned it to the evidence safe at the squad room and it has been there until today when I took it out to bring it to court.

Note: The exhibit is now ready for admission.

Situation 5-9: Videotape equipment used in a surveillance situation. Videotape equipment can be used in various ways, including during surveillance, or to record the speech and actions of an arrested suspect. Rules governing the admissibility of a videotape vary among jurisdictions. You will want to check with your prosecutor concerning its admissibility in your jurisdiction.

The equipment was set up in two locations in a warehouse to be used for an undercover narcotics operation.

Questions by the prosecutor:

Q. Agent McNally, how long have you been employed by your department?

A. Sixteen years.

Q. Do your duties ever involve the use of undercover surveillance equipment?

A. Yes, sir.

Q. Videotaping equipment?

A. Yes, sir.

Q. Have you had any training or instruction in the operation of videotaping equipment?

A. Yes, sir.

Q. What kind of training, and when?

Note: The officer would answer by listing his qualifications.

Q. Have you had occasion, since your training, to operate videotaping equipment?

A. Yes, many times.

Q. Have you used it in connection with surveillance work?

A. Yes, sir.

Q. Did you have occasion to set up video surveillance equipment on December 2nd of last year?

A. Yes.

Q. At whose request?

A. At the request of Agent Bolinger of our office.

Q. Where was the equipment set up?

A. In an undercover warehouse located within the county.

Q. What type of equipment was it?

A. There were two units–both the same, both RCA recorders and RCA 0011 video cameras.

Q. How were they set up?

A. One was set up in the warehouse office and was hidden in an air vent near the ceiling and the other was hidden in an air vent in the bay area of the warehouse.

Q. How were these units powered?

A. By electricity, a 110 volt outlet for each.

Q. Were both of these units operated in the same manner?

A. Yes, sir.

Q. With this type of unit, is the videotape placed into a compartment on the camera or into a separate recorder?

A. These were not camcorders, each component was separate.

Q. Who placed the tape into the recorders?

A. I did.

Q. When?

A. On December 2, 1987 at about 6:30 p.m.

Q. Who turned the equipment on?

A. I loaded and set both recorders on record and started the tapes running.

Q. How long did each tape run?

A. Each ran about the same length of time, about one hour and thirty-five minutes.

Q. Who removed the tape?

A. I did.

Q. I hand you what has been marked as State's Exhibits #16 and #17. Can you identify them?

A. Yes. They are the videotapes I used during the video surveillance on December 2nd.

Q. How can you tell that?

A. Each tape has a sticker and on each sticker I printed the case name, the date and my initials.

Q. What was done with the tapes after their removal from the recorders?

A. I took them to my office and reviewed them to make sure they came out OK, then I placed them in a safe in my office.

Q. Is what you saw on the tapes upon their review a fair and accurate representation of the actual events that took place on that day?

A. Yes, sir.

Q. How do you know that?

A. Because I was with the Defendant the whole time he was in the warehouse, both in the bay and the office.

Q. Is each a recording of the actual events?

A. Yes, sir.

Q. Have the tapes been altered, edited, or damaged in any way since you removed them from the recorders at the warehouse?

A. No, sir.

Q. What was the quality of the recorded tapes?

A. The video on both was excellent, the audio on the recording of what took place in the bay is less than perfect because of the distance between the microphone and the activity.

Q. What was the distance?

A. It varied from as little as seven or eight feet to as much as thirty feet.

Note: The tapes are now ready for admission into evidence.

Situation 5-10: Audio recording of telephone conversations.

The detective instructs a confidential informant to place a phone call from an undercover phone in the detective's squad room to the defendant at his home.

Questions by the prosecutor:

Q. Detective Whitney, did you, in connection with this investigation, cause any telephone call to be made?

A. Yes, sir.

Q. More than one?

A. Yes, sir.

Q. When did they begin?

A. The first call was made on July 18.

Q. From where?

A. From an undercover phone in the squad room.

Q. Were you present when the call was made?

A. Yes, sir.

Q. To whom was the call placed?

A. To the defendant.

Q. Who placed the call?

A. An informant who was working with us on the investigation.

Q. Was there a conversation as a result of the phone call?

A. Yes, sir.

Q. Was any effort made to preserve the conversation?

A. Yes, sir, we recorded it on tape, audiotape.

Q. Did you have the permission of either of the parties to the conversation to make the recording?

A. Yes, sir, we had the informant's permission.

Q. Was it announced to the other party at any time during the conversation that it was being recorded?

A. No, it was not.

Q. Who operated the recording equipment?

A. I did.

Q. What type of equipment was it?

A. It was a standard audiotape recorder with a suction cup extension device.

Q. How does this device work?

A. One end of it is plugged into the recorder in the extension mike intake. The other end had a suction cup with a mike in it. The suction cup is placed on the receiver and the mike picks up what is being said.

Q. Did you test the equipment prior to its use to make sure that it was operating properly?

A. Yes, sir, I did.

Q. And was it?

A. Yes, sir, it was.

Q. And was the recorder loaded and activated when the call was made?

A. Yes, sir.

Q. How long did the conversation last?

A. A little more than six minutes.

Q. Who removed the tape?

A. I did.

Q. What did you do with it after you removed it?

A. When the conversation was terminated, I took the tape and played it back to make sure that the recording was successful; then I locked it in my desk drawer.

Q. I show you what has been marked as Commonwealth's Exhibit #12 and ask you if you can and will identify it?

A. I can. It is the tape used to record the first phone call to the defendant's home on July 18.

Q. How do you identify it?

A. By the markings on the sticker on the tape.

Q. What do the markings represent?

A. I wrote the date and time of the recording, the case name, and I put my initials on it.

Q. Has this tape been kept in your drawer since then?

A. Yes, except to let the defendant's attorney listen to it on October 1st in my office.

Q. Have any changes or modifications been made to the tape since its recording?

A. No, sir.

Q. Has it been damaged in any way?

A. No, sir.

Q. Does this tape contain an accurate and correct recording of the telephonic conversation to which you have just referred?

A. Yes, sir.

Q. I show you now what has been marked as Exhibit #12a and ask you to identify it if you are able.

A. It is a transcript of the phone conversation on July 18th, the first one.

Q. Who prepared it?

A. One of the typists in our office.

Q. Have you reviewed it?

A. Yes, I have.

Q. And have you read it while listening to the tape?

A. Yes, I have.

Q. Is Exhibit 12a an accurate transcript of the recording made on July 18th?

A. Yes, sir, it is.

Note: The tape and the transcript are now ready for admission into evidence subject to a showing of relevance.

3. Witness as an Expert

Situation 5-11: The detective has been assigned to narcotics investigations for six years and has worked as an undercover officer on many occasions. He is being asked about the street purity of cocaine, its value, and his experience in field testing cocaine. He must first be qualified as an expert in the field of narcotics investigations.

Questions by the prosecutor:

Q. Detective Decker, how long have you been employed by the City Police Department?

A. Twelve years.

Q. And to what division were you assigned in September of last year?

A. Narcotics division.

Q. And as a narcotics detective, what were your responsibilities?

A. To investigate narcotics trafficking in the city. Sometimes I work undercover.

Q. Have you been involved in any investigation involving the sale or transporting of cocaine?

A. Yes, sir, many times.

Q. How many times?

A. I'd have no accurate count, but it would be in the hundreds.

Q. How many years have you been a narcotics detective?

A. Six years.

Q. Have you had occasion during that time to work in cooperation with any other departments or agencies?

A. Yes, I've worked with most of the departments in this area and with departments in many of the large cities around country. I've also worked joint investigations with federal and state police agencies.

Q. In connection with cocaine cases?

A. Yes, sir. Cocaine and marijuana seem to be the most prevalent drugs on the street.

Q. Have your investigations involved varying amounts of cocaine?

A. Yes, from as small an amount as one-tenth of a gram to as much as hundreds of kilos.

Q. Have you had any formal training that would assist you in the investigation of narcotics cases?

A. Yes, sir, at the police academy. I've also been to a number of training seminars presented by DEA and US Customs on the detection and investigation of narcotics.

Q. What has that training included?

A. Detection of narcotics, methods of operation, use of undercover surveillance, things like that.

Q. Have you put that training to use?

A. Yes, on many occasions.

Q. Have you been in undercover situations involving the sale or delivery of cocaine?

A. Yes, many times.

Q. And you have had occasion then to make cocaine purchases?

A. Hundreds of times.

Q. What is the largest amount of cocaine that you ever purchased in connection with an undercover investigation?

A. I made a deal to purchase fifty kilos of cocaine.

Q. How many pounds would that be?

A. One kilo equals two point two pounds, so that would be one hundred and ten pounds.

Q. And what was the agreed price?

A. We agreed on thirty thousand dollars per kilo, for a total of one point six million dollars.

Q. Did you ever make the transfer?

A. No, we flashed the money and when they brought out the cocaine, we seized it and placed them under arrest.

Q. Are you familiar with the security precautions taken by drug dealers during their transactions?

A. Yes, sir.

Note: At this point, the prosecutor would release the witness to voir dire or cross-examination with regard to the qualifications of the detective to testify as an expert in the area of narcotics investigations.

5.04 Form of Questions Asked

Most situations call for a question and answer format. Judges prefer it because it allows more control over the witness's testimony and prevents rambling. Prosecutors also usually prefer it for the same reasons. It is clean, crisp, and to the point.

Narrative is a less desirable but sometimes a needed style of questioning. The "what happened then" question is used at times to avoid asking leading questions. When a narrative question is asked, give a complete answer, but do not go beyond the scope of what was asked. If you have a question about its limits, ask for clarification.

A. How to Answer Questions on Direct-Examination

1. Listen to the Question

It is imperative that the witness listen very carefully to the question. As basic as that may sound, it is not an uncommon occurrence for an officer, or any other witness for that matter, to attempt to answer a question they did not hear, or heard incorrectly. This generally results in an unwanted or confusing response to the question. This happens for one or more of a number of the following reasons:

a) The officer is nervous and is concentrating on overcoming his nervousness more than he is on the questions.

b) the officer is distracted by some noise or occurrence in the courtroom.

c) The officer or witness is thinking about the answer he just gave to the previous question and doesn't really hear the next one, though he thinks he knows what that question would be.

Whatever the reason, the officer must concentrate on listening to the question, and should never answer a question he hasn't heard.

2. Pause Before Answering

Before answering any question put to you by either attorney, pause momentarily so that you can gather your thoughts before giving a reply. If you pause before answering every question, on occasions when you need a little more time to gather your thoughts or organize your response, the jury will see you as thoughtful rather than indecisive. Too long a pause, on the other hand, will create the impression that you are searching for a response rather than merely collecting your thoughts. If you are in a situation where you are confused and need a little more time to think of the answer, several options are open to you:

a) You may say that you don't understand the question and ask for it to be repeated. If it would be inappropriate to do that,

b) you may say that you were distracted momentarily and didn't hear the question and ask for it to be repeated.

Note: Don't overuse this tactic.

3. Answer at Your Own Pace

Don't be rushed. A nervous prosecutor may hurrying his questions to you. Don't let that hurry your answers. In answering questions, you should be brief, but complete. Take all the time you need, but don't unduly drag out your answers. Experience will teach you to set your own pace.

4. Answer Only the Question Asked

When the prosecutor asks you a question on direct-examination, he presumably knows the answer and expects a particular response. It is important, therefore, that you not include any unexpected information in your answer. If the prosecutor wants you to elaborate, he will either discuss with you your response prior to the trial or he will ask you to expand your response. Going beyond the limited response expected to the question can cause problems, which may include:
a) the exposure of information which the prosecutor tactically wanted to bring out at a later time;
b) the exposure of information which the prosecutor did not want to share with the defendant, court, or jury;
c) the opening of a matter upon which the opposing counsel may seize during his cross-examination;
d) raising a matter about which the prosecutor was not familiar and which may appear to create inconsistencies in the facts of the case or in the officer's testimony; for example, raising facts which may adversely affect the admissibility of evidence;
e) The prosecutor must, in some instances, plan the admission of evidence based upon his ability to create an assumption of the existence of cer-

tain facts or on a specific sequence of events. By failing to discipline his response, the officer may throw doubt into, or even change, this assumption;
f) Of course, if the prosecutor hasn't confirmed the facts upon which the officer bases his assumption, he has taken an unnecessary risk; or if he asks a question in such a way as to require the officer to disclose the undesired information, there isn't much the officer can do but to answer the question.

5. Don't Appear to be Evasive

Do not be evasive. Each question should be asked for a purpose. That purpose can only be accomplished if it is answered directly and unequivocally; even if it is an "I don't know" response. When an officer unduly hesitates in answering, appears to be unsure of an answer, or is evasive in giving it, not only is the effectiveness of the response diminished from the prosecution's standpoint, but harm can be done both to the jury's perception of the strength of the case and of the officer's credibility. It doesn't take many such responses to create doubt in the jury's mind about the truth or value of the point made, and if that point is crucial or goes to one of the elements of the offense, the case could be lost as a result.

If the officer is sure in his response and appears to be confident of its accuracy, his credibility will be strengthened and any responses which might otherwise indicate a lack of investigative effort or decisiveness will have less of a negative impact on his testimony.

Exception: Answering questions that are harmful and have not been previously discussed.

There will be times when the prosecutor asks a question concerning a matter that he and the officer have not previously discussed. It may be a slip on his part or it may be concerning a matter concerning which the prosecutor did not anticipate a problem. If such a question is asked and the officer knows that the answer will be harmful to the prosecution, but does not involve the type of information which either the law or fairness would require the prosecution to divulge, the officer should, without appearing to be evasive, answer the question in such a way as to tip the prosecutor of the problem. If the prosecutor is thoroughly familiar with the facts, he should be able to pick up the hint, and steer the questioning away from that subject.

If, however, he does not or is unable to signal to the prosecutor that there is a problem, the officer must answer the question the best way he can, constructing his response in such a way as to diminish the harm done by the answer without telling an untruth. There will probably be a price to pay on cross-examination. An understanding of the elements of the offense, the prosecution's theory, and the anticipated defense strategy will be of valuable assistance to the officer when faced with this kind of a problem.

6. Use Plain Language

There are many terms which are commonly used by officers when testifying which are technically inaccurate and which cause confusion about the testimony. Others may be technically accurate, but may be words or terms misunderstood or unknown by the jury members. Technical terms and trade jargon fall into this category and should be avoided when possible. It is the jury that must understand what the witness is saying and what is meant by it. When they do not, they will fault the witness, not themselves. Therefore, it is always wise to use plain, understandable language. When the use of technical language is required, it

should be made clear that the term used is technical and most often used in connection with a specific subject. The term should then be explained to the jury in language which makes its meaning clear to the jury.

Examples:

a) "The subject indicated that he would be at home that evening." There are problems with two of the words in this statement;

1) **Subject:** If the officer is referring to specific person, he should name that person. If the person is unknown, then he should be referred to as such.

2) **Indicated:** Webster says that to indicate is to imply. There are situations which call for the use of the word indicate, but not when the speaker is referring to something that was told to him. What is told, is said.

Corrected version: "Mr. Jones said to me that he would be at home that evening."

b) "The perpetrator was apprehended in his vehicle at twenty-two thirty hours." There are problems with three words or phrases in this statement:

1) **Perpetrator:** The perpetrator is the person who commits or who is guilty of committing an act. When used in a trial referring to the defendant, it is a conclusion and is usually objectionable. When used to describe anyone other than the defendant it takes away the status of the defendant, as being the person accused of the crime. Refer to him as the suspect.

2) **Twenty-two thirty hours:** Many jurors will not know how to translate military time into 10:30 p.m. Others will have to concentrate on figuring it out and may miss some important testimony.

3) **Vehicle:** A very vague term used to describe any means of conveyance. It could mean a truck, motorcycle, automobile, even a bicycle or airplane. The "vehicle" should be described specifically, at least as to its type.

Corrected version: "The defendant (or suspect) was apprehended (or arrested if that is more appropriate) in his automobile at ten-thirty p.m." The officer should be as specific and unambiguous as possible at every point in his testimony.

7. Use of Vulgarity

The officer should not use vulgarity when testifying unless its use is a direct quote attributable to a specific person. One way for an officer to avoid the embarrassment of having vulgar quotes attributed to him is not to use them during conversations with informants or suspects that are relevant to the case. It is not uncommon for an undercover officer, wearing a wire, to use profanity in an attempt to "fit" in better with the suspects. When the tape is played in court or when the officer is asked to restate exactly what was said, the result can be embarrassing to the officer and could adversely affect the officer's image and credibility, especially if the jurors feel that the use of vulgarity was unnecessary.

8. When Not to Answer

a) Never answer a question that you do not understand. Say that you do not understand the question and ask that it be repeated or put in other words.

b) Do not guess at an answer. If you do not know the answer, say so without making a big deal out of it. If you raise a fuss, your testimony will sound suspicious. Never say, "I think so" or "I

guess so." It leaves you wide open on cross-examination. If you're not sure of an answer, simply say "I'm not sure." Then, if you're asked to give your best answer, at least the jury will understand why your answer is less than emphatic.

B. General Rules

1. Do not give memorized testimony. Put the answer in your own words; it expresses a natural response.

2. Do not be afraid to admit that you do not understand the meaning of a certain word. Some defense attorneys tend to employ seldom used words, sometimes in an attempt to embarrass the witness. You can be sure if you don't understand a certain word, there will be someone on the jury who doesn't understand it. They will thank you for asking for the definition.

3. Admit any mistakes that you may have made in your investigation. It is better that the fault lie with you than with the facts. Do not, however, dwell on the mistake and don't let it shake your confidence. I guarantee yours will not be the only mistake made in the investigation, or during the presentation of the case. If you simply admit the error without fanfare or explanation (unless there is a plausible explanation), you will make it seem less important. Do not deny the obvious. There will inevitably be facts in the case which will seem to be unfavorable to the prosecution. You cannot change them and you should never cover them up. Again, the less importance you place on the matter, the less likely the jury is to see it as a major flaw.

4. Correct any mistake in your testimony as soon as you realize it was made.

5. Stop testifying when an objection is made.

6. Stay within your limits.

a) Personality–be yourself. You need not put on a different face to meet the jury. If you do, they will see through it. If you are the quiet, serious, business-like type, use it to your advantage, but don't appear to be the overly stern, schoolmaster type. Conversely, the loose, devil may care, bubbly type must also control his personality without changing it. Every personality has a serious side. The courtroom is a very serious and solemn place. Be your serious self. Do not let your personality dominate your testimony and do not let yourself appear to be unprofessional.

b) Ability and expertise–do not paint a distorted picture of the facts or your ability or expertise to make yourself, or your case, look better than it actually is. Every person has his limitations. The jury understands that and will not see your limitations as a weakness unless they catch you trying to conceal them with exaggeration.

c) Know the prosecutor's style. Understanding the prosecutor's style and personality will help you to better understand what is required of you. For example, if your prosecutor is the type that prepares well for cases, you know that your preparation will be easier. From the well-prepared prosecutor you can expect the Q and A type of direct-examination, which is also helpful to you. The only drawback to dealing with a well-prepared prosecutor is that the officer sometimes tends to get a little lazy in his own preparation. Remember that no matter how easy the prosecutor makes direct-examination for you, you had better be prepared to face cross-examination. Though it is only a small number, some prosecutors are prone to little or no preparation for trial. A few even take pride in trying cases by "shooting from the hip." If this is the case, your job becomes even more difficult because you may expect a lot of narrative questions and should be prepared to lead the prosecutor into the next question. Appear to be fair and impartial. The jury expects you to have confidence in your investigation and the conclusions you have drawn from it, but they also expect you to be fair to the defendant. Don't appear overzealous. You don't have to appear to like the defendant or even to admit the possibility of his innocence, but don't let the jury see that you think a trial is a waste of time. Let them convict the defendant. If the evidence is there and you testify properly, the jury will convict him.

5.05 Elements of Direct Testimony

A. Who? What? When? Where? How? Why?

The answers to these questions will provide the required proof to supply the elements of the offense, without which the prosecution cannot succeed. Such answers will be brought out through physical evidence and the testimony of witnesses. As the officer, you are not expected, in most cases, to be able to answer all of these questions. In some cases, you won't be able to answer any of them. You may only be called as a witness to qualify evidence or to testify as to some other peripheral matter in the case. All of your testimony should be given with accuracy, clarity, completeness, and without speculation, unqualified opinions, or excessive verbosity.

1. Who?

Who you saw, who you spoke with, who you were working with, and who was implicated by whom. All of these who's should be identified by name. If the jury is confused about the who, nothing else will make sense to them.

2. What?

What was the crime committed and what were the facts? What was the criminal trying to accomplish? What did your investigation include and what were the results? Be precise and concise in answering these questions.

3. When?

Include the date, time, and weather conditions (rain, snow, dark, light, etc.); when the police arrived; when the victim called in or when the victim died; and when the victim was last seen, or any other information that will place the facts in the proper time frame for the jury.

4. Where?

Where the crime occurred, where the witnesses and the suspect were at the particular time, and where the evidence was found are all questions that paint a clearer picture for a jury.

5. How?

The modus operendi. How the crime was committed, how entry was made, and how the escape was made are just a few of the important "how" questions.

6. Why?

As pointed out in the section on Report Writing, the "why" is the motive and is not an element of the offense, therefore not required to prove the prosecution's case. It is an important question to answer for the jury, however, if that can be done. You must be very careful when testifying as to the motive. You may provide all of the information from which a conclusion about the motive can be reached, but unless you are specifically asked your opinion, do not give the jury any of your own conclusions.

5.06 Anticipating Defenses

By the time you are called to the witness stand, you should already have given the defense considerable thought and reached some conclusions about the defense strategy. You should be addressing this matter on direct-examination and your testimony should provide facts intended to meet that defense.

A. Denial

In a case where you expect the defendant to deny committing the act with which he has been charged, you should have taken the investigative steps to plug that defense. Be sure that in your testimony you bring out this information. Don't prove the crime and forget to identify the defendant as the guilty party. That often involves collateral facts which may not in themselves identify the defendant as the person who committed the act, but which bring out facts which tend to point to the defendant or which destroy his defense. For example, if when arrested, the defendant states that he was somewhere else when the crime was committed, and if you are able to disprove his statement, it is important to bring that out in your testimony. Also, any successful steps that you have taken to strengthen or corroborate eyewitness identification should be brought to the attention of the jury.

B. Mistake or Ignorance

Mistake and ignorance, of course, are not defenses to crimes that do not require specific intent, but they are matters which the defendant may argue to the jury to make himself seem less culpable. That, in addition to the "family man with no record" image, which the defendant may attempt to build, has set more than one guilty defendant free. If you have anticipated this type of defense, you will have gathered evidence to disprove it. You will have gathered whatever evidence you could find to show the defendant's familiarity with the subject matter, or that he employed a scheme or plan. These, and other facts, should be made known to the jury. They may not be direct evidence of the defendant's guilt but will go a long way to depriving the defendant of credibility when he claims mistake or ignorance.

C. Self-Defense

In an assault or murder case, one of the popular defenses is that of self-defense, especially if the defendant cannot deny presence or claim mistake or accident. This is sometimes a difficult defense to defeat, especially if the victim is a much larger person than the defendant, or was armed. In a homicide case, the pathologist may be able to assist with this, or you may have to reenact the crime to see if the defendant's version is possible. Be prepared to display your work to the jury, perhaps using a live or videotaped demonstration.

D. Accident

Any facts developed through the investigation, or as a result of statements made by the defendant that tend to show that the act committed was no accident, should be brought to the attention of the jury. For example, if the victim was shot in a vital area causing death and the suspect claims that the shooting was an accident, information showing that the victim and the suspect had been fighting earlier or that the victim had provided motive, is evidence tending to show that the act was not an accident.

E. Insanity

Very seldom will you see the insanity defense in cases other then those charging murder. But, in such cases, when there is no other explanation that the defendant can give, or if the facts are particularly heinous, you may expect the insanity defense. If you anticipate this defense, you should have done a number of things at your first opportunity which would tend to prove that:

1. There was evidence that the defendant planned the crime,
2. The defendant carried out the plan in a clandestine manner,
3. The defendant acted in a rational, if brutal, manner,
4. The evidence shows that the defendant was well oriented as to time and place when the crime was committed,
5. The evidence shows efforts by the defendant to conceal the crime after it was committed or to cover himself (as with an alibi defense),
6. The defendant fled after the crime was committed,
7. There is other evidence to show that the defendant was in control of his faculties, knew the difference between right and

wrong, and understood the nature of the offense he committed.

All of the answers to these questions should be given to the jury during your direct-examination. If you don't tell them, what's the use of having done the work to answer them in the first place?

F. Alibi

Almost everyone can find someone who would lie for them in an attempt to provide an alibi. It may be a relative, a spouse, a close friend, or someone who was paid to testify falsely. Any testimony that you can provide that will disprove the expected alibi testimony of defense witnesses will strengthen your chances for a conviction. In most jurisdictions, an alibi defense must be revealed prior to the trial if a timely demand is made by the prosecutor. That should provide you with the opportunity to gather the needed information.

G. Entrapment

Most often found in drug cases, entrapment is what is called an **affirmative defense**. An affirmative defense is an exception to the rule that the prosecution has the sole burden of proof. In using such a defense, the defendant has, in most jurisdictions, the burden of proving his defense, though only by a preponderance of the evidence, not beyond a reasonable doubt. Such a defense will be raised by the defense either on cross-examination of the investigating officer, or through the testimony of the defendant. In anticipating this defense, prepare to present any evidence or testimony which supports your position that neither you nor any other officer illegally enticed the defendant to commit a crime that he would not otherwise have been willing or inclined to commit. A more extensive discussion on

this subject is included in the chapter on cross-examination.

When anticipating the insanity, or some other mental infirmity defense, you should **always** discuss the law in your jurisdiction regarding those defenses.

H. Intoxication

This defense includes alcohol or drugs and can provide, not only evidence of guilt in cases like DUI, but can also provide a defense to other kinds of cases. Some crimes require the element of specific intent. That means that the defendant must have had the ability to, and did, form the specific intent to commit that particular crime (e.g., evidence of premeditation is evidence of the specific intent requirement of first degree murder).

If the evidence does not disprove the defendant's contention that he was in such a condition of alcohol or drug intoxication as to render him unable to form the required specific intent, he cannot be convicted (even though he still may be convicted of a lesser degree of murder, e.g., not guilty of murder, guilty of manslaughter). This defense is most often seen in cases involving crimes against a person (murder, assault) and is sometimes used in connection with the mental infirmity defense (insanity defense) to make the claim that the defendant's intoxicated condition was such that the defendant, reacting to a distorted view of the facts, acted without premeditation or malice. The claim has been made many times in this situation that the defendant, because of his condition and in spite of evidence to the contrary, thought that he was acting in self-defense. In investigating any homicide, rape, or other assault where there is any evidence that the suspect or defendant had been drinking alcohol or using drugs, always look for evidence that would render unreasonable the defendant's contention that use of alcohol or drugs inducing intoxication eliminated one or more of the elements, remembering that merely being intoxicated isn't enough; the defendant must have been so intoxicated as to render him incapable of forming the specific intent required of the crime. Checking with bartenders or getting the defendant to submit to a blood test for drugs or alcohol and gathering evidence of premeditation, intent, clandestine activity, and flight will pay off for the investigator in the courtroom.

Note: Some jurisdictions do not recognize *voluntary* intoxication as a defense to the element of intent. Discuss this with your prosecutor.

5.07 Conclusions

The key to successfully testifying in court lies in the preparation given before taking the stand and in listening closely to the questions, giving brief, but complete, answers and staying alert once you begin giving testimony.

The officer who follows these suggestions will take the stand with confidence in his ability to give his testimony in a competent and professional manner. Consequently, most of the fear and stress usually experienced by the officer on the stand will disappear. His demeanor and delivery will improve and his credibility will be greatly enhanced in the eyes of the jury.

Remember, **there is nothing magical about giving testimony**. Talk to the attorney and the jury in your own way. There are rules to follow, but that should not affect the officer who is well versed in those rules. Be brief, be clear, be truthful, speak plain English, don't get angry or argumentative, and **BE PREPARED**.

Chapter 6

CROSS-EXAMINATION

6.01 Introduction

Cross-examination is usually the primary tool used by the defense attorney to cast doubt in the minds of the jurors as to the guilt of the defendant. As has already been noted, the defendant never has an obligation to testify or to present the testimony of any other witnesses at trial.

A growing number of defense attorneys are now of the belief that in most types of cases it is a mistake to put their clients on the stand to testify. The reason for that is their informed conclusion that jurors are very willing to consider the legal concept of reasonable doubt, and closely examine the prosecution's case for failures in presenting sufficient evidence, right up until the time the defendant takes the stand. From that point on, they believe, the jury throws everything else out and convicts or acquits on the basis of whether or not they like the defendant and whether or not they believe the defendant's version of the facts.

In cases where the defendant does not testify or present the testimony of others during the trial, cross-examination is the only means the defense has to elicit information that will be either harmful to the prosecution, or helpful to the defendant.

The process of cross-examination will begin well before the defense attorney rises to begin his questioning. He will have closely examined any of the officer's reports that

may have been provided him through discovery prior to trial and will be scrutinizing his direct testimony closely. He will know if the witness has prepared himself for court. He will watch the officer's facial expressions, and will listen to the tone of his voice. He will look to see if the witness is confident both in his manner of testifying and in his belief in the evidence being presented. He will watch for and note any nervous gestures and will plan a way to draw the jury's attention to them. He will search for any sign of hesitation or weakness, and when he finds it, he will plan his attack around it. The police officer must be prepared for such an attack. He must learn how to turn it away, or use it to his advantage. The point should be made here that, to a great degree, the extent and style of the cross-examination will depend upon how well the witness has conducted himself on direct-examination. If he has impressed the defense attorney with his thoroughness and professionalism, he will be less likely to risk a wide open attack during cross-examination.

This chapter is intended to acquaint you with the manners and strategies used by defense attorneys on cross-examination, and to instruct you in the proper ways to prepare and present your testimony.

It is the strategies and tactics of the defense that are of primary concern to the police officer about to testify. He is generally confident that his case is strong and that he knows the facts but is often worried that he is playing in the defense attorney's ballpark and that somehow the questioning by the defense attorney will make him appear confused at best or incompetent at worst. If this book accomplishes nothing else, it is my hope that it will provide the tools with which the officer can build confidence in his ability to maintain control over his own testimony. If he has conducted a thorough investigation and has prepared himself to go into the courtroom to testify, the officer should be confident that he indeed controls the situation and it is the defense attorney who is playing in *his* ballpark. Armed with this knowledge and confidence, the officer will be more at ease and better able to think clearly when testifying.

In the succeeding pages you will find, by specific headings, an in-depth examination of the courtroom strategies and tactics employed by defense attorneys and recommendations to the officer on how to combat them and even how to use them to his own advantage. The situations covered are the most common found to be used in criminal trials, and in many instances, are illustrated by sample testimony which includes instructive comments.

6.02 Rules of Evidence

In the conduct of direct-examination, the Rules of Evidence provide the framework within which the attorney on cross-examination may operate. Because the latter is generally less structured than direct-examination, the rules are applied somewhat differently.

On direct-examination, the prosecutor is building his case through the orderly and disciplined presentation of evidence through the direct testimony of witnesses. During direct-examination the rules are intended to

allow the questioner very little opportunity to stray outside very narrow guidelines. On the other hand, during cross-examination the attorney is usually using his opportunity to destroy that which the prosecutor has built. He does this by attempting, through his examination, to discredit the testimony of the prosecution's witness, and in so doing, to raise doubts about the strength or credibility of the case against his client.

In order to insure the defendant ample opportunity to exercise his constitutional right to confront witnesses against him, the rules on cross-examination are designed to allow the defense attorney broader latitude in the manner and content of his questioning.

The area where this is most apparent is in the application of the rules governing leading questions, hearsay, and opinion testimony.

A. Leading Questions

While defined in greater detail in the chapter on direct-examination, a leading question is one which suggests the answer. While leading questions are generally not permitted on direct-examination, they are permitted on cross-examination. Often an attorney will ask only leading questions when on cross-examination. The reasons for this are offered in greater detail later in this chapter.

B. Hearsay

The Hearsay Rule is applied in the same manner during cross-examination as it is on direct-examination. However, practically applied, many judges will often allow broader latitude to the attorney on cross-examination than on direct-examination. Keeping that in mind, when you are on the witness stand under cross, you should be listening closely for questions that call for an answer that you are not able to give from firsthand knowledge. Such questions asked by the defense attorney are usually designed to damage or change the prosecution's position on one or more points.

While the general rule is that the officer should never be drawn into answering questions about which he has no personal knowledge, there are times when the defense attorney, in error, will open a door which will allow the witness to give testimony that he would not otherwise be permitted to offer, and which is damaging to the defense. Experience will usually alert the officer to such opportunities. If you choose to seize upon such a question, do so with caution, always considering the possibility that the defense is laying a trap.

C. Opinion Evidence

Often, trial court judges are more inclined to allow a witness to state an opinion on cross-examination than they are on direct-examination. The officer must be careful of the answer he gives to such a question. If a defense attorney asks for an answer in the form of an opinion, be certain before answering that you have enough information to qualify you to give such an opinion. If you are not possessed of such information, simply tell the defense attorney that you have insufficient information, or that you are unqualified to give such an opinion. *Never offer an opinion that is outside you area of expertise or experience.*

These points will be made in greater detail throughout this chapter by illustration

in sample cross-examination situations.

6.03 Purpose and Scope of Cross-Examination

The primary purpose for cross-examining a police officer is to probe the officer's direct testimony in an effort to weaken the effect of that testimony upon the jury. The extent to which the defense attorney will conduct such an examination will depend in large part on how much damage the officer's testimony has done to the defendant and on how many opportunities for effective cross-examination have been presented by the officer's direct testimony.

If the officer's police report, prior statements, or testimony tends to contradict or to be inconsistent with his direct testimony, the defense attorney will spend a great deal of time bringing that point to the attention of the jury.

The limitations imposed upon the tactics and style employed by the defense attorney will vary from courtroom to courtroom, depending upon the manner in which the judge exercises the broad discretion with which he is empowered. Usually wide latitude is given on cross-examination. That freedom, however, is confined to the legitimate areas of inquiry. Those areas are matters testified to on direct-examination, matters affecting the credibility of a witness, and collateral matters which were not specifically referred to on direct, but which the court, in it's discretion, determines to be proper areas for cross-examination.

A. Matters Testified to on Direct-Examination

Any facts testified to on direct-examination are subject to attack on cross-examination. They could relate to anything from the manner in which the investigation was conducted (to include evidence collection), to conclusions testified to by the investigator, which conclusions were based on statements taken from the defendant or witnesses.

It should be noted that the judge will generally allow cross-examination on matters not strictly covered on direct if those matters are relevant to the conduct of the investigation and are reasonably within the witness's knowledge.

B. Matters Affecting the Credibility of Witnesses

The strength of the prosecution's case depends to a great extent upon the credibility of its witnesses. The defense attorney can seriously damage the case against the defendant by effectively attacking the witness's statements, especially when that witness is a police officer.

For example, by pointing out errors in the officer's written report or by disproving estimated distances used by the officer in describing locations or events, or by successfully attacking the chain or integrity of evidence, the defense will try to shake the jury's confidence in the officer's truthfulness, or competence, or both. These and other such opportunities presented to the defense attorney will be illustrated throughout this chapter.

C. Collateral Matters

Any subject that is relevant to the matters testified to on direct-examination, whether or not specifically referred to by the witness are legitimate subjects for cross-examination. Again, the latitude allowed depends largely on the manner in which the court exercises its judicial discretion. Suggesting that the facts testified to by the officer may reasonably lead to conclusions different from those relied upon by the prosecution is a common tactic seen in criminal trials. The suggestion is that, on the basis of the investigative techniques actually employed by the officer as opposed to those suggested by the defense attorney, the investigation was sloppy or incomplete.

D. Written Reports

It is a common technique of defense attorneys to attempt to discredit the officer's testimony by attacking the police reports. In pursuance of that goal, the attorney will attempt to find a way to gain access to the officer's investigative report during cross-examination. The rules regarding access to a police officer's investigative report vary from state to state. Some jurisdictions, for example, require that the report be given to the defense attorney upon completion of the officer's direct testimony whether or not the officer has referred to the report up to that point. Others do not require that such discovery be provided unless the officer has used or referred to a report or memorandum to refresh his recollection either during his direct testimony or immediately prior to taking the stand (the definition of the word "immediately" is discretionary with the judge). In all jurisdictions, if the officer uses the report or other memoranda or notes during his direct testimony or while on cross-examination, the defense attorney is permitted, on cross-examination, to use that report, or at least that portion of the report referred to by the officer.

One tactic employed by defense attorneys in attempting to gain access to the report is to offer the testifying officer an opportunity to refer to his report. For example, at the first sign of indecision on the officer's part, or the first time the officer responds to a question by saying that he doesn't remember, the attorney conducting the questioning will offer the witness an opportunity to review his report for an answer to his question, and may, in doing so, make it seem that if the officer refuses the offer, he is trying to hide something. If the officer accepts the offer and does refer to the report, the report is given to the defense attorney for further cross-examination. If you, as the testifying officer, have thoroughly reviewed your report in preparation for your court appearance, as you should have, you will know whether or not the information is in the report. If that is the case, you may refuse the offer, telling the attorney that you are familiar with the report and that the information he seeks is not in the report.

The following examples illustrate through sample testimony, many of which were taken from actual trials (although the names, places, and dates have been changed), some of the problems a witness may be required to confront during his cross-examination, and make note of ways to combat those problems.

1. The Officer Is not Completely Familiar with the Contents of His Report

Situation 6-1:
Questions by the defense attorney:

Q. Detective Kerr, on how many of the occasions that you met with my client, Mr. Kokeman, prior to the actual transfer of the drugs on March 5th did you discuss the amount of cocaine to be delivered?

A. I don't recall, exactly.

Q. Was it more than once?

A. Yes, sir, it was.

Q. Would you have had that discussion at half of the meetings?

A. At least half of the time, yes, sir.

Q. Do you recall the total number of meetings that you had with Mr. Kokeman prior to March 5th?

A. No, sir, but there were quite a few.

Q. Detective Kerr, I assume that you wrote a report of your activities during this investigation?

A. Yes, sir, I did.

Q. And, I also assume that you recorded the dates of each of the meetings with my client?

A. Yes, sir.

Q. Did you bring your report to court with you today?

A. Yes, I did.

Q. Where is it?

A. Over there on the prosecution table.

Q. If you reviewed your report briefly, would you be able to answer my questions?

A. I am answering your questions, sir.

Q. But, your answers are that you don't know, and I'm only offering you an opportunity to refresh your recollection about some important facts so that the jury can get the whole story.

A. Yes, sir.

Q. You do want the jury to get all of the facts, don't you?

The Prosecutor: Objection, your Honor.
The Court: Sustained (then to the defense attorney); please confine your questions to the facts and save the argument for summation, counsel.

Q. Thank you, your Honor. Detective Kerr, are you able to answer my questions concerning the number of prior meetings with Mr. Kokeman without referring to your reports?

A. No, sir.

Q. Would you, then, review your reports and

refresh your recollection?

Note: At this point, the officer is in a bad position. He is unable to answer legitimate questions asked of him by defense counsel without referring to his report. He knows that if he refers to his reports, the defense attorney will be permitted to cross-examine him on at least that portion of his reports that deal with prior meetings with Mr. Kokeman. If he refuses to review his reports, he looks bad to the jury. If he had been better prepared, he may have avoided this situation. As it is, he must now answer for the quality of his written report.

2. The Officer Is Completely Familiar with the Contents of His Report

Situation 6-2:

Questions by the defense attorney:

Q. Officer Smith, would you like to refer to your report to refresh your recollection?

A. No, sir, that won't be necessary.

Q. Why not?

A. Because the information would not be in the report.

Q. Wouldn't you rather check it to make sure?

A. No, sir, I am sure. I wrote the report and, a week or so ago, reviewed it. I am completely familiar with what is in there. That information is not in my report.

Q. Why would it not be in the report?

A. Because it is not the type of information I would put in a report.

Q. Why isn't it, sir?

A. Because my report, any report, only includes brief highlights of the events; we do not go into great detail on such matters as that which you have raised.

Note: If the attorney continues along this line of questioning, he will appear to be arguing with the officer and the jury will see that as a weakness in the defense.

Note: The officer's use of the word "we"

when referring to report writing practices makes it clear to the jury that the officer was following an accepted policy set out by the department in the preparation of police reports. If the defense attorney is permitted to use your report while conducting his cross-examination, you may expect him to use various strategies and tactics in his questioning.

3. Failure of the Officer to Testify During His Direct-Examination on Matters Which Were Contained In the Report

Situation 6-3:

Defense strategy:

To make it appear that the officer is trying to conceal from the jury some weaknesses or inconsistencies in the facts of the case.

Tactics:

To interpret that which was found in the report, and not testified to, as being important enough to have been brought to the jury's attention, and that since it wasn't, there must be some error or weakness in the reported item that the officer is trying to hide from the jury.

The defense attorney may attempt to make it appear as though the material in the report was a fabrication. You may expect to be questioned about the reasons why you failed to mention the reported matter in your testimony, especially if he is able to make it seem that the reported matter was important information. The attitude displayed by the defense attorney during this type of questioning will almost always be one of confrontation and the further the questioning goes, the more hostile and accusatory the attorney's questions will become. If he becomes abusive or argumentative, the prosecutor should object. If the court feels that the defense attorney has gone beyond the bounds of fair cross-examination, the objection will be sustained.

The defense attorney will attempt to put

you on the defensive. He hopes you will respond in an angry tone, and he may try to cause you to lose your cool. In many cases, that is more important to him than is the subject of the questioning.

Recommendations:

a) Follow the general rules of responding.

b) Particularly in this situation, keep your cool. Don't allow yourself to get rattled or to show impatience or frustration. Remain the even-tempered professional. This will *always* make you look better.

c) If on direct, you were not asked a question concerning the matters to which the defense attorney is referring, say so. Be sure, however, that there was no question asked on direct which should have, or could have, provided the opportunity to furnish this information. If there was such a question asked, you may appear to have been evasive in your testimony.

d) If you recognize that the omission of such testimony was an oversight or failure on your part, admit it without making a big deal out of it. If you make such an admission without the appearance of being defensive, you will, in effect, be downplaying whatever error you made, and the jury may see it as unimportant.

Situation 6-4:

Questions by the defense attorney:

Q. Detective Adams, on direct examination you have given us your recollection of the sequence of events on April 9th, and indeed have confirmed that recollection on cross-examination, isn't that correct?

A. Yes, sir.

Q. And in preparing to testify, I assume that you went over the events of that day in your mind so as to remember at least all of the important events?

A. Yes, sir.

Q. I ask you now if there is anything that you would like to add to that testimony?

A. No, sir.

Q. I assume then that you are satisfied that your present recollection of the events of April 9th are accurate?

A. Yes, sir, I believe so.

Q. May I assume that you also reviewed your reports before coming here today?

A. Yes, I did that.

Q. And you have your report with you here today?

A. I brought it with me. It's on the counsel table.

Q. I'd like to show you a copy of it. (Then handing the report to the witness) Is that a correct copy of your report?

A. It seems to be.

Q. Would you like to get your original?

A. No, I recognize it as a copy of it.

Q. Fine. Now, I direct your attention to page 6 of that report. Do you have it?

A. Yes, sir.

Q. Do you see where it is written that you instructed the informant to set up a time and place for your meeting with the defendant?

A. Yes.

Q. And, do you see where it is written that you were told by the informant that he had done that, and that the meeting was set for April 9th?

A. Yes, sir, I do.

Q. I assume then on the basis of your answers here today that did not happen?

A. No, sir, you can't assume that. It did happen.

Q. But you didn't say anything about it here today, did you?

A. No, sir.

Q. Why not?

A. I forgot about it.

Q. But, that is an important fact to the investigation, isn't it?

A. Yes, but only because it set up my meeting with the defendant. It had no significance in itself.

Q. But, you said earlier that you were satisfied that your present recollection was accurate.

A. And, it is. I just forgot about the informant's meeting.

Note: The detective has admitted the mistake and made the point that it was no big deal. He didn't get defensive or combative about it. He has left the defense attorney nowhere else to go with it. On the other hand, if you allow your error to be seen as major, it may affect your credibility in the eyes of the jury.

4. Apparent Mistakes In the Report

Mistakes made in the report are almost always avoidable, and when not avoidable, they are almost always correctable. Every report should be reviewed well before the case goes to trial, and when mistakes are found, they should be corrected, either on the report itself, or on a supplementary report. In the two situations shown here, the first mistake involves information supplied by a witness at the scene. The mistake is an understandable one, but it should have been detected during a review and corrected. The second involves a misstatement by the reporting officer, and is more damaging, though it too could have been corrected in a supplementary report.

Situation 6-5: Information mistakenly reported by a witness at the scene.

Questions by the defense attorney:

Q. Now, Detective Dillon, you have testified that the statement in your report that the vehicle which the defendant was driving immediately after the robbery was a white '67 or '68 Chevy, is in error, correct?

A. Yes.

Q. And you are testifying now that it was a dark brown '73 Pontiac LeMans, is that correct?

A. Yes, sir.

Q. Well, forget about the color. Those two cars don't look even remotely alike, do they, detective?

A. No, they don't.

Q. OK, you know that the defendant was in the Pontiac on the day of the robbery because he was arrested in it, right?

A. That's correct.

Q. So, where did the information come from that he was in a white Chevy?

A. From a witness outside the bank.

Q. There is no allegation that the defendant was in on the actual robbery, is there?

Note: This is an attempt to mislead. Here, the defendant was the driver of the getaway car, and never went into the bank. However, as an accomplice, he is just as responsible for the acts of the others as if he himself went inside the bank. Therefore, while the defense attorney is attempting to slide by the witness, he is neatly trying to diminish the defendant's responsibility in the eyes of the jury by insinuating that the defendant wasn't part of the robbery.

A. Yes, there is, he was the getaway driver and, therefore, was charged the same as the ones who went in the bank.

Q. But, no one in the bank was able to identify my client, were they?

A. No one inside the bank was able to see your client. He was waiting outside in the getaway car.

Q. Answer the question, please. No one in the bank identified my client, did they?

A. No, sir.

Q. And, you've established that the outside witness was confused and didn't really see my client, isn't that correct?

A. The one who said he saw your client in the white Chevy was mistaken. He saw another car that he thought was the getaway car, but it wasn't.

Q. Well, maybe it was and maybe my client

wasn't involved in the robbery at all. That's possible, isn't it?

A. No, it isn't.

Q. Why not?

A. Because the other two occupants of the car have been identified by four people in the bank as the robbers and they had the bait money with them when they were arrested.

Q. Why was my client's car stopped? Did someone recognize the other two occupants?

A. No, another witness outside the bank described the getaway car as one similar to your client's Pontiac.

Q. Not the white Chevy?

A. No.

Q. And, how long after the robbery was my client's car stopped?

A. About 45 minutes.

Q. And, where was it stopped?

A. On Interstate 90, about 4 miles west of the intersection with Interstate 79.

Q. And, to get from the bank in Erie to the point where the car was stopped, wouldn't take 45 minutes, would it?

A. It shouldn't.

Q. Who was this witness who described my client's car?

A. I don't know.

Q. You didn't get his name?

A. No, sir.

Q. Why not?

A. I didn't think it was important.

Q. You didn't think that the information which led to my client's car being stopped more than 6 miles from the bank, and which led to his arrest, was important?

A. It was important to us in finding the robbers, but because we didn't know who gave the information, and since they were identified by the bank employees, I didn't think it was necessary to include it in my report.

Q. Isn't it just as likely that the other two men

who may have robbed the bank left in another car with another driver, then later ended up in my client's car 45 minutes later, and more than 6 miles away from the robbery, without my client knowing anything about the robbery?

A. No, sir.

Q. Why not?

A. Because of the description of the getaway car.

Q. Which one? The white Chevy which you mentioned as the getaway car in your report, or my client's '73 Pontiac, which isn't mentioned at all?

Note: Many of the better defense attorneys will ask the "Isn't it possible . . . ?" question, and, unlike the attorney in this example, will not ask the "Why not?" question. With his question and your simple "no" answer, without the follow-up question, the attorney will be able to make an argument to the jury that you had no answer for that question, and that therefore your answer seems unreasonable, under the circumstances. If you are not asked the follow-up question, either try to include your explanation into the answer, or hope that the district attorney asks the follow-up question on redirect.

Note: That was about all the mileage the defense attorney could get out of the point. But, as you can see, he caused considerable damage to the officer's credibility.

Situation 6-6: Misstatement by the reporting officer.

Detectives Fenton and White were working an undercover drug operation targeting a certain known crack house, but no particular person. Eventually, a woman named Nancy McDonald was arrested for delivering an amount of crack cocaine to Detective White. Detective Fenton's report, however, written after the arrest, makes it seem as though McDonald was the target of the investigation. The defense attorney is trying to make it seem that McDonald was already known to the detectives and that she was being set up by them.

Questions by the defense attorney:

Q. Sir, isn't it accurate to say that you indicate in your report that Detective White was to purchase, or hoped to purchase cocaine from a black female?

A. Yes.

Q. And, the allegation in the charge is that he did make such a purchase, isn't that correct?

A. Yes.

Q. And, the person you referred to was the defendant, Nancy McDonald, is that correct?

A. Yes, that's correct.

Q. Now, you testified on direct, and earlier on cross, that you hadn't talked with Detective White prior to his going out into the field, do you recall that?

A. Yes.

Q. And, you had not, at any time prior to the alleged purchase, talked to Detective White about the woman referred to in your report, had you?

A. No, sir.

Q. In fact, you hadn't even heard of Nancy McDonald prior to October 9th, had you?

A. No, but I know her brother.

Q. And, you and Detective White had no one in particular targeted that day, had you?

A. No, we didn't.

Q. Then, how do you account for the statement in your report that White had hoped to purchase cocaine from Nancy McDonald?

A. Well, we identified the defendant after the transaction.

Q. Yes, but at that point he would have already made the purchase, and the report clearly suggests that the defendant was targeted prior to the alleged purchase, doesn't it?

A. Yes, sir, but that isn't the case. I made a mistake in the report. Detective White had intended to make a narcotics purchase, and since he eventually made the purchase from the defendant, I mistakenly wrote what I did.

Q. Don't you review your report before coming to court?

A. Yes, I do.

Q. And don't you, at that time, correct any mistakes made in the report?

A. When I see them, yes, I do.

Q. You didn't notice this mistake?

A. No, sir, I didn't.

Q. That's a pretty glaring mistake, isn't it?

By the prosecutor: Objection, argumentative.

By the court: Sustained.

Q. The defendant wasn't arrested until January 15th, why was that?

A. We were conducting an undercover operation in the area, and arresting the defendant immediately following the buy would have blown our cover and ended our operation.

Q. Were there any surveillance photos taken of the alleged transaction?

A. No, sir.

Note: There were other questions asked concerning the failure of the officers to take surveillance photos of the defendant in an effort to discredit the accuracy of the identification, then the attorney moved on to another area.

Q. Now, in addition to the error made in the report about which we spoke earlier, there was another error made in reporting the location of the alleged transaction, wasn't there?

A. Yes.

Q. Are there any other errors in your report?

A. No, the error regarding the address was made because I wasn't at the scene of the transaction. I was conducting the surveillance from the next block.

Q. May I suggest that both errors were made because my client was your target from the beginning, and whether or not you actually made a but from her, she was the one you intended to arrest?

By the prosecutor: Objection.
By the court: Sustained.

Q. Detective Fenton, you had not seen the defendant between October 9th of last year and January 15th of this year, and you had never seen her before that time, isn't that correct?

A. Yes, sir.

Q. You did not take any photographs of the alleged drug sale which would have assured a correct identification of the dealer, and did not even attempt to get any fingerprints off of the packet, which you say my client sold. Considering all of these errors, isn't it reasonable that you are also mistaken in your identification of the defendant?

A. No, it is not. The person I saw deliver the cocaine to the detective was your client, Nancy McDonald.

Note: There was no discussion on direct about what problems, if any, the detective might have had seeing the transaction from a block away, and the attorney for the defendant never touched the question on cross. He did, however, hit it hard during his summation to the jury. The defendant was acquitted.

5. Matters Testified to Which Were Not Included in the Report

Situation 6-7:
The officer testifies on direct-examination about matters which were not included in the report.

Strategy:
a) To make it seem as though the officer is embellishing his testimony or intentionally adding information about matters which did not occur the purpose of giving the prosecution's case a needed boost.

b) To make it appear that the officer's reporting was shoddy and, therefore, unreliable.

Tactics:
a) The defense attorney will ask you to identify the report as having been prepared by you.

b) He will ask you whether you prepared any other reports or memoranda about the subject matter.

c) He will attempt to have you confirm that you had made certain statements in your direct testimony about matters in the report. Listen carefully to his characterization of what it was that you said. Don't assume that he is attempting to accurately recount it. Be alert! He will ask you to show him, in the report, where the statement is to which you referred in your testimony.

d) If you made a mistake in testifying about what you included in the report, the defense attorney will force you to admit that mistake and in doing so, will attempt to make the error in the report seem to be an intentional misrepresentation.

e) He may ask you questions that make you appear to have failed to follow what you knew were proper procedures in preparing your report.

f) He may also suggest that the report, made when your recollection was fresh, was correct and your testimony incorrect.

Situation 6-8:
The defense attorney misleads the officer regarding what he testified to on direct. The officer was not alert to the attorney's misstatement of his testimony and some damage was done to his credibility.
The defense attorney questions the officer.

Q. All right, Officer Wayne, I am now going

to show you, again, what has been marked and identified by you as being Defendant's Exhibit Number 1 for identification. (The officer takes the exhibit.) Now, I hand you what has been marked as Defendant's Exhibit Number 2, and ask you look at it and tell me if you recognize what that document is.

A. Yes, sir, that's a report of investigation under the same file title.

Q. Do you know who prepared that report and when?

A. It's dated August 26th, and it was prepared by me.

Q. Other than those two documents which are before you now, did you prepare any other reports relating specifically to the events in the Regency Hotel?

A. No, sir, these would be it.

Q. Now, you told me previously that you had noted on your reports somewhere that you overheard a conversation about cocaine and money, and that you wrote it in some report, correct?

A. Yes, sir.

Note: Here, the officer took the defense attorney's word for something that did not occur. The officer never actually said that he, himself, overheard the conversation, but on direct-examination this particular matter was not clarified. The defense attorney knew that the officer hadn't said that, but also knew that the matter was ambiguous enough that, if he could get the officer to say that he had said it, then as far as the jury would be concerned, he had. The officer should have listened more carefully to the question and should not have assumed that the matter was too unimportant to correct right away. Once he said, "yes, sir," it was too late to correct it. What the officer had actually said on direct was that the CI was in the room with the suspect and was wearing a body recorder and that later, he (the officer) listened to the tape and heard the words "cocaine" and "money"

being used. The officer referred in the report to the taped conversation and its contents but did not actually say that he had listened to the tape.

Q. Is that correct, sir?

A. Yes, sir.

Q. Now, officer, will you please show us where in those two reports there is such a statement?

A. In paragraph three of Exhibit 1, it says that the confidential informant did not see any other person in the room with Espinosa during the exchange of money and cocaine. And that what I was referring to when I testified about money and cocaine being discussed.

Q. Isn't it a fact that you have testified under oath here several times today that you, yourself, heard conversation regarding cocaine and money?

A. Yes, sir.

Q. Looking at my copy of the reports, I see nothing in paragraph three, or any other paragraph for that matter, that notes that you overheard any conversation referring to money or cocaine. Do you find anything like that in your report, officer?

A. There is nothing in paragraph three that says that, no.

Q. Look carefully at the entire contents of both reports and tell me if you see it anywhere in there, in any paragraph, on any page.

A. (after a pause) No, sir, it's not in either of these two reports.

Q. Is it in any report that exists in this world today?

A. I don't think so, sir.

Q. Is there any reason why you have told us under oath repeatedly that it existed in writing, when in fact, it does not?

A. I testified earlier that the conversation, . . . I overheard the words cocaine and money in the conversation, but I don't see it in the reports.

Note: Here, the officer should have made it clear that he had heard the conversation on the tape and that he never intended to convey during his testimony that he had overheard the actual conversation.

Q. And, when you first became a police officer, you went to the police academy, didn't you?

A. Yes, sir.

Q. And, at the academy they taught you, among other things, how to write a police report, isn't that correct?

A. Yes, sir.

Q. And the purpose of writing reports is to preserve important matters so that they can be used in the future both by your department and by other departments and agencies with which you may be cooperating, isn't that correct?

A. Yes, sir, it is.

Note: the officer might have given his own statement regarding the purpose of a report rather than to adopt the statement of the defense attorney.

Q. And, in fact, reports were prepared by you on or shortly after the arrest in this case relating to this case, isn't that correct?

A. Yes, it is.

Q. And at that time your memory was fresh, was it not?

Note: Here, the defense attorney makes a general statement that may be true (the officer's memory was fresher when the report was written than it was at the time of his testimony) but was not relevant to his testimony since there was no real conflict between the officer's report and his testimony.

A. It was.

Q. Certainly, it was fresher then than it is now regarding the facts in this case, right?

A. Yes, sir.

Q. So, is there any reason that you give us as to why it is that you left out of your reports the crucial matters about which

you have testified here?

A. I think the transcript of the tapes will better state what the conversation was than what I overheard.

Note: Here, the officer finally recovers and brings to the attention of the jury that the recording, and not his testimony or reports, will let the jury know exactly what was said, and by whom. The defense attorney, not wanting to allow the officer to completely rehabilitate his testimony, decided to go on to another matter.

In the alternative, you may expect to be questioned about the reasons why the matters testified to were not in the report. The defense attorney will probably, in a very subtle and seemingly harmless way, suggest reasons for not including them in the report, and he will use words like "failure" and "neglect" in describing your actions.

Recommendations:

a) Follow the general rules for responding to questions on cross-examination.

b) If what was left out of the report was unimportant, say so. However, be satisfied that it is, because if the defense can illustrate that it was an important matter and that you should have known it to be so, you can be put in a very difficult and embarrassing position.

c) If the importance of a fact was not known at the time that the report was made, say so.

d) Be prepared to explain why that information was not later included in a supplemental report. The excluded fact may have been both important and known at the time of the preparation of the report and yet not included for other reasons:

1) There may be no need to include such information;

2) The information may have been intentionally omitted for some reason or another.

3) If there is such an explanation, give it.

If there is not, say that you didn't feel you needed to note that point in order to remember it.

6. Mistakes In Preparing the Report

Situation 6-9:
The officer has made mistakes in the preparation of the report. The mistakes will usually involve addresses; descriptions of persons, places, or things; names of witnesses; dates and times, distances and sequence of events; but can be about anything reported.

Strategy:
The general strategy is to cast doubt on the reliability of information reported by the officer and, therefore, on his testimony.

Tactics:
The tactics used by the defense attorney will depend, to a great extent, on the nature and number of the errors.

a) If there are few errors and they do not touch on critical areas, the attorney will merely seek an admission that an error was made and go on to other areas, saving the impact of the errors for argument during the summation.

b) If the errors are many, even though unimportant, or if the errors contradict each other, the attorney will spend more time exploring the reasons for the errors while making certain that the jury understands that the errors are your responsibility (even if only typographical). He may attempt to paint your efforts at report writing as shoddy and will later ask the jury to suppose that, therefore, your entire investigation was probably shoddy.

c) If the errors are serious, you may expect a major effort to discredit your testimony and your investigation. You may expect a more confident and belligerent assault by the defense attorney. (For sample testimo-

ny, see Situation 1-1 in chapter on report writing.)

d) If the report includes conclusions based on information received from others, you may expect the defense attorney to challenge the conclusion. (For sample testimony, see Situation 1-3 in chapter on report writing.)

Recommendations:

a) As in other situations, don't allow the mistake to loom larger than it is. Neither should you argue with the attorney about its importance. That puts you in a defensive posture when it is better to remain on the offensive throughout your testimony. Admit the mistake, giving a brief explanation (not excuse) if there is one, and move on.

Situation 6-10: Admitting the mistake. Using the same basic testimony referred to in situation 6-6 with some changes, this testimony illustrates what can happen when the witness is not alert to mistakes in his report that could have been corrected without damage had the officer reviewed his report carefully prior to getting on the witness stand. As it was, the detective was able to avoid serious damage by simply admitting the mistake without trying to dance around it in an attempt to minimize the mistake.

Q. Detective Fenton, isn't it accurate that you indicate in your report that Detective White was to purchase or hoped to purchase cocaine from a black female?

A. Yes.

Q. And the allegation in the charge is that he did make such a purchase, isn't that correct?

A. Yes.

Q. And the person you referred to was the defendant, Nancy McDonald, is that correct?

A. Yes, sir.

Q. Now, you testified on direct and also earlier on cross that you hadn't talked with Detective White prior to his going out into the field. Do you recall that?

A. Yes, sir.

Q. And, you had not, at any time prior to the alleged purchase, talked to Detective White about the woman referred to in your report, had you?

A. No, sir.

Q. In fact, you hadn't even heard of Nancy McDonald prior to October 9th, had you?

A. No, but I knew of her brother.

Q. And you and Detective White had no one targeted that day, had you?

A. No, sir.

Q. Then, how do you account for the statement in your report that White had hoped to purchase cocaine from Nancy McDonald?

A. Well, we identified the defendant after the transaction.

Q. But, at that point he would have already made the purchase, and the report clearly suggests that the defendant was targeted prior to the alleged purchase, doesn't it?

A. Yes, sir, but that isn't the case. I made a mistake in the report. Detective White had intended to make a narcotics purchase, and since he eventually made the purchase rom the defendant, I mistakenly wrote something that makes it seem as though she was the target all along, and that was not so.

Q. The defendant wasn't arrested until January 15th. Why was that?

A. We were conducting an undercover operation in the area, and arresting the defendant immediately following the sale would have blown our cover, and ended the operation.

Q. Were there any surveillance photos taken of the alleged transaction?

A. No, sir.

Q. Now, in addition to that error in the report, there was another error made in reporting the location of the alleged transaction, wasn't there?

A. Yes.

Q. Are there any other errors in your report?

A. No, the error regarding the address was made because I wasn't at the scene of the transaction. I was conducting the surveillance from two blocks away.

Q. May I suggest that both errors were made because of sloppy police work?

By the Prosecutor: Objection, argumentative.

By the Court: Sustained.

Q. Detective Fenton, you had not seen the defendant between October 9th and January 15th, and you had never seen her before that time, correct?

A. Correct.

Q. And, you have not taken any photographs of the alleged drug sale, which might have assured a correct identification of the dealer, isn't that correct?

A. We were not in a position to be able to take any photos.

Q. And, there was no attempt to get any fingerprints from the package allegedly received from my client, which may have either have positively identified or excluded my client as a suspect, correct?

A. The package was handled by Detective White when the transfer was made. Then, he put the package into his pocket. The package would have been completely contaminated and it is very doubtful that any prints at all could have been recovered.

Q. Considering all of these errors, isn't it reasonable that you are also mistaken in your identification of my client as the person who committed this crime?

A. No, it is not. The person who I saw deliver the cocaine was your client, Nancy McDonald.

Note: There was further cross-examination on the subject of the identification, and the quality of the investigation, in particular in the failure of Detective White to wear a body wire, but not concerning the errors on the report.

Note: Other suggestions regarding the admission of errors:

Never use the phrase "I was in a hurry" to explain an error (in the report or anywhere else), it opens up a multitude of opportunities for the defense attorney, and will always hurt your testimony. During an investigation, there are only two times when you should be in a hurry; when you are chasing a suspect and, when someone is shooting at you.

a) Do not get beaten down by your mistake. A mistake is a mistake and we all make them. Keep a positive attitude and you will maintain the jury's confidence.

b) If the opportunity arises, and it usually does, add a positive statement to the admission of the error. This allows you an upbeat finish to your response and diminishes the importance of the error. It keeps you on offense.

Situation 6-11: Witness lessens the impact of a mistake.

The defense has uncovered an error in the report prepared by the witness, Agent Ernest. While it is not recommended that the witness try to undue a mistake that has no explanation, it is advised that, when there is a reasonable explanation for the error, it should be made, and as soon as possible after it is discovered.

Questions by the defense attorney:

Q. Do you have a copy of your report there, Agent Ernest?

A. Yes.

Q. Referring to page two, you have reported that Carlton stated to you that on the 7th of August, he flew Tarkee and Skew from Ft. Lauderdale to Ft. Myers. Do you see

that?

A. Yes, sir. That's an error. It was actually on the 5th of August, and not on the 7th.

Q. Okay, but again, in the same report, you have reported that Carlton flew from Cancun, Mexico to Freeport, Bahamas on August 9th, and your testimony today was that it was on the 8th that he made the flight. Which was it?

A. It was the 8th.

Q. So your report was in error about both flights then, wasn't it?

Note: Here the agent had an opportunity to either say "yes" and just turn his back on the problem or to clarify the reason for the error and show that it was inconsequential. To his credit, he chose the latter.

A. No sir, not about the flights. About the dates. Carlton supplied those dates which I recorded, but later, when we checked flight plans that were filed by Carlton, the correct dates were established.

Note: While the agent probably cut off any negative consequences, he could have avoided the problem altogether if he had filed a supplement to his report, correcting the date and giving the explanation.

c) In the case of a more intense attack by the defense attorney, remain calm. The prosecutor should, and probably will, protect you by objecting to the defense attorney's harassing tactics.

d) Remember, even when the defense attorney has your report for use on cross-examination, the report itself will not go to the jury. Since the jury won't have the opportunity to check on whether the defense attorney is quoting accurately from the report, the officer should insist on having a copy of the document in his possession during cross-examination and never answer a question without first checking the accuracy of the defense attorney's statement about what is in the document. This also applies generally to any testimony you are asked to give about a record, report, or any other document.

e) Care taken in the preparation of reports will, as you have seen, save you from a multitude of serious problems at trial. As the saying goes: "an ounce of prevention is worth a pound of cure."

E. Prior Statements

1. The Law

An adverse party may cross-examine a witness on prior statements made by the witness, whether the prior statements are oral or written. As a practical matter, the defense attorney will not cross-examine the officer on a prior statement unless that prior statement is inconsistent with his testimony at trial, or with other prior statements made by him. Rule 613 of the Federal Rules of Evidence provides that evidence of a prior inconsistent statement of a witness is not admissible unless the witness has an opportunity to "explain or deny the same, and the opposite party is afforded an opportunity to interrogate the witness thereon . . . ." Every state has a similar rule.

2. Judge's Charge to the Jury

In the cases where the credibility of a witness's testimony is a factor to be considered by the jury, the judge will instruct the jury on matters concerning general credibility, including prior inconsistent statements. The charge will usually be similar to the following example:

> In deciding whether you believe or do not believe any witness, I suggest that you ask yourself a few questions: Did the person impress you as one who was telling the truth? Did he or she have a personal interest in the outcome of the case? Did the witness seem to have a good memory? Did the witness have the opportunity and ability to observe accu-

rately the things he or she testified about? Did he or she appear to understand the questions clearly and answer them directly? *Did the witness's testimony differ from the testimony of other witnesses? Did the witness give inconsistent or contradictory statements on a prior occasion?* (Basic instruction 5, 11th Federal Circuit Pattern Jury Instructions).

3. Types of Prior Statements

As the rule states, any prior statement of a witness, whether written or oral, can be used in the cross-examination of that witness. The primary difference between prior written reports and prior oral statements is that, while in his written report, the officer is supplying information on his own initiative, when he makes an oral statement, he is usually responding to specific questions posed by another. Having already considered the effect of the written report in Chapter 1, let's now examine more closely how these prior oral statements will impact on your credibility.

a) *Direct-examination of prior testimony*

Obviously, when the officer testifies at trial on direct-examination, he may be expected to be cross-examined on that testimony. Additionally, when an officer has given prior testimony before a grand jury, or at other pre-trial proceedings, a court stenographer will generally record everything that is said. Transcripts of that testimony may be requested by the defense attorney, and in most cases, the request will be granted.

Obviously, as a witness at trial, your direct testimony will be tested by the defense attorney. At that time, the defense attorney, in an effort to test your credibility, or to develop inconsistencies in your testimony, will probably be in a position to cross-examine you with the aid of any transcripts that may exist of prior testimony you have given on that same case. In addition, any other statements you have made on prior occasions or that are attributed to you, which are relevant to the facts or witnesses in the case, or to your status as an investigator, or to your credibility, will be subject to use by the defense attorney on cross-examination.

By the time the trial begins, you should already have reviewed any prior testimony which you have given and made a mental note of any errors which you made then, or any inconsistencies between that and your present testimony. If you had brought any of these problems to the prosecutor's attention, they may have been dealt with by the prosecutor during your direct-examination. Having done that, the defense attorney's thunder will have been stolen, leaving him no points to make on cross on that matter.

1) Mistakes. Any mistakes that you may have made in any prior testimony should be corrected at your first opportunity. If, when confronted on cross-examination with a transcript of your prior testimony, you are aware of a mistake made by you at that time, admit it readily, but without reaction. On the other hand, if there is an explanation, give it.

Situation 6-12: Here, the witness had testified at a preliminary hearing regarding a surveillance that was conducted. His testimony at that hearing was incorrect as to who conducted the surveillance. He corrects that error in his testimony on direct-examination without giving an explanation, saving it for his answers on cross-examination. Here, we examine how it was done, and whether it was wise to wait until cross to correct the error.

Questions by the defense attorney:

Q. Officer Smith, do you recall testifying at a preliminary hearing on this matter back in May of this year before Magistrate Johnson?

A. Yes, I do.

Q. And do you recall testifying about the incidents which form the basis of your allegations against the defendant?

A. I do.

Q. You have testified here today under questioning from the prosecutor about those same incidents, isn't that correct?

A. Yes, sir.

Q. In your testimony here today, you have stated that there was a surveillance team outside of the building where you met with the defendant, Mr. Talbot. Is that correct?

A. Yes, sir.

Q. And you have identified those men as being Detectives Brown and Jones. Is that also correct?

A. It is.

Q. Officer Smith, I have handed you a copy of a transcript. Do you recognize it, sir?

A. It is a transcript of my testimony at the preliminary hearing.

Q. That's correct. Would you turn to page 67, and go down to line 12, and read from there to the end of the page, please? Out loud, please?

Note: The witness reads the portion of the transcript that he was requested to read, and in it reads that he identified detectives Brown and Baker as the surveillance personnel, and not Brown and Jones. The officer reviewed the transcript prior to trial and confirmed through the Detectives that it was Jones who was with Brown and not Baker.

Q. So, at the preliminary hearing you identified Mr. Baker and not Jones as the second man on the surveillance team. Is that correct?

A. Yes, sir.

Q. Which was it, Jones or Baker?

A. It was Jones, sir.

Q. When you testified at the preliminary

hearing you were under oath, just like you are now, isn't that correct?

A. That's correct.

Q. And you are saying now that is was Detective Jones where before you said it was Baker, correct?

A. That's right.

Q. Obviously, you were in error on one of the two occasions of your testimony on that matter. Would that be fair to say, Officer Smith?

A. Yes, sir, it would.

Note: Notice that Officer Smith offered no explanation. The officer had reviewed the mistake with the prosecutor prior to the trial, and was expecting that the defense would raise it on cross-examination. Instead of offering an explanation, Officer Smith was baiting the defense attorney, waiting to hear the "why" question. If the attorney stops here, the officer must find a way to give his explanation, or hope that the prosecutor asks for it on re-direct. Most defense attorneys, when they feel that they have the witness on the run are often easily led into asking the one question too many. That was true in this case.

Q. How do you know which one was correct?

A. In preparing for this trial, I read that tra script, and when I read that I had mentioned Baker instead of Jones, it seemed to me that wasn't correct because my recollection was that it was Jones. So, I went to the detectives and asked them and they confirmed that it was Jones.

Note: Here, the defense attorney went too far and the officer was able to turn the question to his advantage. The general rule is to correct the mistake at the first opportunity. Officer Smith obviously was getting as much mileage as he could out of the situation by baiting the defense attorney. Fortunately for him, it worked. It may be wise to give the explanation on direct-exam-

ination, or at least at the first opportunity during cross. In this case, Officer Smith was familiar with the defense attorney, and he and the prosecutor were fairly certain about how he would react to Officer Smith's answers.

You may expect that if a mistake was made, the defense attorney will probe it immediately without giving you an opportunity to regroup or regain your composure. All the more reason for you to have prepared well for your testimony.

b) *Inconsistencies*

Situations occur from time to time where the officer testifies on direct-examination about a particular event and on cross-examination testifies about another event that is inconsistent with the first event. In other words, what occurred during the second event is inconsistent with what occurred during the first event. If you are able to explain the inconsistency without speculation, do so. If you are not, then simply state that you have no explanation for it.

Situation 6-13: Inconsistent prior testimony. The officer has testified during a preliminary hearing in a manner which the defense contends was inconsistent with his testimony at trial.

Defense goal:

To shake the officer's confidence in his testimony and to damage his credibility.

Strategy and tactics:

1) The defense will first attempt to get you to agree that you made the prior statement and that it was correct. He may ask the circumstances under which it was made depending upon which version the defense attorney wants you to adopt. He will then try to talk you into adopting his own interpretation of what was said in your prior statement. If he can accomplish that, he will probably have won the

point.

2) You will then be asked questions which point out the differences between the two statements.

3) You may be asked which one of the statements is the truth (the implication being that the other one is a lie). The defense attorney will make it clear to the jury by his questions that you were testifying under oath (if that is the case), when both inconsistent statements were made.

4) By now, the defense attorney will have made his point, but if he has you on the run, he will probably keep after you until he has gotten all the mileage he is able from the situation, or until he is stopped by objection.

Recommendation:

In this situation, the defense attorney will have had an opportunity to outline your prior testimony, determine what in it was helpful or harmful to his case and carefully prepare questions to use during his cross-examination.

1) You must prepare for your testimony. Review all of your prior testimony with an eye out for possible problem areas. Try to resolve those areas if you can. Consider which portions of your upcoming testimony at trial might conflict with your prior testimony. Be prepared to give an explanation for those conflicts.

2) Adopt only what was actually said during your prior testimony and only after reading it yourself. In most instances, the words will be clear and will need no interpretation, but if the statement is unclear or ambiguous, adopt only that interpretation which you know to be consistent with your intention at the time the statement was made.

3) If the two statements cannot be reconciled and you are faced with having to select one as correct, do so without dragging it out, and without excuse.

4) If there is an explanation, give it as concisely as possible. A long dramatic explanation will draw more attention to differences and the longer it goes on the more it will sound like an exercise rather than an explanation. Any time there is a true inconsistency in your testimony, the less said about it, the better.

Situation 6-14: Correcting inconsistent statements made by the witness at a prior hearing.

The defense attorney tries to pin the witness down to prior statements that would seem to dispute her testimony at trial. Actually, the excerpt used was from the witness's prior testimony, but did not refer to the same incident to which the witness was referring during her trial testimony. Here, the witness was prepared, having familiarized herself with all of the facts of the case and her prior testimony. She was able to point out to the attorney that she was referring to the wrong incident.

Counsel for the defendant continued to refer to the transcript of prior testimony, but omits questions which would help clarify the prior testimony and does so in an effort to confuse the witness. The witness doesn't bite, and is finally invited by the court to explain.

Questions by the defense:

Q. Now, ma'am, you testified when the honorable prosecutor was talking with you that you heard a conversation in the co-defendant's room, referring to Mr. Hudson's room, and that, although you were not able to ascertain actually what was said, you heard talk about cocaine and money. Is that correct, ma'am?

A. Yes, sir.

Q. Now, you do recall giving testimony at a preliminary hearing in this matter, don't you?

A. Yes, I did.

Q. And, in fact, that hearing was on July 6th of last year, before the Honorable G. Thomas Morton, isn't that correct?

A. Yes, sir, I believe it is.

Q. And, at that time you were questioned by this very same prosecutor and by my distinguished colleague, Mr. Olsen, isn't that correct?

A. Yes, sir, it is.

Q. And you recall being placed under oath prior to giving your testimony, isn't that correct?

A. Yes, sir.

Q. Now, isn't it a fact that you were asked the following questions and gave the following answers on page 19, Counsel, beginning with line 14. "Now prior to the arrest, you indicated you overheard conversations between these two gentlemen, is that correct?" And you responded, "Yes, sir." And, then you were asked, "And what was the substance of that conversation?" And you answered, "There was not sufficient volume for me to interpret.". Is that correct, ma'am?

A. What conversation are you referring to in that question?

Q. Well, I'm trying to pin down a conversation when the CI was in the room with Mr. Espy, and that apparently, he was only in the room one time, isn't that correct?

A. I don't think that's the same conversation that Mr. Olsen was referring to in my previous testimony. I think that question referred to the conversation after Mr. Hudson left room 1731 and met Mr. Espy in the hallway upon his return form the lobby.

Q. Well, let me go back to page 18 and see if I can put this in context, because this is an important point.

A. Okay.

Q. Question to you: "Is the confidential informant involved in other investigations and other cases as well?". Your answer was, "Yes, sir, he is." Then, the question was, "Ongoing cases?" Answer: "Yes, sir." Question: "And you first met with him with respect to this case on July 15th in regards to this case, correct?". Answer: "Yes, sir." Question: "Did this person actually bring this cocaine from out of the country?"

Note: If the statements with which you are confronted are the words of a news reporter, the source is hearsay and may be objectionable. In any case, they need not be adopted by you unless you are absolutely satisfied that the reporter's words are accurate. Never use the phrase "something like that" when referring to the content of a statement made by someone else, and that you are being asked to adopt. If the defense attorney confronts you with such a news report, you may expect that he has a version which he wishes you to adopt as true and "something like that" suits his plan.

Note: Be careful that when the defense attorney questions you on a prior inconsistent statement that you don't let him lead you into admitting the probability or even possibility of other errors which do not exist. Again, it is the transcripts of any prior testimony carefully prior to taking the stand if you are going to be put in the position of verifying the accuracy of the rest of your report or prior testimony.

Situation 6-15: Here, the witness is confronted with a prior inconsistent statement made at a prior hearing. He admits the mistake but erroneously admits to the possibility of other errors without calling on the attorney to point out each of them.

Questions by the defense attorney:

Q. You now admit, officer, that the statement made by you under oath at the preliminary hearing is inconsistent with your testimony under oath today, is that correct?

A. Yes.

Note: If there is an explanation for the inconsistency, give it, or at least let the jury and the defense attorney know that there is an explanation.

Q. So, it is true then, isn't it officer, that you were either mistaken in your previous testimony or now?

A. Yes.

Q. Isn't it likely, or at least possible, then, that there are other inconsistencies in your investigation or testimony?

Note: The officer is now shaken because the first inconsistency question suggests that the defense attorney is aware of others. There may be others about which you are not aware, especially if you haven't prepared yourself to testify. But, by answering yes, the officer will completely discredit his own testimony and, to some degree, his investigation. The appropriate response is:

A. No, sir, not that I am aware of.

Q. But, sir, you just admitted to one that you weren't aware of. Couldn't there be others?

A. Not that I am aware of, sir. If you know of another one, tell me what it is, and if I have an explanation for it, I will give it.

Note: Even if there are others, unless they are of major import, the jury will see the defense attorney as trying to make a mountain out of a molehill.

5) If the statements were made to the defendant, defense attorney or investigator, you may expect that your words won't come back to you in exactly the same way as you gave them. Be extremely careful about this type of statement, especially if the statement was the result of a conversation between you and the defense attorney. You don't want to get into a "yes you did–no I didn't" type of dialog with the attorney. If your statement was different from that which the attorney has attrib-

uted to you, say so, correct the statement, and stop. Don't argue with the attorney.

c) *Statements to the media.*
   Situation 6-16:
   Occasionally, a police officer will be asked to make a statement to the media. Often the media will interpret the officer's statements rather than reporting them. When statements made to newspapers, radio, or TV conflict with the officer's testimony in court, he may expect to be confronted with those statements on cross-examination. The officer should be careful not to accept the media's interpretation of his statements unless he was correctly quoted. If he does, it will surely come back to haunt him during the trial.

Questions by the defense attorney:

Q. Officer, didn't you tell the newspaper reporters on June 14th that Charlie Baggs, the man you arrested on June 12th, was the one you had suspected all along?

A. No, sir, I was asked if we had suspected Mr. Baggs from the beginning of the investigation, and I told them that he was one of the people we were looking at but that we hadn't zeroed in on him until there were enough facts and evidence to lead us to believe he was the perpetrator.

Note: The defense attorney was trying to make it look as if the police were focusing on his client to the exclusion of all others, thereby making it look as if there were other viable suspects that the police never considered. The officer, however, cleared the matter up nicely, and answered the question in such a way that, not only did he avoid losing points by the question, but actually came out further ahead.

d) *Statements made to the defendant, his attorney, or his investigator.*
   There are times in the post-arrest stages of the proceedings against a defendant, when the officer will say things to the defendant, or

one of his representatives, that may not accurately express the officer's true position. Most often, these statements come during efforts to get a defendant to cooperate against another suspect and may be in the form of promises.

Example: Police officer speaking to the suspect or defendant: "If you cooperate with us, we can make this case go away for you."

Example: Intentional misstatements regarding the defendant's culpability in the offense: "We know you weren't the driving force behind this crime. We know you just went along for the ride. We know it was Joey's idea and we want you to help us prove it."

Note: The defendant may not tell his attorney about these statements, although it is likely that he will. If he does, or if you have made those statements, or statements like them, in the presence of his attorney or other representative, you will have to explain them on cross-examination. If you made such statements, admit them. There is nothing wrong with such statements if, as in the first instance, they were intended to solicit the defendant's assistance, and if the offer was sincere, or if the statements were used as an interrogation technique. In that case, you should explain to the court and jury that allowing the suspect to transfer some of his guilt to another in order to induce him to admit his own guilt, is an accepted, and widely used, interrogation technique.

4. Strategies and Tactics of Defense Attorney

Whenever there are prior inconsistent statements present in any of the above situations, you may expect the defense to employ cross-examination techniques intended to create a doubt in the minds of the jurors concerning the credibility of your testimony.

Strategy:

To shake the officer's confidence in his testimony and to damage his credibility.

Tactics:

a) The defense will first attempt to get you to agree that you made the prior statement and that it was correct. He may ask the circumstances under which it was made depending upon which version the defense attorney wants you to adopt.

b) The attorney will then try to talk you into adopting his own interpretation of what was said in your prior statement. If he can accomplish that, he will probably have won the point.

c) You will then be asked questions which point out the differences between the two statements.

d) You may be asked which one of the statements is the truth (the implication being that the other one is a lie). The defense attorney will make it clear to the jury by his questions that you were testifying under oath (if that is the case), when both inconsistent statements were made.

e) By now, the defense attorney will have made his point, but if he has you on the run, he will probably persist in his line of questioning until he has acquired all the mileage he is able from the situation or until he is stopped by objection.

Recommendation:

In this situation, the defense attorney will have had an opportunity to outline your prior testimony, determine what in it was helpful or harmful to his case, and carefully prepare questions to use during his cross-examination.

1) You must prepare for your testimony. Review all of your prior testimony with an eye out for possible problem areas. Try to resolve those areas if you can. Consider which portions of your upcoming testimo-

ny at trial might conflict with your prior testimony. Be prepared to give an explanation for those conflicts.

2) Only adopt what was actually said during your prior testimony and only after reading it yourself. In most instances, the words will be clear and will need no interpretation, but if the statement is unclear or ambiguous, adopt only that interpretation which you know to be consistent with your intention at the time the statement was made.

3) If the two statements cannot be reconciled, and you are faced with having to select one as correct, do so without dragging it out and without excuse.

4) If there is an explanation, give it as concisely as possible. A long dramatic explanation will draw more attention to differences and the longer it goes on the more it will sound like an exercise rather than an explanation. Any time there is a true inconsistency in your testimony, the less said about it, the better.

5) If the statements with which you are confronted are the words of a news reporter, the source is hearsay and may be objectionable, but in any case need not be adopted by you unless you are absolutely satisfied that the reporter's words are accurate, not "something like that." If the defense attorney confronts you with such a news report, you may expect that he has a version which he wishes you to adopt as true and "something like that" suits his plan.

6) Be careful when the defense attorney questions you on a prior inconsistent statement that you don't let him lead you into admitting the probability, or even the possibility of other errors which do not exist.

7) If the statements were made to the defendant, defense attorney, or investigator, you may expect that your words won't come back to you in exactly the same way as you made them. Be extremely careful about this type of statement, especially if the statement was the result of a conversation between you and the defense attorney. You don't want to get into a "yes you did–no I didn't" type dialog with the attorney. If your statement was different from that which the attorney has attributed to you, say so, correct the statement, and stop. Don't argue with the attorney.

F. Memory

Apart from matters to which you are already previously committed in writing or in testimony, the defense attorney will, if the opportunity presents itself, attack you on the basis of details about which you did not testify on direct and which the defense attorney will argue should have, if true, been brought out by you in your direct testimony. The idea, of course, is that your testimony will lose credibility if you remember some details, but forget other material details. In order for the forgotten details to have the effect desired by the defense attorney, they must be more than minor or unimportant.

1. Details Omitted on Direct-Examination

Situation 6-17: During his direct testimony, the police officer, in recounting the events of an undercover meeting between the defendant and him, does not mention the fact that the defendant left the meeting for a period of approximately five minutes (the entire meeting lasted for over an hour and several people came in and left during that time) and that shortly after his return, he produced the cocaine which he then gave to the officer.

Strategy:

To make it seem that the detail of the defendant's temporary absence prior to the transaction was an important matter and was omitted because it is information that would have been favorable to the defendant.

Tactics:

a) To establish that the defendant did temporarily leave the meeting.
b) Establish that prior to the defendant's leaving, the officer had not seen the cocaine.
c) Confirm that the officer saw the cocaine for the first time after the defendant returned.
d) Ask whether or not the officer knew where the defendant went, whom he met, and when he left.
e) Inquire as to why the officer did not attempt to learn the answers to those questions, making it seem that those are important matters or that the officer would like to have known those answers.

Recommendations:

a) If the matter involves something that you left out unintentionally and if the statement of the defense attorney is accurate, confirm that it did occur and that you did not mention it.
b) If you are asked if you "forgot" to mention it, be sure that is the accurate description of what happened, because you should never admit to forgetting something when you omitted it for some other reason. An admission that you "forgot" something will do some damage to your credibility and the more important the matter, the more damage will be done. You may not have mentioned the event if you thought it unimportant or if it had no effect on what you were attempting to accomplish. For example, you may have had some slight curiosity as to where the defendant had gone but declined to inquire as the question may have raised suspicions about you. If that was the reason, say so. Don't be led into one difficult

situation just to get out of another.

G. Opportunity to Observe

If your testimony includes facts derived from observations you have made, you may be certain that the defense attorney will question your opportunities for accurate observation.

Depending on the circumstances, you may expect questions regarding:

1. Adequate Light

Whether or not there was adequate light to permit you to accurately observe that about which you have testified. If the observations were made at night, were they indoors or outdoors? If outdoors, were they made by the light from a building, a lamp post, automobile headlights or some other form of artificial lighting?

Situation 6-18: The defendant was seen by a police officer moving away from a house that was later found to have been burglarized at about the time that he was seen. The officer ordered the defendant to stop, then had to pursue. The officer lost sight of the defendant for several minutes, but then found him in an alley and placed him under arrest. The incident occurred in dimly lit alleyways in a crowded tenement area of the city during the early morning hours.

Questions by the defense attorney:

Q. How far away were you from the person in the alley when you first saw him?

A. You mean your client?

Q. I mean the person in the alley that you've identified as being my client.

A. About 20 or 30 feet.

Q. And what time of night was it?

A. About 2:10 a.m.

Q. And this was in the back alley known as Fisk Alley?

A. Yes, sir.

Q. I've been to that area and there are no street lights on Fisk Alley. Would you agree with that?

A. There's one on the corner of Fisk and Arsenol.

Q. But Arsenol is the main street and the light really hangs over it and not Fisk, doesn't it?

A. Yes, but the light also shines onto Fisk.

Q. How far would you say that lamppost was from the spot where you say you saw the defendant standing?

A. I was about half way between the street lights and the defendant, so about 40 feet.

Q. Or 60 feet?

A. Could be.

Q. Or more?

A. I doubt it.

Q. Did you measure it?

A. No, sir.

Q. OK, well, you ordered the person to stop, but he didn't, did he?

A. No, he ran.

Q. And, I assume that he ran in a direction away from you?

A. Yes, sir.

Q. And, you gave chase?

A. Yes.

Q. On foot?

A. Yes.

Q. And, how far did you chase this person?

A. Three or four blocks.

Q. Well, you approached my client on Dundirk Way, didn't you?

A. Yes.

Q. What if I told you that I checked and found the distance to be five blocks, not three or four?

A. Could be five blocks.

Q. It is five blocks. Anyway, you lost sight of the person that you were chasing, didn't you?

A. Momentarily.

Q. OK, you chased the person to the end of Fisk, then lost sight of him until you got to the corner of Fisk and Lawrence, here on the map, correct?

A. Yes, sir.

Q. Then, you saw the same person running down Lawrence Avenue and turn up Elder Street, one block away, right?

A. Yes, sir.

Q. How do you know it was the same person?

A. He was dressed the same and had about the same build.

Q. And he was running, yes?

A. Yes.

Q. How was the person dressed that you saw on Fisk?

A. Same as he was on Lawrence.

Q. Fine, how was that?

A. Blue jeans and a dark shirt.

Q. But, when you arrested my client, did he have on a dark shirt?

A. No, he had taken it off and thrown it away.

Q. How do you know that? Did he tell you that?

A. No, we found the shirt on Hargrove Street, near Tripp Street.

Q. And that's about a block away from where you saw and arrested my client, isn't it?

A. Yes, sir.

Q. Anyway, when the man you were chasing turned up Elder, you lost him again, didn't you?

A. For a minute or two.

Q. Well, unless my client is the same man, you didn't see him at all again, did you?

A. Your client is the same man.

Q. But, if he wasn't?

Prosecutor: Objection, your Honor, counsel is calling for speculation.

Defense attorney: It isn't I who is speculating, your Honor, it's Detective Allen.

The Court: I'll sustain the objection. Do you wish to ask any more questions, Mr. Gross?

Defense attorney: Yes, your Honor, I do.

Q. Other than the light from the lamppost at Fisk and Arsenol, was there any other source of light by which you could see the man you were chasing?

A. Yes, other street lights on Lawrence and from several passing cars.

Q. Those were all when the person was running away from you though, isn't that so?

A. Yes.

Q. You found my client wearing a white T-shirt in an alley over three blocks from where you last saw a person running away from you in a dark shirt, is that about it?

Note: The defense attorney is trying to put words in the officer's mouth by stating half-truths that the officer really can't disagree with, but stating the facts in a light most favorable to the defendant. The "is that about it" part of the question provides the officer an opportunity to add facts that were previously unmentioned.

A. Almost. I saw your client in Fisk alley and gave chase. I caught him, as you say, five blocks later in Dunkirk Alley. The light available was more than enough to get a good enough look at the defendant to recognize him when I saw him on Dunkirk and even though the night was cool, the defendant was perspiring.

2. Distances

If the observation was made from any substantial distance away from the subject you were observing, you will be questioned about that distance. You may expect the defense attorney to ask the questions in such a way as to make the distance of your observation seem farther than it actually was. If you have measured such distances prior to testifying and are able to relate them to distances which will give the jury the ability to perceive them (e.g., "What I saw, sir, occurred about as far away from me as the distance between you and me, now"), you will insure that the distances will not be distorted by the defense. In short, don't allow the defense attorney's estimate of the distances to be the one that the jury goes out with.

3. Obstructions

Seldom is the observation of a suspect totally unobstructed for the entire time of the surveillance. If what you saw during the surveillance becomes an issue, you may expect the defense attorney to ask questions about any obstructions to your view, and to try to put you in the situation of testifying that at least part of the time you were unable to see exactly what the suspect was doing.

Situation 6-19: Surveillance; controlled narcotics buy: A police officer testified on direct that he observed the defendant pass to the confidential informant an aluminum foil packet that later was retrieved from the informant and tested for cocaine with positive results. The distance was about 20 yards across a street, at dusk. The informant had been searched prior to the contact with the defendant and was not in possession of the packet then. The officer wears glasses. No surveillance photographs or body recorder were used.

Strategy:

a) To establish that the conditions were such that it is questionable that the officer could have seen that about which he has testified.

b) That he is really assuming that the packet was passed, since the informant went to the meeting without the packet and returned with it.

Tactics:

a) Establish the distance to be as far from the transaction as possible.

b) Establish that there were obstacles to the officer's ability to observe (cars passing, poles, parked cars, etc.).

c) Pin the officer down on exactly how the search of the informant was conducted, whether the informant was out of sight at any time between the search and the meeting with the defendant, whether it was possible for the informant to have come into possession of the packet between the search and the meeting (this question is used only if the answers to the others point to such a possibility).

d) Establish that there were places on the informant's person where small items such as the packet may have been hidden without being detected by a search of the type conducted.

e) Question whether or not the defendant's hands and the informant's hands were in sight the entire time.

f) Go over with the officer every movement of the informant while he was with the defendant.

g) Establish that the officer could not have seen all of the simultaneous moves of both the informant and the defendant at the same time.

h) Establish that the lighting permitted no better than fair visibility.

i) Question the officer about his eyesight and need for glasses, when he wears them and if he was wearing them at the time of his observations.

j) Ask whether fingerprints of the defendant were found on the packet.

k) Establish that the officer could not remember every movement made by both parties.

l) Question the officer as to the exact length, in time, of the meeting.

m) Question the officer as to what the informant's reasons were for cooperating with the police: money, assistance with a legal problem, etc.

n) Establish that the informant would have motive for setting up the defendant and that he was not above doing so.

Situation 6-20: Defense is alleging that the officer used an informant who lied about his transaction with the defendant.
Questions by the defense attorney:

Q. Detective Kirk, when you say that you searched the informant prior to his going to meet with my client, what do you mean?
A. I mean that I searched his pockets.
Q. Did you check his underclothing or his socks?
A. No, sir.

Note: The defense attorney might have stopped questioning on this point since he has established that there are places on the informant's person that were not searched that might have hidden a small amount of cocaine. If he had, the officer should keep what was said in the back of his mind and when the opportunity arises, point out to the attorney that the informant did not reach inside his clothing except to get the money out of his pocket, and he did not bend over to remove anything from his sock.

Q. Why did you not do that?
A. Because I didn't think there was any need. Besides, if he had reached for anything in either place, I would have seen him.
Q. But, you did not check?
A. Correct.
Q. Now, detective, when the informant left to meet with the defendant, did you see where he went?
A. Yes, sir, across the street.
Q. Was any portion of the informant's body hidden from you at any time?

Note: The defense knows that when the informant went across the street, he went between some cars and that once on the other side, cars passing on the road obstructed the officer's view, but he's hoping that the officer will be afraid to admit that the informant was out of sight at all.

A. Well, sir, first of all, it wasn't nighttime, it was only 7:00 p.m. on July 28th, and it wasn't even starting to get dark yet.

Q. OK, excuse me, evening.

A. No sir, on that particular day, there was only very light traffic.

Q. How many cars passed between you and the spot where the informant and my client were standing?

A. I don't know, sir, I didn't count them, not many, certainly not enough to make me miss what was going on over there. If I couldn't have seen them and what they were doing, I would have moved.

Q. How far would you put the distance between you and where the informant and my client were standing?

A. About thirty yards.

Note: The most critical question in any surveillance is whether or not the circumstances were such that the officer could reasonably see that about which he has testified. In addition to the amount of light that was available, and the condition of the officer's vision, and the obstacles which may have blocked his vision, the amount of distance between the officer and the subject upon which he was conducting the surveillance is always a critical issue. Knowing that to be the case, the detective should have measured the distance before going to court. Since he did not, he should estimate at the farthest distance that he would agree it might have been. If he tries to shorten the distance, and then agrees that it might have been farther, the distance could then become an issue and the defense attorney could suggest that it could have been thirty-five yards, or forty or forty-five or fifty yards. At some point, the distance would put some doubt in the minds of the jurors as to whether or not the officer was close enough to have actually observed

as his testimony suggested. Pretty soon the jury would question the detective's ability to see from the distance suggested by the defense attorney.

Q. Could it have been farther than that?

A. No, sir, but it could have been less.

Q. But, you didn't measure the distance, did you, detective?

A. No, sir.

Q. So, you're not sure how far it was, are you?

A. No, sir, but I know it couldn't have been further than thirty yards.

Q. How do you know that?

A. Well, sir, I've been judging distances for a long time and, if anything, I always overestimate the distance.

Q. Why do you do that?

Note: The detective recognizes a perfect opportunity to expose to the jury what it is that the attorney is trying to do.

A. Well, sir, what you're trying to do is to make this distance to be as far as possible. . . .

By the defense attorney: Objection, your Honor, he's not being responsive to the question.

By the prosecutor: Excuse me, your Honor, but the defense has asked the question "why" and now, like it or not, he must let the witness respond.

By the court: I agree, you may continue your answer, detective.

A. Thank you, your Honor, and, ... well I estimated the distance to be the farthest possible so as not to be unfair to the defendant, but as I said, it was probably less than thirty yards.

Q. I notice that you are wearing glasses, detective. Do you have trouble seeing without them?

A. Yes, sir, otherwise I wouldn't be wearing them.

Q. OK, were you wearing them on the

evening of July 28th.

A. If you mean was I wearing them when I saw your client give the cocaine to the informant, yes, I was.

Note: The more times the jury hears that the defendant did what he was accused of doing, the greater the chances are that they will believe it. Here, the officer took advantage of the situation to remind the jury of what he saw.

Q. Did you see every movement of my client and the informant while they were across the street?

Note: This is an impossible question to answer with a yes or no, and the detective shouldn't even try. "Every movement" technically includes even the smallest movement of a foot or a finger. The detective should make the defense attorney be specific.

A. Well, if you're asking if one or the other could have moved his foot or shifted his weight slightly, I guess I might have missed some movements. I was looking to see if the defendant was going to hand the cocaine, on that table there, to the informant, and he did.

Q. Could either man have handed something to the other that you didn't see?

A. No.

Q. You're sure?

A. I'm sure.

Q. Speaking of the packet on the table, State's Exhibit #3, did you have it processed for fingerprints?

A. No, sir.

Q. Why not? Wouldn't that have confirmed that my client was the one who handed the cocaine to your client?

Note: This question is intended to put the officer on the defensive. By answering yes, the detective would be allowing the defense attorney to suggest that the investigation wasn't complete. The attorney also has asked a double question.

A. The reasons that I didn't submit it were that first, there was no need. Four people, the informant, Detectives Stringer and Knoll and I, all clearly saw and recognized your client and, secondly, the packet is very small, and by the time the informant took the packet, put it into his pocket, then took it back out to give it to me, there would only have been smudges of the defendant's prints at best.

Q. But, you don't know that for sure. There might have been detectable prints on the packet, right?

A. Highly unlikely.

Q. But possible?

A. I don't think so.

Q. This informant, is he what you call a confidential informant?

A. Yes.

Q. So, you wouldn't be willing to reveal his name to us, would you?

Note: The defense attorney doesn't really want the detective to give him the name. The defendant knew the informant and although he didn't know him to be an informant, he knew that it was to the informant that he sold the cocaine. If the detective refuses to identify the informant after he testified that the informant knew the defendant, the jury might be confused and wonder about the informant's identification.

A. Well, I should say he *was* a confidential informant. As soon as your client was arrested, he knew that Mr. Polk was the informant. They had known each other for some time.

Q. Well, wasn't Mr. Polk having troubles of his own with you?

A. Yes, sir.

Q. What kind of troubles?

A. He had sold some cocaine to an undercover agent.

Q. Some? He sold quite a bit, didn't he?

A. I think the total was just shy of three ounces.

Q. That involved more than one sale, didn't it?

A. Yes, sir, I think three sales altogether.

Q. And he had some promise from you, if he was willing to help you, didn't he?

A. Yes, sir.

Q. But before he would get his break, he had to help you set up buys of cocaine, didn't he?

A. Yes, sir.

Q. And, in return for his setting up these people, I assume that his cooperation led to the arrest of more than one person?

Note: The defense attorney is actually trying to get a "yes" response for his "setting up these people" statement by asking the question about other arrests. The detective should not give him a blanket "yes."

A. There were other arrests as a result of our work with the informant.

Q. And, if the informant had not been willing to help you, he wouldn't have gotten the break he did, would he?

Note: The defense attorney continues to mention the break that the informant received. In this case, it's a good idea for the witness to tell the jury what the break was. In other cases where the break was a giveaway, the defense attorney will tell the jury himself.

A. Well, sir, what the informant got wasn't really very much. He pled guilty to all of the charges against him and we informed the court of his cooperation at sentencing.

Note: The defense attorney isn't getting anywhere with this detective, and he moved on to another line of questioning.

Recommendations:

a) Establish, by measurement, the exact length of relevant distances.

b) Don't allow the defense attorney to dictate the distances. If you haven't measured the distances, say so, and give *your* best estimate of what they were. If the distance suggested by the defense attorney differs substantially (what was "substan-

tial" would be determined by the facts of the case) from your own, reject it, even if the attorney suggests that he had the distance measured. If he did, he wouldn't be trying to get you to agree with his estimate, he'd be doing just the opposite and then, with his own witness, establish that your estimation was incorrect.

c) Testify to what your recollection is of what you saw and be firm about it. Don't be talked into agreeing to the possibility of something happening that you didn't see happen. For example, if asked whether it was possible that the defendant's hands were out of your sight during the time you conducted surveillance, you might respond that "I was watching the defendant very carefully, paying particular attention to the movement of his hands because of the nature of the transaction (narcotics) and because of the possibility that he might be armed with a knife or gun, and I would remember if I had lost sight of the defendant or his hands."

Note: When the officer testifies that he was concerned about a weapon, he reminds the jury of the dangerous nature of drug transactions. The detective lets the jury know this isn't a school yard game; it's a serious matter, and it's in the detective's best interest, both from an evidentiary standpoint, and from a safety standpoint to be ever conscious of what is happening.

d) Regarding your ability to observe, if there were obstacles to your unobstructed vision, make clear what they were and what effect they had on your ability to see what was going on. If the lighting was sufficient to see what you testified to observing, say so, no matter how poor the lighting might have been for other purposes. It is important that you maintain control over this situation and not allow your recollection to be shaken by the defense attorney's suggestions.

e) Regarding the length of the meeting, if you noted the exact time that the meeting began and the time of its termination, as you should have, you will have no problem with cross-examination on this point.

f) If questioned about the informant's motives, be sure to point out any information that would contradict a suggestion that the informant is inclined or motivated to lie about what he said happened.

H. Weaknesses in the Case

Weaknesses in a case may arise from the facts or from a piece of evidence. They may come from the bias of one witness or from the physical handicap of another.

The officer will find that once the defense attorney finds an area that he feels to be a weakness, or hears something in the officer's testimony that he believes gives him an opening, he will attack that point immediately without allowing the officer an opportunity to regain his composure.

It is important during these times for the officer to remain calm, collect his thoughts as quickly as possible and, if he realizes his mistake and is able, to retract his statement or correct the error immediately.

When the police officer discovers the weakness, and most can be spotted during the investigation, he should do whatever possible to remedy the problem. If he is able to do so before getting to court, he will find the matter much easier to deal with on cross-examination.

If the mistake is one that cannot be remedied, the officer should try to explain why the mistake happened, if it is possible to do so, but should never try to cover it up. If there is no reasonable explanation, the mistake should be admitted without hesitation or apology. If the mistake was in your testimony, your response will depend upon the type of error that was made. You may have misunderstood the question that brought the response that has been incorrectly interpreted. If this is the case, correct the impression immediately, even if you're not called on to do so. Do not let it stand, thinking that it is unimportant because the defense attorney didn't follow it up. He is probably well aware of the error and doesn't want to give you the opportunity to correct it. He'll address it in his closing argument to the jury when it's too late to make the correction.

I. Bias or Prejudice Against the Defendant

1. The Problem

One of the more popular tactics of cross-examination is the attempt by the defense attorney to discredit the officer's testimony by showing or suggesting a bias or prejudice against the defendant.

By using this tactic, the attorney is attempting to make it appear to the jury that the officer has a motive to exaggerate or lie in his testimony, or even to fabricate evidence against the defendant in order to convict him of a crime he did not commit.

a) Prior contact or history with the defendant will provide subject matter for cross-examination if the nature of that prior contact could make it appear that the officer could have it in for the defendant. For example:

1) If you have arrested the defendant on prior occasions, especially if those arrests were frequent enough for the defendant to claim that they amounted to harassment, or if the defendant was cleared of any of them. If such a situation is a potential problem, you should:

i) research the defendant's past record and make yourself familiar with the crimes for which he was arrested so that, in the event of such an attack, each arrest may be justified to the jury. If the defense uses this tactic, and you handle it properly, not only will you defeat the insinuation that the arrest was based on some bias or prejudice, but you will have been provided an opportunity to furnish for the jury the defendant's complete criminal history, something you may not otherwise have been able to do.

    ii) Make a list of arrests made of the defendant by other officers without your assistance or input. This will show the jury that the defendant has been able to get arrested on his own, without your help.

2) You have had problems in the past with other members of the defendant's family. This is often more harmful to the defendant than helpful, for by opening the way for you to bring before the jury any criminal activity conducted by members of the defendant's family, you will have gone a long way in stripping the defendant of the presumption of innocence. Juries tend to believe that "crime runs in the family." If criminal conduct has brought you in contact with the defendant's family on prior occasions, let the jury know exactly what they were, giving the impression that you have dealt fairly with his family in the past. If, in the past, a member of the defendant's family was falsely accused, make that clear to the jury without having it brought out by the defense attorney. Suggest to the jury that, indeed, that incident made you even more cautious during this investigation to insure that there was an abundance of evidence gathered against him prior to the decision to arrest him.

Also, if making the arrest was a decision reached by someone else, or by oth-ers with you, let the jury know that. It will defeat any attempt to suggest that you decided to arrest the defendant because you had it in for him.

2. Racial Prejudice

Obviously, if the charging officer and the defendant are of different races, there is a strong possibility that the defense will attempt to show that the development of the defendant as a suspect was at least partially motivated by racism. This will especially be the case where:

a) The victim and the defendant were of different races,

b) There was a struggle during the arrest,

c) There have been allegations of racism or excessive violence against you in the past.

Note: Racial prejudice will also become a question in **suppression hearings**, when, for example, a black defendant was walking along the street or was in a car when the officer's suspicion was aroused, and the defendant was stopped. In these kinds of cases, the defense often files a **Motion to Suppress** on the basis that the defendant was stopped, not because of a reasonable suspicion, but rather because of his race. This, obviously, becomes an issue more often when the defendant and the officer are of different races.

This can be a difficult issue to handle if there have been accusations against you in the past concerning prejudice, but rarely is an officer retained on any police department when such an allegation has been justified. If you are confronted with this, and if your department investigated it, and if you were cleared, let the jury know about it. Everyone has had false accusations made against them at one time or another, and they will sympathize with you if they know that such allegations were false.

If there are officers on you force who are

of a different race than you, and if you have successfully worked with them in the past, point that out to the jury.

Example:

Questions by the defense attorney:

Q. Officer Jones, isn't it true that you resent black suspects, and tend to believe them to be guilty even without sufficient evidence to justify such a belief?

A. No, that's not true.

Q. Isn't it true that you have had at least one complaint filed against you by a black citizen alleging that an arrest you made was racially motivated?

A. Yes, and it was investigated, as are all such complaints, and the investigation showed that the arrest was not motivated by race. The defendant was convicted by a jury.

Q. Is that the only such complaint brought against you in that regard?

A. Until the one you're trying to make now, yes.

Note: This cross-examination and the answers appear to be of no consequence, and that's just the way you hope they look to the jury. Here, the officer gave simple answers, without getting defensive, then zinged the attorney with his last answer. The attorney was left with nowhere to go with this line of questioning. Remember, what the attorney, who has nothing specific to blast you with, is trying to do is to get you to react in such a way as to lead the jury to believe that there must be something to it for you to react as defensively as he hopes you will.

3. Collateral Matters

Anything else about the defendant, or yourself, which might leave you open to attack by the defense as being biased or prejudiced against the defendant.

In any such situations, remain calm and answer the questions that are not objected to by the prosecutor. Let the defense attorney be the one who appears to be in a rage. Give simple, but sincere answers to the questions. So do not, as some have done, try so hard not to look defensive, that you appear to the jury to be cocky or too nonchalant when answering the questions.

J. Facts Favorable to the Defendant

1. The Law

I am aware of no jurisdictions which do not require that any evidence which is favorable to the defendant, or is exculpatory in nature, be provided to the defendant at or before trial (see *Brady v. Maryland,* 373 U.S. 83 (1963). Though jurisdictions may apply the rule differently, the bottom line is that any evidence which tends to exculpate the defendant *must* be provided to him within sufficient time for the defendant to be able to incorporate the information into his defense. In cases where the evidence has not been discovered until just before the trial, or even during the trial, the defendant will probably be entitled to a continuance before the trial begins, or some kind of a recess during the trial. If the court believes that the prosecution has been withholding such information from the defense, the entire case will be put in jeopardy, and if such deception is discovered after the trial is over, any conviction resulting from the trial will probably be overturned by an appellate court. The best rule to follow is to turn over to the prosecutor any and all information you believe may be exculpatory, and in situations where you're not sure as to whether the information is exculpatory, give it to the prosecutor and let him make the decision as to whether it needs to be provided to the defense.

This information can be in any form, or come from any source. It may come from physical evidence or from witnesses. It may physical evidence or from witnesses. It may be positive information which tends to support a defendant's alibi or other defense, or it may be negative information which seems to contradict the prosecution's evidence. It may be information about the facts of the case, or it may be information about one of the prosecution's witnesses. Examples of such information are:

a) Statements by witnesses which tend to support the defense, or tend to disprove the prosecution's case;

   1) "The man I saw was much taller than the man you arrested."

   2) The witness picks out, in a line-up, a person other than the suspect.

   3) "I saw the whole thing, the other guy started it."

   4) A witness against the defendant is promised immunity from prosecution, or some break in connection with potential charges against him (even if only by promising to inform the court of the witness's cooperation at the time of his sentencing) in return for his testimony.

   5) Information concerning a witness's prior record.

   6) A statement, taken early in the investigation from the victim, in which he names another person as the possible perpetrator of the crime.

b) Physical evidence;

   1) A fingerprint found in a conspicuous place which does not belong to the defendant, and which has not been matched with anyone else whose prints may be expected to by found in that place.

   2) Evidence that the victim may have injured the perpetrator, such as hair or skin under the fingernails in a homicide case, or a victim's bruised knuckles along with a witness's statement, "Yeah, he hit him pretty good." If the

defendant suffered no wounds which are consistent with the evidence, that information is exculpatory, and the defendant is entitled to have it.

   3) Any other physical evidence found at the scene, or any place else, which tends to exculpate the defendant.

Note: There is a natural reluctance, in a case where the investigators are certain of the defendant's guilt, to turn over evidence which may help him escape justice. That is understandable, however, the point cannot be made strongly enough that the failure to do what the law requires in this regard may seriously and adversely affect the prosecution's case, and worse, could result in disciplinary, or even criminal, actions taken against the investigator who violates these rules. When the defendant is guilty, and there is sufficient evidence to convict him, the existence of exculpatory evidence will usually not be sufficient to cause an acquittal, especially if the investigator is able to find and use other evidence which tends to negate or explain the exculpatory information.

2. The Trial

Quite apart from the requirements of discovery, information which is, or appears to be, favorable to the defendant is often uncovered by the defense attorney, especially on cross-examination of the police officer. It may arise from something testified to by the officer concerning some incriminating fact pointing to the defendant which the defense attorney is prepared to refute on cross-examination, or it may be some fact unknown to the prosecution which tends to exculpate the defendant.

Situation 6-21: Defense attempts to lessen the impact of evidence offered by the officer.

The officer testifies about a piece of evidence which he believes tends to prove the guilt of the defendant. The defense attorney has information, or other evidence which tends to refute the officer's conclusion regarding his evidence.

Strategy:

To exaggerate the importance of the evidence in question to the prosecution's conclusions regarding the defendant's guilt. To establish that without that particular piece of evidence, the defendant would not have been charged.

Tactics:

Once the officer has identified the piece of evidence and established its relevance during his direct-examination, the evidence will be admitted. Then, on cross-examination, the defense attorney will attempt to lure the officer into his trap.

a) The officer will be asked by the defense attorney to once again identify the piece of evidence.

b) The officer will be asked again to establish the relevance of the piece of evidence.

c) The defense attorney will overemphasize the importance of the evidence, but in such a way as to allow the officer to agree with the defense attorney's evaluation of it rather than to alert the officer to the exaggeration.

d) Once the defendant's attorney has the officer going in the desired direction, he will take the matter farther and farther until the officer eventually agrees that without that particular piece of evidence, the defendant would not have been charged or at least that without that evidence the prosecutor's case would be significantly weaker.

Questions by the defense attorney:

Q. Agent Driscoll, the photo which you have identified and which has been admitted into evidence is an important piece of evidence from your point of view, is that correct?

A. Yes, I would say it's a very important piece of evidence.

Q. I would agree. If the man you have identified in the photo is indeed my client, that would be pretty conclusive evidence that he was on board the Gulf Breeze on August 12th of last year, don't you agree?

A. Absolutely.

Q. You were there when the photo was taken, correct?

A. Correct.

Q. So, you're certain that the man in the photo here (pointing) is my client, correct?

A. I am. Don't you think so, too?

Q. Well, it certainly looks a lot like him, but it is taken with a telephoto lens from a long way off. Did you testify that you were about 60 yards away?

A. More or less, that's right.

Q. And, if that was my client, that would be pretty important evidence in this case, wouldn't it? Oh, I'm sorry, you said it would be very important evidence, didn't you?

A. I'm not sure, but I would say so.

Q. Can you think of any other evidence which would be more compelling evidence against my client than this photo and, of course, the other photos?

A. Probably not, no.

Q. And, of course, the other photos were taken at about the same time and from the same distance from the boat as was this one, correct?

A. That's correct.

Q. And, really, this photo is the only physical evidence you have that puts my client in Cancun on August 12th and on that boat, correct?

A. There's the testimony of the informant.

Q. Excuse me, Agent Driscoll, but I asked you if this was the only physical evidence. The testimony of your snitch isn't physical evidence.

A. Yes, that's the only physical evidence we have of your client's presence on the boat on that day.

Q. Thank you. Now, without these photos, you would have had only the testimony of your informant, Mr. Hoya, correct?

A. Concerning the presence of your client, yes.

Q. And without these photos, having to rely solely on your informant's testimony would have significantly weakened your case, wouldn't it?

A. But, we don't have to rely solely on Mr. Hoya's testimony. It happens that his credibility is bolstered by the photos.

Q. Right, thank you.

e) The defense attorney will suggest to the officer the possible fallibility of the evidence, expecting the agent to resist such a suggestion.

f) Finally, the attorney will make the point he has been leading up to. He will point out the weakness in the evidence about which the agent was testifying and argue that the now refuted evidence clearly exonerates the defendant.

Situation 6-22: The defense attorney has in his possession information, previously unknown to the prosecution, which tends to exculpate the defendant.

Strategy:

To induce the agent to commit to the completeness of the investigation, then to introduce new evidence intended to shake the agent's testimony and confidence in his investigation, thereby casting at least a reasonable doubt in the minds of the jurors as to the defendant's guilt.

Tactics:

a) To question the agent about the investigative steps taken to secure the evidence, inducing the officer to commit to the thoroughness of the investigation.

b) To ask questions which led into the agent's gaining the photos taken, attempting to show that the identification of the defendant in the photo is based solely on the agent's visual identification.

c) In this case, the defense attorney had done something with the photo which will strongly and adversely affect the agent's testimony. The attorney may make indirect reference to the type of evidence he is preparing to introduce, and ask the agent if he had examined the photo closely enough to be certain of his identification. He may phrase his questions in such a way as to force the agent to defend his investigative techniques.

d) The officer may expect to be asked whether or not evidence such as suggested by the attorney might have, if it existed, changed the thinking about the defendant's status as a suspect. If the answer is "yes," the damage has been done and the defense attorney will confront the witness with the evidence to which he made reference during the cross-examination. If the officer answers "no," the attorney will back the officer into a corner trying to defend his response.

Situation 6-23: Exculpatory photo.

Questions by the defense attorney:

Q. (Handing the photo to Agent Driscoll) Agent Driscoll, looking at the photo, can you tell me that you are certain that the man in the photo is my client?

A. I have said so several times. Yes, that is your client.

Q. And are you as sure about that as you are about every other part of your investigation?

A. I am.

Q. But, this photo was taken from quite a long distance away; are you sure you are able to identify this man as my client?

A. I am.

Q. And, you spent some time there observing the person you suggest is my client, isn't that correct?

A. I spent four days watching your client and others both at the hotel and at the dock. On several occasions, I was much closer to your client than I was in the photo.

Q. Fine. Have you had occasion to consider examining this photo under any magnification?

A. No.

Q. Is that because you felt there was no need to do that?

A. That's correct.

Q. Wouldn't you consider that to be contributing to less than a thorough investigation?

A. I would not.

Q. (The defense attorney hands the agent another photo.) Agent Driscoll, please examine this photo. (Then waiting for the agent to complete his examination) OK, agent Driscoll, would you agree that this photo is a blown up portion of your photo?

A. (The agent is silent, still examining the photo.)

Q. Agent Driscoll?

A. Yes, it is.

Q. And would you agree that in this blown up photo, the identity of the people in it is much clearer?

A. Yes.

Q. And now, looking at the man in this photo that is the same person in the other photo that you identified as my client, would you agree that you have made a mistake in your identification of my client?

A. Yes, sir.

Q. So, this then is not the defendant, is it?

A. No, it isn't.

Q. And the defendant is not anywhere in this photo, or in your photo either, is he?

A. No, sir, he isn't.

Q. But, you were so sure, Agent.

Prosecutor: Objection, you Honor.

The Court: Sustained. Move on Mr. Carhart. You have made your point.

Note: This exchange took place in an actual case involving the illegal importation of 500 kilos of cocaine. There were other problems with the case, but this mistake contributed greatly to the jury's distrust of the government's case, and all seven of the defendants were acquitted.

Situation 6-24: The defense attorney has information in his possession tending to refute the prosecution's evidence, and exculpate the defendant.

Questions by the defense attorney:

Q. Alright, sir, I am now going to show you again what has been marked as Defendant's Exhibit Number 2, and I ask you to look at it and tell me if you recognize it.

A. Yes, it's a report of investigation.

Q. Who's report is it?

A. Mine.

Q. Good. Now, other than this document, and exhibit one, which you identified earlier, did you prepare any other reports relating specifically to the events in the Hyatt Hotel?

A. No, I think those are the only reports I generated about the events in the Hyatt that day.

Q. Alright, sir. Now, you told me previously that you had noted on your reports somewhere that you overheard a conversation about cocaine and money, and that you wrote it in some report. Is that correct?

A. Yes.

Note: Here, the agent took the defense attorney's words for something that did not occur. The agent never actually said that he, himself, overheard the conversation. However, on direct-examination this particular matter was not clarified. The defense attorney knew that the agent hadn't said that, but also knew that the matter was ambiguous enough that if he could get the agent to admit to saying that, the jury would accept it as true. The agent should have listened more carefully to the question and should not have assumed that the matter was too unimportant to correct right away. Once he said, "yes, sir," it was too late to correct it. What the agent really said was that the CI was in the room with the suspect and was wearing a body recorder, and that later the agent listened to the tape and heard the words cocaine and money being used. The agent referred in the report to the taped conversation and its contents, but did not actually say that he had listened to the tape.

Q. Is that correct, sir?

A. Yes.

Q. Now, sir, will you please show us where in those two reports there is such a statement?

A. In paragraph three of the exhibit, it says that the confidential informant did not see any other person in the room with Espinosa during exchange of money and cocaine. And that's what I was referring to when I testified about money and cocaine being discussed.

Q. Let's just wait one minute, sir. Isn't it a fact that you have testified under oath here several times today that you, yourself, heard the conversation regarding cocaine and money?

A. Yes, sir.

Q. Now, sir, may I see that document? You are referring to paragraph three. I'm looking at it now, and I see no mention in there that you overheard anything regarding money and cocaine. Do you?

A. It doesn't say that I heard the words.

Q. Well, please, then show us anywhere in this report, or in any other document in the whole world where you have made a notation confirming what you have told

us here today under oath.

A. There is none. It's not in there.

Q. Is there any reason why you have told us under oath repeatedly that it existed in writing, when, if fact, it does not?

A. I testified earlier that the conversation . . . I overheard the words cocaine and money in the conversation, but I don't see it in these reports.

Note: Here, the agent should have made it clear that he heard the conversation on the tape and that he never intended to convey during his testimony that he had overheard the actual conversation. He probably believed that he was in so far that he couldn't get out without seriously affecting his credibility.

Q. And, when you first became an agent about a year ago, you went to agent school, didn't you?

A. That's right.

Q. And, in agent school, they taught you, among other things, how to write reports, isn't that correct?

A. Yes, that's correct.

Q. And the purpose of writing reports was to preserve important matters so that they can be used in the future, both by your agency, and by the government, and the court. Isn't that correct?

A. That's right.

Note: The agent should have given his own statement regarding the purpose of a report rather than adopt the statement made by the defense attorney.

Q. And, in fact, reports were prepared by you on or shortly after the date of the arrest in this case, isn't that correct?

A. That's correct.

Q. And at that time, your memory was fresh, probably more fresh than it is today, is that correct?

Note: Here, the defense attorney makes a general statement that may be true (i.e., the agent's recollection was fresher when the report was written than it was at the time of his testimony) but was not relevant to his testimony since there was no real conflict between the agent's report and his testimony.

A. Yes.

Q. So, is there any reason that you can tell us why it is that you left out the crucial information from your reports?

A. I think the transcript of the tapes will better state what the conversation was than what I overheard.

Note: Finally, the agent refers to the taped conversation, stating that the tapes are a better record than his recollection. The defense attorney, not wanting to allow further explanation, switches to another subject.

Recommendations:

1. Though it is proper to defend the quality of your investigation, never say or insinuate that your investigation was so thorough that no evidence could have remained undetected at its conclusion. You are expected to put forth your best effort in conducting your investigation, not to guarantee its conclusions or that every piece of evidence that existed was discovered and collected.

2. Where the case was solved by the conclusions drawn from a number of pieces of evidence and information, as the vast majority of cases are, never be led into any statement which might allow an assumption to be drawn that any one piece of evidence was so critical that without it the case against the defendant might not have been made. Some articles of evidence carry more significance than others, but it is rare that one particular fact or exhibit standing alone is the whole case against the defendant. Do not allow the defense attorney to overemphasize the

importance of one fact or article of evidence over another. Assure the jury that, while the evidence to which the attorney refers is important because it points to the guilt of the defendant, it is only one of a series of things from which the conclusion as to the defendant's guilt can be drawn.

3. Never exclude the possibility of more evidence than was found. If the defense attorney suggests the existence of a particular piece of evidence, you may respond that you have done your best to uncover all of the evidence and that you are unaware of such evidence as the defense attorney suggests.

4. There are very few instances where you should admit that if a certain fact was true, the defendant could not have been the guilty party. Even in cases where such would be the case, your response should be that you are not aware of any such evidence. If the attorney persists in advancing his theory, you might point out that such a fact would fly in the face of all of the other evidence and that the likelihood of the veracity of such a fact would be almost non-existent. Do not base an answer on the speculated existence of certain evidence. The intention of the defense attorney is to get you to give an opinion or draw conclusions favorable to the defendant.

5. If the defense is in possession of evidence damaging to the prosecution or favorable to the defendant, and if you have been satisfied as to the actual existence of such evidence, it would be foolish for you to deny that some importance should attach to that evidence. Your response might be to accept the existence of such evidence and to suggest that its importance must be weighed in with all of the other evidence against the defendant.

6. Never admit the likelihood of other exculpatory evidence solely because of the dis-

covery of the evidence with which you have been confronted and with which you were previously unaware, but never deny the possibility of the existence of such evidence.

7. If the defense attorney has confronted you with an important piece of exculpatory evidence, the natural reaction is to be a bit shaken. That is what the defense attorney is counting on. His hope is that he can break your confidence in your case and persuade you to make an admission of that to the jury. You must maintain your composure on the stand and even if the evidence has shaken you, don't let the jury see that it has. This is another situation where the importance of the evidence may be lost to the jury unless, by your response, you bring more importance to it than is deserved.

K. Motive for Exaggeration or Distortion

In every case where the officer's testimony is crucial to the facts, or otherwise important to the credibility of the evidence, the defense attorney knows that, for his client to prevail, he must be able to provide some reason for the jury to question the credibility of the officer.

As you have seen, anywhere there is the slightest crack in the prosecution's case, the defense will try to slip through, and where there is none, they will try to create one.

One of the more popular defense tactics intended to create doubt as to the officer's testimony is to suggest that the officer has some reason to lie or exaggerate about the defendant or the facts or evidence discovered during the investigation.

1. An Oral Confession Made to the Officer Is One Type of Evidence Which

Provides the Defense with an Opportunity to Create such a Doubt

Situation 6-25: The investigating officer is also the arresting officer and the case against the defendant consists of some circumstantial evidence, but the primary evidence is the oral statement made to the same officer following the defendant's arrest. The statement was not taped and the defendant refused to sign a written statement, and now denies making the statement.
Strategy:

The defense will attempt to convince the jury that you are lying about the statement and that you are doing so because of your belief in the defendant's guilt. He will argue to the jury that the prejudices developed by experienced police officers against suspects leads them to believe that all defendants are guilty, and that you knew without the statement, the evidence against the defendant was not strong enough to convince a jury of his guilt.

Tactics:

The tactics used by the defense in this situation will vary, depending on the type of case, the defendant's background, and the defense attorney's evaluation of you as an investigator and witness. Basically, however, in attempting to achieve his aim, the defense attorney will:

1. Ask questions regarding your status in the department making it appear that if you wish to become a detective or attain higher status in your department, you must clear your cases and that the more convictions you get, the greater your chances for advancement. The emphasis will be on convictions rather than on arrests;.

2. Attempt to inflate the defendant's importance to you, either because of who he is or because of the importance of the case.

3. Get you to admit that the most important and damaging evidence against the defen-

dant is the statement he gave you. Beyond that, he will try for an admission that without the statement, the case would be a weak one, challenging you on each of the remaining pieces of evidence and pointing out that regarding some of the evidence, the court and jury have only the officer's word for the source of the evidence.

Recommendations:
1. In response to suggestions by the defense attorney that the way to get ahead in the department is to get convictions, you might say that good, professional police work is what is rewarded in your department and not perjury or framing suspects, and that all you can do is to bring your evidence to court, the question of conviction or acquittal is one for the jury.
2. Regarding the defendant's importance, you might say that the defense attorney has not underestimated the importance of the case and that is exactly why it was so important to insure that the guilty person was charged, and not to rush to judgment just to make an arrest. Point out that, if the wrong suspect is arrested, the person who really committed the crime is still out there prepared to victimize others.
3. If the statement given by the defendant led to other evidence, or if the statement included information that only the person who committed the crime would know, then when asked about the importance or value of the statement made by the defendant, work that into your answer.
4. At any suggestion that, even in another case, some officers must be motivated to fabricate evidence or lie under oath in order to nail a person they truly believed to be guilty, your answer should be that such action by a policeman is never justified and you might add that you and all other policemen are sworn to uphold the law, not to break it. If the question is

asked whether or not you've ever known any policemen to do that kind of thing (the question will probably be objected to and the objection should be sustained, but if it isn't), your response should be whatever is appropriate (you have or you haven't) and if you have, what action was taken against that person.

Situation 6-26: Here, the defendant was arrested and charged with burglary. The only evidence against him at the time of his arrest was the statement of an ex-girlfriend who said that the defendant had told her that he had done the burglary. The defendant had been arrested as a juvenile on the same type of burglary, and actually was a suspect prior to the information received from the girlfriend. With few exceptions, most jurisdictions do not allow proof of prior arrests unless the defendant testifies, or where the prior crime can be shown to be part of a pattern or chain of crimes of which the present crime is a part. Here, though neither of the exceptions apply, the defense attorney, by his questions, opened the door.
Questions by the defense attorney:

Q. Detective Wilson, at what time did you take the defendant into custody?
A. You mean when we arrested him?
Q. Yes.
A. On May 5th at about 8:30 p.m.
Q. And, you picked him up at his house?
A. Yes.
Q. You knew when you went to his house that you were going to arrest him, didn't you?
A. Yes.
Q. And, you were armed with a warrant, correct?
A. Yes.
Q. Why did you wait so late in the day to pick him up?
A. I was occupied on another matter that

day.

Q. You could have waited until the next day to arrest him, couldn't you?

A. I guess so, yes.

Q. Why didn't you?

A. Because, I had called the township officer earlier and told him that we would pick up Mr. Belcher as soon as I was finished working on the other matter, and it was that time before I got to it.

Q. And, you testified on direct that you had intended to interrogate him immediately after the arrest, isn't that correct?

A. We had intended to question him, yes.

Note: Avoid the use of the word interrogation where possible. It conjures up negative images to the jury. The words "question" or "interview" are less harsh and adequately describe the procedure. Avoid becoming defensive about the use of the word interrogation, however.

Q. You had talked with Officer Young of the Rushton Police Department about questioning my client, prior to picking him up, hadn't you?

A. Yes, we did.

Q. Getting a statement from my client was very important to you in this case, wasn't it?

A. A confession of guilt is always a valuable piece of evidence, yes.

Q. But, maybe more so in this case than in others, isn't that true?

A. What do you mean, more so?

Q. Well, you had very little else to go on. There was no physical evidence at the scene implicating my client, was there?

A. There was not.

Q. And, there were no eyewitnesses, were there?

A. No.

Q. And, you never recovered any of the stolen items from my client, did you?

A. No.

Q. In fact, all you had was the statement of an ex-girlfriend who told you that my client committed the burglary, isn't that so?

A. No, that isn't all. The MO used by the burglar made your client a suspect before we received any information naming him as the perpetrator.

Note: By answering in this way, the officer hasn't broken any rules, and yet has let the jury know that the defendant has been involved in criminal activity on at least one prior occasion.

Q. That isn't evidence against him in this case, detective. Let's stick to the evidence here. The point is that a confession was very important in this particular case, and you knew it, isn't that true?

A. Yes.

Q. And, you knew that if you got such a confession it would be very valuable evidence before the jury, didn't you?

A. That's true, yes.

Note: This is a good answer. Trying to sidestep the importance of the confession would be foolish. Almost any juror would realize how important a confession is, and to minimize it to the jury, or to try to dance around the question would cause you to lose some measure of credibility as a witness.

Q. And, you also knew that when you came to court armed with such a confession, you would have to prove that it was voluntary, right?

A. Yes.

Q. And truthful, right?

A. Yes.

Q. And that, in fact, it was given at all, correct?

A. I don't understand what you mean.

Q. I mean that you have some responsibility to prove to this jury that my client made the statement at all, isn't that right?

A. Yes, of course.

Q. And you knew that then, didn't you?

A. Yes, I did.

Q. Detective Wilson, how long did you say you have been a police officer?

A. A little over seventeen years.

Q. And, during that time, I assume you have conducted many interrogations?

A. I have interviewed many people, both suspects and witnesses, yes.

Q. And, when you get an admission, do you sometimes put it on tape or in writing?

A. In writing; not very often on tape.

Q. You do have a tape recorder at your officer, don't you?

A. That's correct. There is a tape recorder there.

Q. Probably more than one?

A. Maybe.

Q. And, I assume you have access to those recorders?

A. I would have access to a recorder, yes.

Note: It's amazing how many officers, who have access to a tape recorder, don't choose to use one in taking a statement. What better evidence can you have than the defendant confessing to the crime in his own words on tape for the jury to hear? It is always a mistake to pass such an opportunity.

Q. Then, why on earth would you not use the recorder?

A. No reason.

Q. Did you even ask my client if he would allow the conversation to be recorded?

A. No, I did not.

Q. But, you would agree that if you had, and if my client had agreed, then the jury could have heard for themselves what he said, that is whether or not he actually admitted to the crime, rather than merely taking your word for it, wouldn't you?

By the Prosecutor: Objection, argumentative.

By the Court: Sustained.

Note: Notwithstanding the fact that the officer did not have to answer the question, the jury heard the question, and may well have been asking themselves the same question.

Q. Do you often take written statements?

A. Fairly often.

Q. And, of course, you prefer the statement to be written, don't you?

A. It doesn't matter to me.

Q. Well, then, why ever go to the trouble of getting a written statement?

A. We like to get a written statement if the defendant will give us one, but your client refused to give a written statement.

Note: Normally, mention of the defendant's refusal to provide any statement by exercising his Fifth Amendment rights will cause an immediate mistrial. However, when the defendant's attorney asks questions about it, he opens the door for the officer to make comment on such a refusal. In this case, the defendant was willing to make an oral statement, but he would not write it out and he wouldn't sign a statement written by the officer. You will find that often the defendant who is not willing to give a written or recorded statement, will often be willing to sign a paper stating that he was willing to make an oral statement but not a written or recorded one. Here, the defense attorney realized he had gone too far, and that to go any farther would be counterproductive. However, for the purposes of this exercise we will assume that the attorney decided to continue along this line of questioning.

Q. And, did my client not agree to provide a written statement?

A. That's correct. He was asked to provide a written statement but refused.

Q. Did he say why not?

A. No, he didn't say, but it's not uncommon for a suspect to freely give an oral statement but not be willing to put it in writing.

Q. But, if you could have it in writing, it would be better, wouldn't it?

A. Yes, sure.

Q. Then, there would be no doubt in the jury's mind that the defendant said what you allege, correct?

Note: The officer should be careful here not to make it appear that his own testimony isn't enough. On the other hand, he should not get defensive, either. He should stay positive and confident.

A. If your client would have been willing to follow up with a written statement, of course, it would have been to our advantage. But, he was unwilling to do that, and that's why I'm here, under oath, testifying about what he said to me.

Note: Because of the officer's poise and preparation, the defense attorney has failed in his attempt to attack the confession, even though it was not written. He may argue to the jury that his client never gave the statement, but he has shown no reason for the jury to disbelieve the officer's testimony.

L. Officer's Personal History

Everyone has mistakes in their past, but few are called to task on them as are police officers. When the officer testifies in court, his credibility is on the line, and open to attack by the opposition. Anything in the officer's past which might affect his credibility or reflect on his professional ability will be probed on cross-examination.

1. Officer's Past Mistakes

Situation 6-27: There were investigative mistakes made in the past by the officer (search and seizure errors resulting in the suppression of evidence, arresting the wrong persons, misidentifications, etc.) which affected the outcome of cases, and a departmental reprimand and court sanction were placed against the officer.

Strategy:

To weaken the officer's credibility by pointing to past mistakes or reprehensible actions of the officer.

Tactics:

1. To raise the prior mistakes or conduct asking the officer to confirm the truth of the allegations.

2. If the officer denies the allegations, the defense attorney may point to it as an example of where a person can be falsely accused. This tactic has turned more than one officer into a defense witness.

3. If the officer admits the mistake or action, the defense attorney will question him in detail about the mistake, especially if it was a serious one or of a type that would affect the instant case were the same mistake to recur.

4. The attorney will suggest that if a mistake was made once, it could happen again, forcing the officer to admit that since he has made mistakes in the past, he is susceptible to mistakes in the future and that he will indeed make mistakes in the future.

5. The officer will be asked if it is not, therefore, possible that he has made a mistake in the instant case.

Recommendations:

1. If you have any information the type of which might be used by the defense to impeach your credibility, tell the prosecutor about it *prior* to trial. It may be irrelevant and objectionable. If the prosecutor is aware of it, he may be able to anticipate it and stop that line of questioning before any damage is done.

2. When confronted with a past mistake, your response will vary depending on the nature and circumstances of the error.

   a) Questionable error.

      One which may or may not be an

error, depending upon how it is viewed. Don't let the defense attorney talk you into admitting to an error that you didn't commit. Often the attorney will not seek an immediate admission, but will ask you to confirm the action taken. He will portray the action in such a way as to make it appear to some to be an error. It may only vary in a small way from the way you would describe it, but usually that small difference will allow the defense attorney to portray the action in such a way as to make it appear to some to be an error. This will occur after he has asked a series of questions, each designed to change the facts ever so slightly. His goal is that, after having been led to accept the defense attorney's version of the fact, you are forced to admit that your action was in error. Always be aware of this tactic, not only concerning errors in conduct, but in reference to any matters addressed on cross-examination.

b) Obvious error.

If you are confronted with a past error about which there is no question, you have only two choices, admit the error and give an explanation (if there is a plausible one), or admit the error without an explanation.

In this regard, you must use sound judgment. There are no stock answers. If you made a mistake in the past, it should be obvious that the defense attorney is trying to make the point that if you have erred once, especially if it was a serious one, it is not unreasonable to assume that you could error again. That, of course, may be true, but the worst thing for you to do is to go on the defensive by attempting to point out the difference between the mistake committed and the one suggested. Let

the prosecutor do that, either on re-direct-examination or during his closing argument, while you remain cool and above being drawn into an argument with the defense attorney. You will come off looking a lot better to the jury.

Situation 6-28: The officer has been disciplined in the past for physically abusing a prisoner. The defendant has given you a written statement that he now claims he only made because of threats of, or actual physical abuse made upon him by the officer.

Strategy:

To suggest to the jury that you are the type of person who would not hesitate to threaten or commit a violent act to achieve a purpose.

Tactics:

To question you about the facts of the situation which led to the disciplinary action taken against you and to suggest to the jury by his questions that on the occasion of your questioning of his client, you employed such tactics to get him to tell you what you wanted to hear.

Recommendations:

1. Obviously, if another person witnesses the interrogation and could testify counter to the defendant's allegations, his position would be weakened considerably. Most police interrogation specialists know that a one-on-one interview with a suspect is the most effective method of obtaining a statement against interest, and would, therefore, reject the idea of a witness unless that person was monitoring the interview from another room while, either watching through a two-way mirror, or listening to what was being said through a hidden microphone in the interrogation room.

An acceptable alternative is a technique taught by many instructors in the field of witness interview and interrogation (notably John Reid of Chicago). The technique involves activity occurring after a successful interview. The interviewing officer calls another person into the room, often a woman (a woman is usually less suspect to charges of brutality) and repeats to her essentially what the suspect has told him, asking the suspect to acknowledge the truth and accuracy of those statements and that he was neither forced nor threatened into giving the statements.

2. Discuss the problem of your prior disciplinary action with the prosecutor prior to trial. He may have specific advice that will relate to your particular situation, or he may be able to prevent the defendant from probing that area on cross-examination.

3. If confronted with this problem by the defense attorney, it is wise to simply admit your transgression, making it apparent to the jury, without actually saying so, that you feel remorse for the prior act and that the action taken against you has taught you a lesson. For example: "Yes, I did that once, some time ago and have paid the price for it. What I did was unprofessional and I have not since done anything to bring shame on my badge. I was overzealous and allowed my personal feelings about that suspect and his crime to get the best of me."

By making such an admission, the officer has defused the situation and his immediate and straightforward answer will go a long way in enhancing his credibility with the jury.

6.04 Confidential Informants

Any time a confidential informant is employed in the investigation and, either testifies in court or provides information upon which the investigator relies and acts, the officer may expect that the defense attorney will devote a portion of his cross-examination to the informant's background, motives for cooperating in the investigation, and incentives to lie under oath.

A. Attacking Informant's Credibility

Situation 6-29: A confidential informant, working on behalf of the police, without surveillance or a "body bug," encounters the defendant who makes statements to him about his participation in criminal acts which are the focus of an ongoing police investigation. Acting upon information supplied by the defendant to the informant, the police recover several pieces of evidence. The informant has been promised considerations regarding charges against him in return for his cooperation. Following his arrest, the defendant admitted providing the information to the informant, but said that he was only passing on information that he had heard elsewhere and denies ever telling the informant that he was involved in the commission of the crime.

Strategy:

To make it plausible to the jury that the informant has lied about the admissions of the defendant, the defense attorney will attempt to make it appear that the informant has good reason to lie by suggesting that the greater the cooperation he gives to the police, the more consideration he gets in return, and by pointing out that his background is such that he would have no qualms about lying to the police or to the jury. This, of course, is to suggest that the officer should have suspected the same thing and taken steps to substantiate the informant's testimony (e.g., video or audiotape surveillance).

Tactics:

1. To question what the officer knows about the informant's background;
2. To obtain a statement from the officer that the informant was not "totally" trustworthy;
3. To question the officer about precautions taken to substantiate statements by the informant concerning what occurred during his meeting with the defendant;
4. To suggest to the officer, and to gain an admission from him, that the statements made by the informant about his meeting with the defendant are, or should be, suspect if for no other reason than the informant's motives to lie;
5. To put the officer in a defensive posture if he does not concede at least the possibility that the informant has lied;
6. To castigate the officer for sloppy investigative procedures concerning such an important phase of the case.

Recommendations:

1. Without suggesting that this informant lied, it may be conceded that an informant is capable of lying, just like a suspect.
2. Point out that other evidence corroborates the informant's version of the facts.
   Example: "Of course, the informant is capable of lying, but in this case, that is highly unlikely in light of the other evidence which supports the informant's statements."

3. When questioned about the informant's motive for lying, point out other information given to you by the informant that was verified to be accurate. Your ability to ward off the defense attorney's attack on your informant will depend a great deal on the informant, his character, his past performance, and the amount of evidence supporting his statements.
4. Always make it clear that the informant understood that he was to be truthful in all matters, and that lying would only get him into more trouble. Also, explain that the informant understood that his function was to assist in the investigation, not to guarantee the results.
5. Avoid being put in the position of testifying that you relied exclusively on the uncorroborated statement of the informant in making an important move in an investigation. That is almost never the case. There is always something which led you to accept the information given by the informant:
   a) past performance of informant;
   b) an existing knowledge or suspicion about the truth of the information before it was received from the informant;
   c) independent evidence or corroboration supporting the informant's statements.

B. Attempts to Uncover the Informants Identity

Situation 6-30: The prosecution and the police wish the identity of the informant to remain confidential, and have argued, in the face of the defendant's request for disclosure, that, in light of the informant's limited participation in the investigation, and the fact that he was neither a participant in, nor a witness to, the illegal transaction, the law does not require that the informant's identity be disclosed. The court has allowed cross-examination on the matter of the extent of the informant's involvement in the investigation.

Strategy:

To extract information from the officer which will convince the court that the informant's identity should be divulged.

Tactics:

1. To ask questions of the officer about what the informant knew or saw of the criminal activity.
2. The defense attorney will attempt to lead the officer into admitting that he himself doesn't know, of his own knowledge, what the informant saw or where the informant was at the time of the activity in question. This will open other doors for him in his efforts to obtain the identity of the informant.
3. The attorney will speculate as to the possibilities concerning where the informant may have been and what he may have seen, seeking to lead the officer into testifying that the informant may have been a witness to the transaction by showing the court that since no one but the informant can testify as to what he saw, his identity must be disclosed.

Recommendations:

Only testify as to what you know of your own knowledge. Do not allow yourself to be led into speculation about what the informant saw or didn't see. The prosecutor should know how to protect you on the stand and, if in your pre-trial preparation you covered this area, the prosecutor will know what to expect from your testimony. Your part is to prevent the defense attorney from playing games with you. What you do not know, say you do not know. When the defense attorney wants to avoid the "I don't know" response, he will make it appear that

such an answer would be indicative of poor police procedure, or of an unprofessional job on your part, hoping to force you to avoid embarrassment by speculating.

If you fall into that trap you may lose the point and be put in the position of having to give up the informant's identity on your case.

6.05 Entrapment

A. The Law

All states and the federal government recognize the defense of entrapment. The law forbids any law enforcement officer, or any person acting upon the instructions of a law enforcement officer, from inducing, enticing, or persuading any person, who is not otherwise disposed, to commit a crime.

Often, in the conduct or an investigation or arrest, there is a certain amount of deception involved. An undercover police officer may, for example, approach a known or suspected drug dealer and, posing as a user or another dealer, propose an illegal drug transaction. It is not the deception that raises the defense. Rather, there must have been inducement of such a nature as to persuade a person, not otherwise inclined to violate the law, to commit a criminal act.

B. Strategies and Tactics

Entrapment is a defense often used in drug cases, especially if the defendant has no prior record, or if the defendant had to obtain the drugs from a third party in order to complete the illegal transaction. You may also see the defense in any case where, in committing the crime, the defendant has acted as the agent of another.

1. Entrapment Defense

Situation 6-31: Entrapment defense

An undercover police officer has purchased narcotics from the defendant who, after having been approached by the officer, had to obtain the drugs from another, unknown source. The defendant was known as a suspected dealer but had no prior record.

Strategy:

To use the facts and the deception employed by the undercover police officer to make it appear that the defendant was induced to commit a crime which, without prodding from the officer, he would not have been inclined to commit.

Tactics:

1. To establish that the defendant was approached by the officer.
2. To establish that the officer is the person who first raised the subject of the drug transaction.
3. To ask questions which attempt to establish that the defendant did not seem willing, at first, to enter into the illegal activity. If the attorney can coax the officer into saying that the defendant wasn't bubbling over with enthusiasm at the prospect of making the deal, he will try to take it a little farther with the next question, and the next. He will attempt to wear the officer down to the point where the officer is less willing to resist the attorney's suggestions.
4. He may pose questions suggesting that if the defendant had been a dealer, as he was suspected to be, he would not have had to go to a third party to obtain the drugs.

Recommendations:

1. Do not be influenced by questions posed in such a way as to make it seem that because you approached the defendant, rather than vice versa, you entrapped him. Most drug arrests are the result of just such action taken by the police and there is nothing illegal or unfair about it in the eyes of the law. The defense attorney is aware of that but is attempting to put you off balance, hoping that you will make a mistake.
2. Do not allow yourself to be worn down. Often, the officer, faced with a constant pounding by the defense attorney, will give the answer the defense attorney wants, thinking that the response is not damaging, and that it will get the attorney to move on. The "OK, if you say so, now let's move on" type of response is often more damaging than the officer knows. The answer itself may not be damaging, but if the attorney can get the officer to make several such responses he may be able to paint the officer as being confused and less than firm in his convictions or recollections about the facts of the case.

Situation 6-32: Drug sale, no audio surveillance.

Here, the defendant is accused of selling a controlled substance to an informant. Questions by the defense attorney:

Q. Detective Pike, you have been an undercover narcotics officer for how long?

A. Four and a half years.

Q. And, prior to that, you had been a police officer for how long?

A. Eight years.

Q. For a total of twelve years?

A. That's correct.

Q. And, during those twelve years, especially the last four and a half, you've seen quite a few narcotics addicts, I would suspect.

A. Yes, I have.

Q. And, they can be a pitiful sight, can't they, detective?

A. Yes, they can.

Q. Do you feel sympathy for some of them?

A. Sometimes I feel for some of the addicts, but not for the dealers.

Note: Here, the detective is anticipating one of the defense tactics, and is, by his response, placing the dealer in a category apart from the user.

Q. Yes, I understand that, but might you try to help an addict?

Note: Be sure you understand the manner in which the question was asked before answering. His definition of "help" may be different from yours.

A. In what way?

Q. Might you try to talk to him about his condition, or perhaps suggest to him that he get treatment?

A. I might. In fact, I have on many occasions.

Q. Would you secure dope for an addict to ease his pain?

A. No, sir, I wouldn't.

Q. Under any circumstances?

A. Under no circumstances.

Q. And, why not?

A. Because it's against the law.

Q. But, you are aware that addicts give, not sell, to each other on occasion when one sees that the other needs help?

Note: The officer, if he understands the law of entrapment, and if he has anticipated the possibility of an entrapment defense, should be starting to see where the defense attorney is going with these questions, and should avoid being led into trouble.

A. No, sir, that does not happen occasionally. I would say it almost never happens. Addicts are almost always in need of more drugs, and they sure can't afford to give their supply to someone else.

Q. But, if one had enough, might he be willing to share some of it if he saw someone who was really hurting?

A. I suppose it's happened, but that would be very rare.

Q. What is your definition of a dealer of narcotics?

A. Someone who delivers drugs, or who conducts drug transactions.

Note: This is not a good response. The detective is playing into the hands of the defense attorney who is trying to define the dealer as one who is in the "business" of selling drugs.

Q. Selling drugs can be very financially profitable for a dealer, can't it?

A. Yes, very profitable.

Q. And, of course, those in the business of selling drugs are motivated primarily by profit, wouldn't you say?

A. Yes, I would say so.

Note: The experienced defense attorney probably won't push the definition any farther. He's obtained what he wanted from that, and he doesn't want to risk the chance that the detective will back off if it is suggested that one who would give to another to help the other would not be considered a dealer. He will rely on an assumption that the jury has already been left to understand that he would not be considered a dealer. He wishes to leave this impression because if he is successful in making it seem that the defendant was enticed into doing something admittedly illegal, he was not one who was predisposed to do so—Entrapment.

Q. Detective Pike, you personally observed the defendant giving the heroin to your informant, didn't you?

A. Yes.

Q. But, you weren't close enough to hear what was said, were you?

A. No.

Q. Were any other surveillance detectives close enough to hear the conversation?

A. No.

Note: Some officers have the habit of answering that kind of question by saying "Not that I know of." That would be a bad answer in this situation. The officer testifying was the lead investigator on the case, and as such she would, or should, have known what surveillance was taking place. To answer this way would tend to lead the jury to believe that you were hedging on your answer. This detective answered the question correctly: definite and straightforward.

Q. And there were no listening or recording devices used, were there?
A. No, there were not.
Q. So, we have only the informant's word for what was said at that meeting, isn't that correct?

Note: The detective should stay alert for opportunities. It is always desirable to put the defendant in the position of having to take the stand in his own defense, or looking bad for not doing so. Here the defense attorney has provided an alert witness with an opportunity to put the defendant in such a position.

A. I suppose, unless the defendant gives his version of what was said.
Q. You had never met or spoken with my client on January 3rd or at any time prior to that, had you?
A. No, sir.
Q. And, what information you do have about the defendant comes from the informant, isn't that so?
A. Yes, sir.
Q. The defendant has no prior record, does he, detective?
A. Not that I know of.
Q. Well, I'm sure that you made a records check and an NCIC check, didn't you?
A. Yes, sir.
Q. Requested an FBI sheet, I assume?
A. Yes, sir.
Q. And according to your information and that of the FBI, the defendant has no record here or anywhere else in the United States, does he?

A. No record.
Q. Fine, but with the information supplied to you by the informant, who by the way does have a prior record, you decided to try to make a buy from my client, didn't you?
A. Yes.
Q. And you instructed your informant to meet with my client for that purpose, didn't you?
A. Yes, sir, we did.
Q. And your informant met with my client on January 3rd, didn't he?
A. Yes.
Q. But, no delivery was made, was there?
A. No, the defendant didn't have any heroin with him on that occasion and couldn't reach his supplier. At least that's what he said.
Q. But, that information came from your informant, correct?
A. Correct.
Q. Did he tell you that he told my client that he was short and needed some heroin because he was in bad shape?
A. No, he did not.
Q. But, you don't know that he didn't say that, do you?
A. Yes, I know that he didn't.
Q. How do you know that?
A. We completely debriefed the informant after the meeting and determined exactly what transpired during the meeting.
Q. But, again, we have to take the informant's word for that, correct?
A. Correct.
Q. OK, so you sent the informant in again to talk to the defendant on the 5th, correct?
A. Yes, that's correct.
Q. And, again, no deal, correct?
A. Correct.
Q. Why not?
A. The defendant had no heroin with him.
Q. Wasn't it your understanding that the meeting for the 5th was set up on the 3rd?

A. I don't understand.

Q. Well, the informant couldn't make a bust the first time because the defendant had no heroin, correct?

A. Correct.

Q. That's a waste of your time and the taxpayer's money when that happens, isn't it?

A. We'd rather not have to do it a second time.

Q. Exactly, so you certainly wouldn't want to have to do it a third time, would you?

A. We would not.

Q. So, you were hoping to make the deal on the second try, right?

A. Right.

Q. I can only assume then, that the informant tried to find out when he could come back and get some heroin, correct?

A. No, the meeting wasn't set up like that, strictly as a drug buy.

Q. What, then?

A. The informant said that he'd just stop over to see the defendant, without having any prearranged time or deal.

Q. I see, the informant was a friend of the defendant?

A. No, not exactly.

Q. OK, anyway, no deal was made on the second try, was there?

A. That's right.

Q. And, again, no listening devices or recording equipment, correct?

A. Correct.

Q. And, again, only the informant's word for all this, correct?

A. Correct.

Q. Did the informant tell you that he pleaded with the defendant to help him get some heroin, that he needed some badly?

A. No, he did not.

Q. And, finally, on the 8th the informant was finally able to talk the defendant into getting him some heroin, correct?

Note: Notice that throughout the questioning, the defense attorney never mentions money and hasn't really provided the detective an opportunity to mention it, himself, until now. The detective should seize the opportunity to show that the defendant wasn't giving the informant heroin to help him out but was selling it to him.

A. The informant didn't have to talk your client into giving it to him, He had to pay him for it and I watched your client count the money before giving the heroin to the informant.

Note: The defense attorney was unable to sneak that last question by the detective. He was counting on the detective being off balance as the result of the earlier questions, but the detective remained alert and unaffected by the earlier problems and took his shot when the chance came. If you stay alert and poised, there will almost always be an opportunity to turn the tables on the defense attorney.

6.06 General Tactics

In addition to tactics employed in specific case situations, there are tactics which we shall call general tactics which can and will be used in almost any type of case. They are intended, not so much to attack the officer's testimony as his manner of testifying, his style, and his demeanor while on the stand. In short, we have already seen in this chapter how the defense attempts to make the officer's investigation look incomplete at best, and incompetent at worst; now we will see how he attempts to make the officer himself look ineffective or inept. He will attempt to confuse him, frustrate him, and cause him to lose his composure. If the defense attorney can accomplish that, he will have taken a giant step toward creating reasonable doubt in the minds of the jury that will result in his client's acquittal.

The following is a list of the tactics most often employed by defense attorneys on cross-examination. A complete list is impossible, as the number of tactics is limited only by the imagination of the defense attorney. The type of tactics employed will depend upon the situation and the personality of the cross-examiner.

A. Intimidation

1. Standing Position

The experienced attorney will always stand when addressing a witness. He knows that it is a position of authority and one which demands the attention of everyone in the courtroom. The attorney who remains seated at counsel table loses the effect that moving from place to place in the room creates. He wants to be the center of attention, drawing attention to the witness only when it is to his advantage to do so.

2. Proximity

There are several situations in which the closeness of the cross-examiner is intended to affect the testimony of the witness. He may stand close to you, either to show the jury that he does not fear you, or to attempt to intimidate you. This intimidation factor does not necessarily involve fear but more likely will cause an uneasiness in the witness much like the uneasiness an interrogator attempts to instill in a suspect by moving closer to him as the interrogation progresses. Most of us have seen this tactic at airports when the Krishnas attempt to instill an uneasiness in the person they approach in order to get money. Their tactic is to get inside your space, make you feel so uncomfortable that you'll give them money just to get them away from you, yet they are any-

thing but offensive as they approach you, since they want to make you feel uneasy, not angry or violated. If the attorney does this, you may politely ask him to step back from you a little bit. The attorney may decide to take the issue farther by asking questions about the effect of his closeness on you. For example:

Q. Does my closeness make you nervous?
A. No, but it is distracting.
Q. Why so?
A. I'm not sure, probably for the same reason that most people become distracted if the person talking to them is too close.

The jurors will understand, since most of them will have experienced that feeling at some time in their life.

The defense attorney may also vary his proximity to the witness to emphasize a point. For example, if he wants to dramatically confront the officer with a fact which he feels is favorable to the defendant, he may quickly move closer to the officer when posing the critical question or when making his point. Do not let the attorney's flair for the dramatic affect your composure.

3. Tone of Voice

The attorney will vary his tone of voice during the course of a cross-examination. He will do this to affect the composure and response of the officer and to make his position known to the jury. All of the following tactics are common.

a) *Bored tone of voice.*

The attorney is signaling the jury and you that your testimony is not truthful or is not important. This tactic is usually used when the attorney wishes to create this impression with the jury in situations where your testimony is damaging, but not devastating.

b) *Soft or inquisitive tone of voice.*

The attorney using this approach may be trying to sneak something past you by lulling you into a false sense of security.

c) *Loud and threatening tone of voice.*

Your testimony has seriously damaged the defendant and the defense attorney, taking even the smallest discrepancy or inconsistency in your testimony, is trying to build a mountain out of a molehill. He will try to make you defensive and combative, hoping to blow a small matter out of proportion. Before he can effectively raise his tone of voice and keep it raised, he needs your cooperation. If you listen carefully to what was asked rather than how it was asked and respond in a calm, professional manner, the attorney will be the one who appears to the jury to be in a panic, not you.

d) *A tone of disgust.*

The attorney has not been successful in his attempt to shake you, but wants to create the impression in the jury's mind that he has done just that, so he attempts to belittle your testimony by dismissing you from further questions by showing disgust or disdain for you and your testimony. Do not respond to this tactic. You have won.

4. Pace of the Question

This can indicate a number of things. A quick pace could be an indication of nervousness on the part of the defense attorney, or an attempt to confuse the officer by not giving him a chance to think and answer at his own pace. This happens most often when the attorney thinks he has you on the spot. Do not allow yourself to be driven to his pace. Take all the time you need to digest the question, and answer it completely. If you are interrupted during your answers, the prosecutor should object. If he does not, just tell the attorney that you haven't yet finished your response.

B. Multiple or Complicated Questions

A fairly common occurrence in court is the cross-examiner asking multiple or complicated questions. This may be done accidentally or with purpose. When it occurs by accident, it is usually because the attorney is confused or is not completely clear on the facts or your testimony. When it is done with purpose, it is usually intended to confuse the witness.

1. Multiple Questions

A question which actually asks two or more questions. When that happens, you may say that you have been asked two questions in one, then answer them. Do this only when there are no more than two questions in one, and when they are fairly simple questions. When there are more than two questions in one, or when they are complicated questions, or when each requires a lengthy answer, do not attempt to answer, simply ask the attorney which question he would like answered first.

Example: Two simple questions.

Q. What were you doing in front of my client's house and why were you there?

A. There are actually two questions there, sir, but I can answer that I was in front of your client's house conducting a surveillance and I was there because we had information that your client was dealing drugs at his home.

Example: Two complicated questions.

Q. Officer, tell us who you saw going in and out of my client's home and what investigative steps you took in each instance?

A. I'm sorry sir, your question is confusing. You have asked me a number of questions at once. If you will break them into separate questions or tell me which you wish me to address first, I will be able to answer.

C. Leading Questions

The defense attorney will almost always ask questions that are leading. This allows him better control over the witness. The purpose of this tactic is to prevent the officer from expanding his answers in a narrative that could damage the defendant and destroy the impression that the defense attorney wants the answer to have on the jury.

If, when faced with this situation, you feel that an explanation for your testimony is necessary, you should answer the question first and then offer the explanation (as in a question that calls for a "yes" or "no" answer that could be misleading without explanation). If your explanation is interrupted by the defense attorney prior to finishing it, and the prosecutor doesn't object, you may have, at least, alerted the prosecutor to return to the same area for further explanation on redirect-examination.

D. Leading the Witness into a False Sense of Security

It is always to the defense attorney's advantage for the testifying officer to be led into a false sense of security. It causes the officer to relax and become more sure of himself. He loses his fear of the cross-examiner and he lets down his defenses. When that happens, the officer gets careless in his answers and is more likely to fall into traps set for him by the defense attorney. Several approaches are used by the attorney, depending on his assessment of the officer's personality and the nature of the information about which the officer is testifying:

1. Feigning Ignorance

The attorney may ask questions in such a way as to indicate an ignorance of the subject matter, or he may come right out and tell you that he has little expertise in the area of your testimony. This is intended to lower the officer's guard and give him the false sense of security. This, the defense attorney hopes, will play into his hands.

2. Appearance of Being Fair and Courteous

When the defense attorney goes out of his way to appear to be fair and courteous, the officer should beware, the attorney may well be trying to put him at ease for a reason. Most of the time, when the officer takes the witness stand to face cross-examination, he is prepared for an attack and is keen and alert for tricks and confrontation, but when the attorney leads the officer to believe that there will be no such attack or confrontation, the officer loses his edge and starts to relax. That is when the officer can make serious and far-reaching mistakes.

Don't allow yourself to be lulled into a false sense of security; remain alert and on guard. Listen carefully to each question before answering.

E. Building Block Questions

The defense attorney's cross-examination may be divided into segments, each segment having it's own goal. The questions in each segment will be directed toward that goal, and each is intended to provide an answer which follows a sequence that the cross-examiner hopes will end with his goal being achieved.

In doing this, the defense attorney will employ several of the other tactics we have already addressed. This is an opportunity for us to see how they are used in combination to achieve a result.

1. The attorney will usually begin with the most innocent questions. This is unlike the situation where the defense attorney spots an error and goes right for the throat. Here the attorney is attempting to build your testimony in a way that best suits his client. As in almost all types of questions asked on cross-examination, these will be leading and will be put in as unsuspecting and delicate a manner as possible. The intention is to cause the officer to build his testimony in the direction desired by the defense.

2. The defense attorney will call the officer's attention directly to the facts about which he wishes the officer to testify and will try to "con" the first few answers out of the witness by putting him at ease so that his guard is down. He will probably mix these questions in with other innocent questions to leave the impression that he is not looking for anything damaging to the prosecution.

3. With each answer, the defense attorney will take the officer further and further away from his original testimony and away from what the officer knows the true facts to be. Each answer will strengthen the preceding one and the officer's position becomes increasingly untenable.

4. Finally, the officer is put into a position where every time he tries to change his position, he finds that he is so deeply tied to his previous answer that his situation is impossible and he is in danger of being successfully impeached.

Situation 6-33: The witness is a state police officer. In this murder case, he went to the crime scene where the victim was beaten and strangled and left in an automobile in a ditch on the side of a country road. The night before the car was located, there had been a fairly heavy rain, and the roof of the car was wet. The automobile contained evidence which included blood and fingerprints on the roof, hair samples inside, and two empty beer cans in a pool of blood on the floor behind the passengers seat. This is a classic example of what not to do during the evidence collection process.

The prosecutor qualified the officer as an expert without objection, and elicited testimony on direct. Then, the officer was turned over on cross-examination.

Questions by the defense attorney:

Q. Trooper Aikens, if I understand the opinion you gave yesterday, you said that the palm print found on the roof of the car was either placed in blood that was already on the roof of the car, or the palm had blood on it when it made the print on the top of the car, is that correct?

A. That is correct.

Q. Now, that's a very crucial piece of evidence, isn't it?

By the prosecutor: Objection. What is crucial or not crucial is for argument and for the jury to determine.

By the court: Sustained.

Q. You understand the importance of that evidence, don't you?

By the prosecutor: Objection.
By the court: Sustained.

Q. Well, you do have a report that sets forth in writing this opinion that you gave yesterday, correct?

A. No, I do not.

Q. You did not do a report on that?

A. I did a report on the findings of the palm print, and the comparison of the palm print.

Q. Yes?

A. I did not do a report on that because I was

not qualified to say that it was blood at the time. I had to submit that to a lab to find out if it was blood or not.

Note: The officer actually starts out doing pretty well. The attorney tries to make the officer look bad for not doing a report on a subject in which the officer was not qualified. Had the officer not stated that he was not an expert in analysis, the attorney might have succeeded in putting the officer down one point with the jury. There were some other questions of no consequence to us, then the attorney moves to another set of questions.

Q. All right, so tell me, again, why you reached your conclusion that this print was in blood rather than the blood being on top of the print? What is the basis for that conclusion?

A. Well, as I stated yesterday, if a substance such as water or any other—grease or anything like that, I've come into contact on many occasions when I was lifting latent prints, if that substance would have been applied after the print was there, it would have obliterated the print, would have gone inside the ridge detail and completely obliterated it.

Q. You say water is one of those substances?

A. If it comes down heavy enough or lays on it long enough, it can obliterate it, yes.

Q. You arrived at the scene of the crime at what time?

A. 5:55 hours in the morning.

Q. And there had been a lot of other people there prior to your arrival?

A. I don't know how many, but there were people there, yes.

Q. Yes, Harmonsville Police Department, couple of men from emergency medical teams, couple of boys who found the car in the first place, and some other state police officers, correct?

A. I think that's right, yes.

Q. I see. You don't know what they did or what they touched in the meantime, cor-

rect?

A. They gave me an idea of what they touched. I can't say exactly because I wasn't there.

Q. I see. So except for what you heard from them, you don't know what they touched or what they moved or what they did, correct?

A. That's correct.

Q. Okay. Now, by the way, when you saw the car at first, and when you had the photograph_by the way, this is the photograph that was taken there, at the scene before the car was removed?

A. That is correct.

Q. And, there's a lot of water on the top of that roof, isn't there?

A. It's a dew. It's a dew on there. Yes, it is.

Q. Isn't dew water?

A. Yes.

Q. So, there's a lot of water on top of this roof, right?

A. Not—not per se. It wasn't raining when I arrived, but there is dew on the roof.

Q. There's a lot of water on this roof. Am I correct or not?

A. As far as to say a lot of water, I can't say. It's just—it was dew.

Note: This was the first mistake made by the officer. The photo, which was taken of the car prior to its removal, clearly shows that there were large beaded drops of water all over the roof. It's not clear why the officer tried to conceal that fact, when he must have known that the jury would eventually get a look at the photos.

Q. Well, you were there?

A. Not like it's poured on there.

Q. Sir?

A. It was dew on the roof.

Q. Well, you were there?

A. Yes.

Q. You saw it, and there was a lot of dew. The whole thing was covered with it, wasn't it?

A. There was dew on the roof, yes.

Q. Okay, you don't want to answer the question?

By the prosecutor: Objection. He has answered the question.

By the court: I think he's answered it two or three times, and he's not going to say anything else, apparently.

Q. Did you search the inside of the car before you moved it to the barracks at Kerry?

A. No.

Q. Do you know who the people were who took the victim's body out of the car?

A. Yes.

Q. Did you see them there?

A. Yes, I did.

Q. Did you take hair samples from those people?

A. No, I did not.

Q. So, you weren't able to compare their hair with any of the hair that you found in the car?

A. I don't do comparisons. I just collect the evidence.

Note: By using the word "just," the officer sort of diminishes the value of the expertise which the prosecutor took so much time to establish. He should have said something like, "I don't do comparisons. My field of expertise is in the collection and preservation of evidence."

Q. (For the next segment of questions, the attorney reviewed some of the officer's qualifications)

Q. Yes. And then, finally, at the Kerry Barracks or at the Municipal Building, you had some training in crime scenes, correct?

A. That is correct.

Q. Okay. In this training that you've taken, you've learned that once a crime scene is altered it can never again be put back the way it was before, correct?

A. That's correct.

Q. Right. And that's why it's important to process the scene before anything is moved, right?

A. That's correct.

Note: This officer should have seen where the attorney was going with his questioning, and never should have given an unqualified "yes" to the question. As we shall see, this answer cost the officer, and the prosecution, dearly.

Q. All right. So, you would agree, then, that when you examine a crime scene, the integrity of that scene is of primary importance, correct?

A. That's correct.

Q. Because you never know when the specific location of a particular piece of evidence is going to be important, may be crucial to the case, right?

A. That's correct.

Note: Again, the officer wasn't thinking. In this particular case, there was nothing that was left at the scene which was of any importance to the prosecution, at least not anything that was found then or after. The officer should at least have made that point during his answer.

Q. And, of course, at the time you came upon the car at the scene, you didn't know what was going to be important or what wasn't going to be important, did you?

A. That's correct.

Q. And, of course, while at the crime scene, you are the man in charge, correct?

A. Well, I wasn't the highest ranking officer at the scene.

Q. Yes, but you directed all of the activity at the scene, correct?

A. Basically, I guess you could say that.

Q. I did say that, would you say that?

A. Yes.

Q. So, then, basically you made the decisions

about the evidence and what to do with it, correct?

A. That's correct.

Q. And one of the reasons it's important to process the scene before it's tampered with is because anything that's moved can be contaminated, isn't that correct?

A. That's correct.

Q. And it can become, indeed, worthless as evidence because of that, right?

A. In circumstances, yes, that's correct.

Q. And, of course, if that were the case, then that would invalidate, or at least cast some doubt on any examinations or tests on evidence that was done after the evidence was moved or tampered with, correct?

A. That's correct.

Q. Ok, now I think you said on direct that all steps were taken here to preserve this crime scene so that you could process it with its integrity preserved, correct?

A. Within reason that we could, yes.

Note: Again, the attorney provided the witness an opportunity to somewhat rehabilitate his work. Unfortunately, the officer, rather than take the opportunity to explain why certain things weren't done exactly by the book, merely provided basically an unqualified "yes" answer and putting himself further in the hole he must have known he was digging for himself. Worst of all, the prosecutor wasn't in a position to help the witness out of his problem. He could only sit and watch his witness's testimony be taken apart.

Q. And, you took steps to make sure that no one touched the car until you processed it, correct?

A. That's correct.

Note: You have noticed that many of the questions asked to this point were "building block" questions intended to put the officer at comparative ease and to elicit soft answers regarding procedures which the attorney knew weren't followed here. The attorney

was hoping that the officer would not react to those questions and would, instead, answer them as casually as they were asked. The witness did exactly what the attorney hoped he would do, and has left himself open to the confrontational part of the cross-examination, for now, the attorney having completed all of his building block questions, is prepared to change his demeanor and the style of his questions in order to emphasize the mistakes and their effect on the evidence, and to embarrass the witness in the bargain.

Q. Now, you did not process the car there, did you?

A. No.

Q. And, in this case, the car was the crime scene, or at least a significant part of it, correct?

A. That's correct.

Q. Now, when you went to the scene, if I'm not mistaken, you said you took all of your processing equipment with you?

A. That's correct.

Q. You were completely prepared and equipped to process the car at the scene, correct?

A. That's correct.

Q. At some point, you made the decision to take the car back to the Kerry Barracks before being processed, correct?

A. I didn't make that decision. My superiors made that decision.

Q. I see, who was that who made that decision?

A. Probably our on-scene commander there, who was Lt. Chatterly.

Q. Is he a forensic scientist?

A. No, he's not.

Q. Well, I don't understand. You said you were in charge of the evidence at the scene, and that you made the decisions about it? Why did you allow him to do that?

A. He was the commanding officer at the

scene. It was his call.

Q. No, you said you were in charge of the evidence. I asked if you directed all of the activities at the scene, and you said yes. Then I asked if you made the decisions about the evidence and what to do with it, and you said yes, again. I can have the court reporter read it all back to you if you wish.

A. I don't need to have it read back to me. I know what I said. The commanding officer made the decision.

Q. Did you discuss with your commanding officer the importance of processing the car there instead of moving it?

A. At the time, the importance was to preserve it so it didn't let anything happen to it. We had to have it in an area where I could process it, and it was covered.

Q. You mean you had to have it processed in an area where you would be comfortable instead of having to do it out on a cold, wet, 5:30 in the morning isn't that correct?

By the prosecutor: Objection, argumentative.

By the court: Sustained.

Q. So, in other words, the answer to my question is no, you didn't tell him of the importance of processing it there, did you?

A. I agreed with his decision to take it back to the barracks.

Q. You did?

A. That's correct.

Note: By answering the question that way, the officer has signaled the attorney that he no longer wishes to resist, and that he is almost willing to agree with anything the attorney says.

Q. I see. Okay, so you agreed that the car should be pulled out of the ditch with a winch, and then loaded up onto an uncovered flat-bed truck, and carried a distance of about 30 miles at speeds of up to 55 miles per hour (the truck operator had already testified that way) with the wind blowing over the blood and rain drops, or as you said, dew drops on the roof, then rolled back down off the truck and pushed into a warehouse or garage at the barracks to be processed two days later. Is that about it?

A. No, I started–initiated processing it that night.

Q. What did you do that night?

A. As far as the–I took samples, blood samples from inside the vehicle, I took possible semen samples and hair, and then I initiated processing for latent fingerprints.

Q. Inside or outside the car?

A. Everything I did was inside the car the first night.

Q. This is a photograph of the roof of the car that was taken before the trip to Kerry, right?

A. That is correct.

Q. Do you have a photograph of the roof similar to this showing a nice close-up of this area after the car went through this 55 mile per hour trip to Kerry?

A. I don't believe I have one, no.

Q. Why would you not take a photograph of it then?

A. I didn't feel I needed to have a close-up of that at that time.

Q. Oh, really. I take it the idea of taking the photo in the first place was to show the area that was to be processed later, correct?

A. Yes.

Q. But, you already said that once evidence is moved, it's changed forever, and can't be put back the way it was?

A. Yes.

Q. So, what use was the photo taken before the car was moved when, in fact, that area had changed during the trip to Kerry?

A. It shows the roof of the car when I first

saw it.

Q. But this blood, the blood that is shown on the photo taken before the car was moved, wasn't there when the trip was over, was it?

A. I wasn't there when the car arrived. When I got there, no, it was dried.

Q. Well, it's wet here, and bubbled?

A. Yes, that's correct.

Q. You don't think that a car going 55 miles an hour with the wind blowing across it would move that blood?

A. It would move the blood.

Q. Sure it would.

A. Were there any efforts made to protect the roof of this car while it was traveling over the roads of Campbell and Acker Counties?

A. Not that I know of.

Q. And, by the way, this was toward the second half of September, correct?

A. Yes, it was.

Q. When leaves are falling from everywhere, right?

A. That's correct.

Q. And, there's a lot of rain during those days, right?

A. On the days that we had this, I don't know if there was rain or not.

Q. You're not aware that it had rained almost all night before you arrived that morning?

A. No, I am not.

Q. Did you not hear the testimony of Trooper Bailes about how it had rained the night before?

A. No.

Q. All right. But the leaves fall that time of year?

A. That's correct.

Q. And sometimes they fall on the roofs of cars, don't they?

A. That's correct.

Q. As they drive along on the highway with the trees hanging over, don't they?

A. That's correct.

Q. And sometimes, when they fall on the roof of the car, they might get blown off and take whatever was there with it, correct?

A. I'm sure it can happen.

Q. But, you didn't follow this car, or ask them to keep the speed down, or go with it to make sure it was carried in a way as to best protect the roof, and unloaded properly and put in the place the right way so that nobody could touch it or do the wrong thing to it, did you?

A. No, I went with the body.

Q. I didn't ask you that. Did you go with the car?

A. No, I did not.

Q. You've already testified that your chief concern was the integrity of this crime scene, correct?

A. That's correct.

Q. Do you know who unloaded the car?

A. No, I do not.

Q. Do you know how it was pushed into the garage?

A. No, I do not.

Q. Do you know who pushed it into the garage?

A. No, I do not.

Q. Do you know if anybody brushed against any part of the roof while they were pushing it into the garage?

A. No, I do not.

Q. Before the car was moved, did you know that there was a beer can under the seat?

A. No, I did not.

Q. So, you didn't even look under the seat for anything or look inside the car, search it for evidence?

A. No, I did not.

Q. Did you collect the beer can that was on the floor of the car in the back before the car was moved, or did you leave it there?

A. I left it there.

Q. You don't know whether or not, during the trip this beer can rolled back and forth or whether the beer can on the floor might have been moved when the car was moving or bumping or anything else, do you?

A. No, I don't know that.

Q. And, of course, with the beer can rolling around in the area where the blood was in the back seat, that might have damaged any possibility of getting prints because it could be, and I believe was, contaminated from rolling over and over on the floor of the car, correct?

A. That's possible, yes.

Q. Well, you weren't able to get any prints off of the beer cans, were you?

A. No.

Q. So, then it seems it was more than possible, doesn't it?

A. Yes, I suppose it is.

Q. Do you have an explanation as to why you took 35 photographs of the car at the scene, and didn't take any photographs of this very important part of the car after you got back to Kerry?

A. At the time when I got back to Kerry, before I found the palm print, I didn't know that it was going to be an important part of the car. I took everything on the car I thought was important.

Q. You didn't think blood found on the roof of the car would be important?

A. At that time I didn't know if there was blood on any other part of the car, either, so I was going to wait.

Note: This cross-examination went on for over two hours, with the officer continuing his answers in the same way: listless and sloppy. For some reason, this was considered to be a very tight case for the prosecution when the trial started. There was plenty of evidence pointing to the defendant as the perpetrator, but the testimony of this officer clearly showed that the investigation was conducted in a sloppy and unprofessional manner. His work so contaminated the pros-

ecution's case that, even though the trial lasted for five days, the defendant was acquitted in less than one hour.

F. Misstatement of Previous Testimony

Often a defense attorney will go over the officer's testimony on direct-examination with him, and, in restating some of that prior testimony, will change one or two words which, in effect, will change the meaning of the entire statement. He will put the statement in such a way as to draw your attention away from the subtle changes he has made. He will then ask you to confirm the statement as your testimony on direct-examination.

You should listen carefully to the questions that are asked before answering and, no matter how innocent the error may seem, if the defense attorney misstates your prior testimony, say so. Do not adopt his version. If he asks if you recall testifying in a certain manner on direct and you know that is not exactly what you said, your answer should be: "No, sir, that's not the way I recall my testimony" or "No, sir, that was not my testimony." He may then attempt to rephrase his version and ask you again to adopt it. Again, if it is not what you testified to, do not adopt it. For example, if he suggests:

Q. Officer, even though those may not have been the very words that you used, isn't that what you meant by your testimony?

A. No, sir, I meant what I said.

By answering the question that way, you have put the defense attorney in a box because, if he wanted you to repeat what you said earlier, he wouldn't have changed the wording in his questioning, yet he has made an issue of what was said. If he asks you to repeat what it was that you said, you are in the driver's seat; if he does not, he will look bad to the jury. In either case, you have kept control of your testimony and, therefore, the situation.

G. Personalizing the Defendant

The defense attorney wants the jury to believe that the defendant is really a nice guy in spite of the evidence of his guilt. Accomplishing that can have very positive results for the defendant. For example, if the charge, in the minds of the jury, is a minor one (e.g., retail theft, DUI with no accident) and if they like the defendant, they may, even though they believe him to be guilty, excuse him, or consider him worthy of a break and acquit him. Even where the charge is more serious, juries have been known to convict on a lesser included offense because the defendant was "a nice guy."

What better place for kind words about the defendant to come than from the investigating or arresting officer. People seldom refer to others by their first names unless they like them. Therefore, you may expect the defense attorney to refer to the defendant by his first name hoping to get you to do the same; or he may refer to the defendant in endearing terms or say things about him that make him look good, or at least like something less than the monster that the crime suggests.

The attorney will seek confirmation from you of his statements about the defendant. The officer should always be aware of this tactic and not allow himself to be made into the defendant's "character witness." If the defense attorney wants to put the defendant's best foot forward, let him put the defendant on the stand.

Situation 6-34: The officer had neither met nor heard of the defendant prior to the investigation which led to the arrest.

Questions by the defense attorney:

Q. Now, officer, isn't it true that you've never had any trouble with Bill (the defendant) prior to this occasion?

Note: The defense attorney would like you to simply say "that's true." That sounds as if you may have known the defendant in the past, or at least creates the impression with the jury that the defendant has been a law abiding citizen.

A. Sir, I never met the defendant prior to the time he sold me the cocaine.

On the other hand, you should not deny information about the defendant that you know to be true. If you are asked to confirm a fact about the defendant, and if there has been no objection to the question, you should confirm that fact if you know it to be true. Be careful, however, not to confirm a statement that draws a conclusion about the defendant.

Situation 6-35: Confirming a fact.

Q. Officer, isn't it true that Bill is married with two children and has a steady job?

A. I don't have any personal knowledge of that, but I am told that he does, yes.

Note: Here, the officer confirms that he is aware of the defendant's marital and occupational status without making it seem that he personally knows him. This separates the defendant from the officer, which is what the prosecution wants.

Situation 6-36: Conclusion.

Q. Officer, you know the defendant personally, do you not?

A. I have met him before and know who he is, yes sir.

Q. And you know him to be a law abiding citizen, don't you?

A. Sir, prior to the commission of this crime, I know of no prior record of the defendant.

Note: The officer has answered the question without satisfying the defense attorney's wish that he personally confirm the law abiding status of the defendant.

H. Improbabilities in Officer's Testimony

There may be certain portions of your testimony that deal with matters which go against the laws of probability. You may expect the attorney to highlight those facts in such a way as to show that your testimony is inconsistent with the experiences of the average person. These are matters that every officer has to deal with from time to time. In criminal investigations, things don't always make a lot of sense and don't always follow a logical order. There is nothing you can do about that. Do not be drawn into admitting the improbability of your testimony. That is a conclusion that the defense attorney can argue to the jury. It is not for you to add credibility to his argument. You might contradict defense counsel's suggestion by pointing out that in the area of criminal activity, improbabilities are a regular occurrence.

1. Improbabilities a Regular Occurrence Among Criminals

Situation 6-37:
Questions by the defense attorney:

Q. Officer, doesn't the sequence of events, as you have testified to them, seem odd to you?

A. I'm not sure I understand what you mean, sir?

Q. Well, what I mean is that they seem to go against common sense, wouldn't you say?

A. No sir, I would not.

Q. You wouldn't? Are you suggesting to this jury that the statements made by you about the facts in this case should square with their common sense?

A. Sir, what I am saying is that many things that may not make sense to the average law abiding citizen occur regularly among criminals. Many things that criminals do, do not make sense, but they do them anyway. Often that is the reason they get caught.

Situation 6-38:
In this situation, the officer has testified on direct-examination that his investigation shows that the defendant was at a certain location at about 2:30 a.m.

Q. Detective Martin, on direct-examination, you testified that according to your report and notes, you arrived at the scene at 2:33 a.m., and that you were told by witnesses that my client, Mr. Swift, had left the scene at the corner of Chestnut and Market Streets only moments before your arrival. In fact, I believe the longest estimate was about three minutes, correct?

A. Yes, sir.

Q. And, you have also testified and have produced a receipt to support your testimony that your investigation shows that Mr. Swift was at the Crumbly Hotel from 2:45 a.m. on for the rest of the night, isn't that correct?

Note: If the officer answers yes, the defense attorney will probably desist from further questions on that matter, and move to another because he will have accomplished his goal of turning an improbable factual situation into an inconsistency on the officer's part.

A. Well, sir, the evidence shows that the defendant was at the Crumbly Hotel at 2:45 in the morning. The parking lot time clock registered that as the time the defendant's car entered the hotel parking lot and a number of witnesses have stated that they saw the defendant inside the hotel at about that time. It is also true that witnesses at the crime scene have put the defendant there at about 2:30 a.m.

Q. Would you agree that it is highly unlikely and probably impossible that your investigation is correct?

A. Sir, it is unlikely that the witnesses at the crime scene were correct in their estimation of the time of the defendant's departure from the area, however, my investigation which merely reports that estimate, clearly proves that the defendant was at the area of Chestnut and Market when the fatal shot was fired and further that your client was the one who fired that shot. Therefore, my conclusion is that the defendant left the area enough before 2:30 in the morning to allow him to travel the distance to the Crumbly Hotel by 2:45.

Note: At this point, the defense attorney is in a bind. He can't ask the officer to list the evidence which proves that conclusion (fingerprints on the murder weapon, descriptions of the defendant's car leaving the scene and statements of witnesses that they saw the defendant fire the shot that killed the victim), that would be too damaging, and he has failed in his attempt to open even a slight crack in the prosecution's case, so he moved on to another area of cross-examination.

I. Contradiction in the Officer's Testimony

Any time a person tells a story more than once, there are bound to be some inconsistencies, no matter how carefully the story is told. In recounting events which have occurred, use your best recollection and when confronted with an inconsistency, explain it if you can. If you cannot, simply tell the cross-examiner that your present testimony is your best recollection. If, in confronting you with prior statements made by you that are inconsistent with your present testimony, your recollection is refreshed and

it is your feeling that your earlier statement was correct, admit to the error and adopt the earlier statement. You'll take some heat over it, but don't let that mistake affect the rest of your testimony. Pre-trial preparation will minimize problems like this.

J. Attacking the Undercover Investigator's Credibility

If the defendant can successfully attack the investigating officer's credibility, he will have gone a long way in creating a reasonable doubt about his guilt. We have already seen an example of the defense attacking the officer on the basis of the improbability of the events about which he has testified, and in the contradictions that sometimes exist in the officer's testimony, as well as others. Sometimes the officer is involved in matters which give him license to lie during the investigation. This is especially true during undercover or drug operations. The following is an example of how the defense typically probes the very core of the officer's profession to find a way to cast doubt upon his credibility.

Situation 6-39:
Questions by the defense attorney:

Q. Officer Tripp, you have already testified that you are attached to the department's Narcotics Squad, is that correct?

A. That's correct.

Q. And as a member of that squad, you have occasions to operate in an undercover capacity, is that also correct?

A. Yes, sir, that's correct.

Q. And when you are working undercover, you don't wear the traditional uniform of a police officer, do you?

A. No, sir, we don't.

Q. In fact, you try as best you can to blend into the environment in which you are working, correct?

A. Yes.

Q. And that entails dressing and appearing in ways that are intended to disguise your true position as a police officer, correct?

A. Of course, yes, sir.

Q. You might wear your hair longer than you would otherwise?

A. Yes.

Q. And, your hair was much longer during this investigation than it is here in front of this jury, isn't that correct?

A. Yes, that's correct.

Q. And, unlike now, you were wearing a beard, correct?

A. Yes.

Q. And your clothes were not what you would normally wear even in your private life, correct?

A. Yes, I wore a leather jacket with zippers, chains. I tried to look as much like your client did then as I could.

Note: Here the officer made the point that the defendant didn't look then like he did in the courtroom, either, and that the purpose of the facade was to blend in with the defendant and his companions.

Q. When you're working in an undercover capacity, you don't use your real name, do you?

A. (the officer chuckles, but doesn't overdo it) No, sir, I don't. That's part of being undercover.

Q. So, you make up a false name, is that correct?

A. Yes, I do.

Q. What name did you use in this case?

A. (the officer checks his report) I used the name Bob DeVain.

Q. And that never was your real name, was it?

A. No, it never was.

Q. And, on other occasions, you use still other false names, correct?

A. That's correct.

Q. And when you meet people during the course of your investigations you tell them things about yourself and your activities that aren't true, isn't that also correct?

A. Yes, that's correct.

Q. What, for example, is a typical story that you make up?

A. It depends on where I'm working. I do a lot of work around student age people, high school and college, so I may tell them that I'm a night student and that I have a job during the day.

Q. And, do you tell them that you use drugs?

A. Yes, if I'm doing a drug investigation, that's what I tell them.

Q. And, do you use drugs when you're not involved in such investigations?

Note: This is a trick question. The defense attorney is trying to gain a tacit admission that you may use drugs during the investigations. The officer should be on guard against such an attempt.

A. No, sir, I don't use drugs at any time, even during my investigations.

Q. But, how do you convince them of your sincerity, then?

A. I will sometimes, even often, pretend to use the drug.

Q. Really, you pretend to use drugs?

A. Yes, I pretend.

Q. And this is with people who often use drugs themselves?

A. Yes.

Q. And they don't know that your faking it?

A. No, they don't.

Q. Do you at times pretend to use marijuana?

A. Yes.

Q. And marijuana is a drug that is inhaled, correct?

A. That's correct.

Q. Otherwise the user wouldn't get anything out of the marijuana, would he?

A. That's right.

Q. Do you smoke cigarettes?

A. No, I don't.

Q. Have you ever smoked a cigarette?

A. Yes.

Q. I mean inhaled it?

A. Yes, I have inhaled regular cigarettes.

Q. And after you inhale the smoke, you have to exhale it, right?

A. Yes, that's correct.

Q. And, of course, the smoke looks different coming out after inhaling it than it does coming out if you don't inhale, correct?

A. I'm not sure what you mean.

Q. That's okay, I think the jury does.

By the prosecutor: Objective, argumentative.

By the court: Sustained.

Q. In any case, all of what you tell them about yourself, your fondness for drugs, and your use of drugs is false information, isn't it?

A. Yes, it is.

Q. And, you know it's false when your doing it, don't you?

A. Yes.

Q. And, you intentionally lie about these things, because that's part of your job, isn't it?

A. Yes, that's right.

Q. So, misrepresenting things is part of your job, isn't it?

A. That's right.

Q. So, part of your job is to deceive other people, correct?

A. That's correct.

Q. And the better you are able to do that, the more successful you can be, correct?

A. That's correct.

Q. And, you have had a lot of success, haven't you?

A. Yes, I'm proud to say, I've been able to have a positive impact in the fight against the business of drug distribution and use.

Note: Here, the officer was able to turn around, in the last answer, all that the defense attorney was trying to accomplish in

trying to label the officer a liar.

K. Questions Containing Half-truths

As already stated, most cross-examination will come through leading questions. It is not uncommon for those questions to suggest information which is only half true. Such questions often seem plausible and tempt a "yes" or "no" response that would be inaccurate. Do not allow the defense attorney to testify in your place. If a question is not totally accurate, say so and give whatever explanation that is necessary.

Situation 6-40:

Questions by the defense attorney:

Q. Officer Smith, is this a copy of your report?

A. Yes, it is.

Q. Did you prepare it?

A. Yes, I did.

Q. And, what is your report? What does it consist of?

A. It is made up of information and data gathered over the course of the investigation

Q. So, it's kind of a written history of the investigation, correct?

Note: The officer should be suspicious of the manner in which this question was asked. Even if the officer isn't sure where the defense attorney intends to go with this question, he should suspect a trap. What the defense attorney is attempting to do with this question is to change the answer given to the prior question, or at least to qualify it in terms that the defense attorney will find more suitable to his goals. The witness should not restate an answer already given into terms that the defense attorney will find more suitable to his goals. If an answer must be explained in other words, the witness should make sure that he is the one supplying the words.

A. No, sir, it is what I said it is, information and data gathered over the course of the investigation.

Note: The defense attorney has lost this one and must satisfy himself with the officer's answer since it is both clear and concise.

Q. OK, Officer Smith, it is what you said it was. We'll work with that definition. What kinds of information and data go into the report?

Note: Whenever the defense attorney asks this kind of a question, you can be sure he has something specific in mind. Until he gets more specific, you shouldn't be, either.

A. Information and data concerning the investigation, witnesses and evidence.

Q. Yes, Officer Smith, but specifically what kinds of information?

A. It depends on the investigation, sir.

Q. How about this investigation, sir?

Note: The attorney is obviously beating the bushes looking for you to either volunteer something that he can hang his hat on, or to nail you down to a position that he can attack. Most often, when this occurs, the attorney will be thinking of some information which he will want to make seem important that was not in the report. Think before you answer these types of questions.

A. I'm sorry, sir, I don't understand. Are you referring to something in particular?

Note: The officer is holding fast. Since the witness has not taken the bait, the defense attorney must now, himself, state what it is he is trying to bring out.

Q. OK, let me try to ask it another way. In your report, you write information about the investigation, is that correct officer?

A. Yes, sir?

Q. And this information is important or it wouldn't be in the report, isn't that a fair statement, Officer Smith?

Note: Whenever the attorney makes a statement and then asks if what he said was a fair statement, he is injecting new information. It may be a fair statement, but just as likely, it is not. Be careful not to be led into agreeing with the attorney just because he is being nice and polite and because you don't want to look disagreeable. If it is a fair statement, say so; if it is not, say so. Additionally, any time the defense attorney tries to categorize your actions during the investigation, you should suspect his motives. The defense attorney will try to turn you into his witness by doing that.

A. No, sir, it is not a fair statement.

Q. What is unfair about it?

A. All of the information that goes into the report has a purpose, but not all of it could be classified as important.

Q. But, it is true that all of the important information goes into the report, isn't it?

A. No, sir, that is not true.

Q. Well, let me see if I have this stated correctly. Unimportant information goes into the report, and important information does not. Is that about it, Officer Smith?

Note: The defense attorney is baiting the witness and trying to get him to explain his way out of what the attorney is trying to depict as a dilemma. If the officer is made to feel that he has said or insinuated what was stated in the defense attorney's question, the officer will often be put on the defensive, and will try to explain his way out of what he sees as a difficult situation. Actually, there is no situation, and no problem. The officer knows that he did not say what was suggested by the attorney and there is no need to react.

A. No, sir, that is not about it.

Q. Well, what do you mean? Isn't that what you said?

A. No, sir, that is not what I said.

Q. Did you not say that information that is unimportant goes into the report?

A. On occasion, some information that is not of particular importance to the investigation, but has some other purpose, will be included in the report. Other facts which are thought to be important at the time turn out to be unimportant also end up in the report.

By the prosecutor: Objection, argumentative.

By the court: Sustained.

Q. Would you agree that a report is, or should be, a record of all of the important events, conversations, and procedures of the investigation?

A. No, sir.

Q. Well, then, Officer Smith, you tell us what a report is, please.

A. Yes, sir. A report is a formalization of notes written by an officer of events or other matters about which the officer felt he would need to record for later use.

Q. And, that would include all of the highlights of the investigation, wouldn't it?

A. No, sir, not necessarily.

Q. Give me an example in this case of something of importance that occurred that was consciously omitted from the report.

Note: The officer should always be prepared to answer a question like this because every time the defense attorney gets access to the report, he will ask it. It is a good habit to get into selecting such a piece of information prior to taking the stand so that if the question is asked, you won't have to grope on the stand trying to remember a fact that fits the situation.

A. Yes, sir. Well, for one thing, I felt no need to include your client's description in the report even though his appearance is an important fact in this case.

Note: The officer has turned this situation

to his advantage. Now, the officer is inviting the defense attorney t ask him what the defendant looked like at the time of the observation. The chances are the defendant has cleaned himself up considerably for trial to make a good impression on the jury and isn't going to be anxious for the jury to hear what he looked like at the time of the offense. It shouldn't be overdone, but it is not improper to remind the jury in this way that the defense attorney is perhaps more interested in the defendant's welfare than in justice.

In this case, the defense attorney determined that he was not going to be able to lure the witness into his trap, and went on to a different phase of the cross-examination.

Many times witnesses are led to believe by the person examining them that every question must be answered "yes" or "no." This is frequently untrue. Many questions cannot be answered accurately with such a simple response because they contain half truths or ambiguous phrases which can be misinterpreted later if answered that way. These are questions which call for an explanation and in response to which you should state the facts of what happened in your own words. If the defense attorney asks you to answer with a simple "yes" or "no," you are entitled to tell him that it can't be answered that way without the answer being misleading. If he insists, the prosecutor should object, and the court would probably allow you to give the answer with an explanation. If the prosecutor does not object, repeat your response. If he still doesn't object, answer with yes or no, but add that without an explanation, it would be misleading. The court will almost always allow an explanation where one is necessary. If an explanation is not allowed on cross-examination, the prosecutor should revisit the matter on redirect-examination.

L. Questions Outside the Officer's Area of Knowledge

At times, a police officer is asked questions on cross-examination that are police related, but that don't fall within the expertise or knowledge of the testifying officer. Often these questions are put in such a way as to make it seem that, if the officer admits to a lack of knowledge or expertise about a particular matter, he is a poor policeman who hasn't done his homework. Generally, of course, this is not the case, but many officers feel trapped by this approach and try to answer questions that they are not qualified to answer. This almost always leads to trouble. The officer should say that this particular area of law enforcement is not within the area of his expertise or that he didn't deal with that particular phase of the investigation, and that his only information about it is hearsay. The officer should not apologize or make excuses for his lack of knowledge or expertise.

M. Asking for or Attacking Conclusions

Defense attorneys, when it suits their purpose, often during cross-examination, try to either elicit opinions from police officers or attack conclusions reached by the officer during his investigation. They might include a multitude of subjects, such as the value of a piece of evidence or the credibility of a witness. They ask the officers to draw conclusions about such things as the ability of a person to see certain things under specific conditions: poor lighting, heavy weather, or from great distances, for example. Or, they may attempt to question the officer's basis for conclusions already made in an attempt to discredit the conclusion.

Again, the attorney will try to lead the witness down the path gently so that he is in

deeper than realized by the time the defense attorney reaches the conclusion he wants.

It is important to remember in this, and other situations under cross-examination, not to volunteer information not directly requested. The defense attorney is not there to pass the time of day with you. He is trying to bring out, any way he can, information that will be favorable to his client.

Situation 6-41: This case involved a drunk driving charge. There was an accident and the defendant suffered slight bruises. The defendant neither asked for, nor appeared to require medical attention. No photographs were taken of the automobiles. The defendant refused a breath test, and there was no video taken of his actions or responses to questions.

Questions by the defense attorney:

Q. Trooper Strong, when you arrived on the scene, what was the situation?

A. Other than the two vehicles involved in the accident, I was the first at the scene.

Q. And what time was that?

A. Approximately 2:45 a.m. (Notice the officer stayed away from using military time.)

Q. Were the cars still on the road?

A. Yes, it was apparent to me that the collision had occurred only minutes prior to my arrival.

Q. Were you called to the scene?

A. No, I was on patrol in the area and just came upon the accident.

Q. What did you do when you saw it?

A. I stopped my vehicle, radioed my position, and immediately went to see if there were any injuries.

Q. Did it appear from the condition of the automobiles that there might be injuries?

Note: In any collision, no matter how slight, there is the possibility of injuries. Here, the defense attorney wants the trooper to testify that he was checking for injuries because of the seriousness of the accident. If the trooper answers "yes," the jury may have an image of badly damaged automobiles. This would play into the hands of the defense attorney, since he will later attempt to create the impression that the defendant's apparent condition was the result of an injury, and not an intoxicated condition.

A. No, sir. The damage to the cars was only minor, but checking for possible injuries is standard procedure.

Q. On direct-examination, you gave testimony about your observations of the defendant and that your observations led to an opinion that the defendant was intoxicated, isn't that correct?

A. Yes, sir.

Q. And, it was on the basis of that conclusion that the defendant was arrested?

A. Yes.

Q. Before, or after you placed him under arrest?

A. Before.

Note: The defense attorney wants to establish that the reason the trooper wanted the breath test was to confirm for him that the defendant was intoxicated, and that, therefore, the officer wasn't certain of the defendant's condition.

Q. And, did he agree to take the breath test?
A. No, he did not. He refused.
Q. Then, you placed him under arrest?
A. Shortly after that, yes.

Note: Be careful not to answer in such a way as to allow the defense attorney an opportunity to suggest that you arrested him, not because of your belief in his client's condition, but because of his unwillingness to cooperate.

Q. I'd like to ask you about those observations, if you don't mind. You said that there was an odor of alcohol on the defendant, correct?

A. No, sir, on the defendant's breath.

Q. And you described the odor as moderate; what does that mean?

Note: The term moderate is an ambiguous one, and the defense attorney is counting on the officer's inability to adequately define it. The officer should not get wrapped up in semantics but should use it as an opportunity to otherwise describe the defendant's condition.

A. It means that the odor is consistent with someone who has had more than just a couple of drinks.

Note: That response will have hurt the defendant. The officer appears to have been fair to the defendant by describing the odor as moderate rather than strong, which point the prosecutor had already made on direct-examination, yet his definition of the term moderate still describes a person who has had too much to drink. The defense attorney may choose to abandon this point and move on, or he may choose to question more intensely on it, challenging the officer's statement with questions such as, "At how many drinks does the odor go from slight to moderate?" If he does, the officer should answer that there is no particular point at which that occurs, and the it's an impression based on years of dealing with drinking drivers. He should, at all times, keep his poise. If he does, the jury will see the defendant as the wounded party, not the officer.

Q. But, you didn't conclude from that that the defendant was intoxicated, did you?

A. Not by that fact alone, no sir.

Q. And you've described his gate as unsteady?

A. That's correct, the defendant was unsteady in his movements..

Q. Unsteady how?

A. He was unable to walk a straight line, and he put his hand on the side of his car as he moved to the rear of the car. It appeared as though he was doing that to maintain his balance.

Q. He didn't fall over, though, he was just unsteady when he walked?

A. He did not fall over, but he came close several times.

Q. And, did I hear you say that his speech was slurred?

A. Yes, it was.

Q. Could you understand what he was saying?

A. Part of it.

Q. Was his speech disjointed, in other words, did his sentences end before they were finished, or did he change subjects in the middle of a sentence?

A. No, sir. He was slow in his speech, his words were garbled, and though he appeared confused at times, he did not do what you asked.

Note: It would have been easy, and tempting, for the officer to simply answer yes to the question, but by answering the way he did, the officer made two things clear to the jury: he was being fair to the defendant in his description of his actions and words, and the defendant was still intoxicated.

Q. How about his eyes, you didn't say anything about them. I assume from that that there was nothing unusual about them?

A. Sir, I believe I testified that his eyes were glassy.

Q. I'm not sure what you mean by glassy. Did they have a look of pain?

A. No, sir.

Q. What, then?

A. There was little or no movement in them, and he seemed to be looking past me. They just didn't seem to be focusing on anything, and the had a glaze about them.

Q. As though he were dazed?

Note: The word dazed is defined as stunned, as with a heavy blow or shock, and is usually used when referring to a physical injury. The defense attorney will use this or other terms to put the witness in the position of agreeing that the defendant's condition was caused by injury.

A. I wouldn't say dazed, no.

Q. Why not?

A. Because being dazed involves more than a certain look in the eyes. I associate it with someone who is wandering around like he's lost. They also usually complain of a head injury. Your client didn't act that way, and made no complaint about a head injury, and he gave no sign that he had suffered one.

Q. Disoriented, then?

A. No, sir, intoxicated.

Q. Your opinion?

A. Yes, sir, my opinion.

Q. Based, in part, on the moderate odor of alcohol?

A. Yes, sir, in part.

Q. Again, your opinion.

A. Yes, sir.

Q. You would agree that opinions on matters like this may differ from one individual to another, correct?

A. I'd say that was true.

Q. And another officer may have described the odor differently?

A. That's possible.

Q. Another officer might have described the odor as slight, correct.

A. I doubt slight. More likely, strong.

Q. But maybe slight.

A. Yes, sir, that's a possibility.

Note: Again, the temptation is to deny that possibility, but the officer did the right thing. He made the point that the point that the difference would most likely be between moderate and strong, while admitting the mere possibility that it might have been described as slight. Answers like this are far more valuable in establishing the officer's credibility than they are simply for the answer. Jurors often look for overkill from police officers, especially in the area of drunk driving. By handling the answers the way he has, the officer's conclusions are enhanced in the eyes of the jury.

Q. So, if reasonable officers might differ in their opinion regarding such things as balance, speech, and the odor of alcohol, it's also reasonable to assume that they might also differ on the matter of intoxication, isn't that correct?

Note: With this question, the officer should only answer for his own conclusions. No attempt should be made at speculation regarding the ultimate conclusion of intoxication.

A. Sir, I have been a state trooper for over nine years. I have seen many people who suffered head and other injuries as the result of all kinds of things, and I've seen how they react to them. I have also been with many other officers when they have made such observations and reported on them. I have also seen a lot of people who were intoxicated, and how they reacted. Your client was intoxicated.

N. Broad, Sweeping Questions

Most often broad, sweeping questions are asked for one of two reasons: when the questioner lacks information about the facts surrounding the subject matter of the examination, or when the examiner is on a fishing expedition, hoping to hear information that he wasn't aware of until the answer was given.

Sometimes, the defense attorney will ask a very broad question in order to get a commitment from the witness and, at the same time, mislead the witness as to the meaning of the question, then, later on during the examination, use the answer to that question to attack an answer to another question. Usually the first question will not be a critical one, but the one set up by the first question does concern a critical, or at least, and important matter.

Situation 6-42: Broad and misleading questions.

Questions by the defense attorney:

Q. Have you told us all that you heard?

Note: The question presents a problem because it's too broad. The witness may have testified to all that he heard from one source, the one that he was asked about on direct, but not about what he may have heard from another source, even at near the same place and time. The witness may answer that he has told all of what he has heard, thinking the question referred to that which the previous questions were limited, when, in fact, the attorney was looking for a broad, unqualified answer that would have started the witness off in a bad position. You should be warned by such questions and answer them carefully; otherwise a trap can be set.

A. Yes.

Later, the defense attorney asks:

Q. Was there any commotion in the connecting room while you were talking to Wit Baker?

A. Yes, there were loud noises, like arguments, coming from the next room.

Q. And you could hear those noises?

A. Yes.

Q. And could you understand what was being said?

A. Yes.

Q. Why then did you not testify about these noises before?

A. Because I was not asked about them.

Q. I asked you earlier if you had told us all that you had heard. Would you like the reporter to read back your answer?

A. No, I misunderstood. I thought that you were referring to what Wit Baker had said.

Note: The intent of the attorney's question is to imply to the jury that the witness is trying to add something that didn't happen which he thought would hurt the defendant. This answer tends to, at least, cast the witness in a less than professional light. The defense attorney's point is that if the officer couldn't understand a question as simple as the one asked, there are some serious questions raised about other parts of the officer's testimony and even about his investigation in general.

A more appropriate answer to the question would have been:

A. I have told you all that I heard Mr. Baker say inside that room on April 5th.

Another example:

Q. Is that all that was said?

Note: Here the defense attorney may be trying to put you in conflict with the testimony of another witness. The question seems to really ask, "Is that all that you heard said?" and the tendency may be to respond as if that were the question.

Example:

A. Yes.

Then later the defense attorney asks:

Q. Are you aware that Mr. Baker testified that the defendant said he was going to kill the victim?
A. Yes.
Q. And that the defendant said that on April 5th in his apartment?
A. Yes.
Q. But the defendant did not say that, did he?
A. Well, I don't know, Mr. Baker must have heard him say that when I was out of the room.
Q. But you testified earlier that you went to the apartment at about 3:15 p.m. with Mr. Baker and that you both left at 4:00 p.m.
A. Yes, but I went into the other room momentarily to use the restroom.
Q. Why did you not testify to that earlier?

A. Because I was not asked that question.

Note: Again, the witness has put himself in a position to be criticized for not being precise or for attempting to withhold information until the defense attorney brought it to light. This will act to discredit the witness in the eyes of the jury and is intended to make it seem as though it is the defense, and not the prosecution, that is really seeking the truth.

Other similar questions that require care and thought in answering:

Q. Are you sure you have described all of the persons present?
Q. What you have told us in response to the prosecution's questions is everything that you know about what took place on that date. Are you quite certain of that?

6.07 Traps

Defense attorneys dream and scheme of ways to trap witnesses, especially police officers, while they are on the stand testifying. It is important for the officer to know this because if he is able to spot the trap, he will most often be able to avoid it, and sometimes be able to turn it back on the defense.

Defense attorneys will use many different tactics and styles while setting up the trap. The following is the typical approach employed by the attorney with discussion of the various tactics used:

A. Setting Up the Witness

Before the defense attorney gets to the questions which he hopes will cause the damage, he will try to set you up, putting you in a position where you are unable to escape the trap. In doing this he will:

1. Evaluate the Witness

The defense attorney will be watching you as you testify looking for anything in your facial expressions, voice tone or inflection, or any other mannerisms, that will provide a clue to help him determine how to lead you into his trap.

2. Keep the Witness Unaware

The attorney will most likely start his questioning in a friendly, perhaps even flattering way. It is intended to put you at ease, making it possible for him to manipulate you. He will be very polite and may even appear to be confused or unfamiliar with the area of your testimony. This should alert you to his real purpose. No competent defense lawyer is going to fumble through an area with which he is unfamiliar and allow the witness to maintain the superior position. The area in which he feigns his unfamiliarity is probably the area in which he hopes to slam you. You should remain on guard, though not defensive, and carefully answer each question only when you are certain that you understand it.

3. Building the Questions

The attorney will begin to probe the area by asking innocent questions in the area about which he wants you to testify. He will be very careful not to expose his plan or purpose. In using this "kid glove" approach, he will try to force you to conform each answer to the previous one, but he will slowly change the picture being painted by your testimony. Each change will be slight and will seem unimportant. The attorney will try to talk you into accepting the facts included in his question, even though they are not totally accurate. By having "befriended" you at the beginning, he is hoping that rather than risk a confrontation or a change in his demeanor, you will accept this "innocent" inconsistency with the true facts. The defense attorney neither befriends a witness who gives testimony damaging to his client, nor asks innocent questions on cross-examination.

B. Getting the Commitment

By successfully molding your testimony as described above, the defense attorney will have placed you in a position where you have little choice but to commit to a statement of fact that is the defense attorney's interpretation of the subject matter of your testimony. Your only other choice would be to expose yourself to impeachment by changing the answers you were maneuvered into giving earlier. By now, the defense attorney will be using a little harsher tone of voice and generally will be a little more intimidating in his demeanor. He will refer back to the answers which you previously gave and will try to get you to admit that if the answers to the previous questions were as you gave them, the answer to which he seeks your commitment now must be as he suggests.

If you find yourself in this situation you must refuse to commit to the attorney's misstatement and, when reminded of your previous answers, correct them as best you can. You may cause some damage to the case, but not nearly as much as if the attorney is successful in closing the trap on you.

C. Closing the Trap

Once the attorney gets you to commit to his answer to the crucial question he will either confront you with the irrefutable information which will disprove your position, or he may move on to another subject without further questions or confrontation. If he chooses the latter course, it will be because he does not wish to expose his proof immediately, thereby avoiding any possibility of an explanation by you which might lessen the effect of his effort. Or, he may be intending to move into another area where he hopes to trap you again and, therefore, doesn't want to alienate you by unnecessarily embarrassing you in front of the jury. He may, however, delight in doing just that at a later time.

Situation 6-43: Traps may be set up by using evidence outside the officer'stestimony, or by using the officer's own testimony against him. This is a situation involving evidence outside the officer's knowledge and testimony.

The defendant was arrested on board the Southern Comfort, a 60-foot trawler, smuggling cocaine into Florida. The boat had come from Cancun, Mexico. While in Cancun, the boat and its crew were photographed by a DEA surveillance team from a distance of about seventy yards. At the trial, a DEA agent testified from the photo that one of the men on board the boat was Cal Faller, one of nine defendants charged in the conspiracy to smuggle, thereby placing him on the boat at the time the cocaine was loaded on board. The defendant claims that he wasn't there when the boat was loaded, and wasn't aware there was cocaine on board when the boat was stopped upon its arrival back on the west coast of Florida. Questions by the defense attorney:

Q. Agent Stauffer, referring to government's Exhibit number 35-D, the photo from which you testified when you identified my client, Mr. Faller, what does it appear toyou that the five men in the photo are doing?

A. They appear to be working on the forward deck in the area of a storage bin at the base of the Wheel-house where cus-

toms agents eventually found the entrance to the concealed, refrigerated storage area where the cocaine was found.

Q. And, how many people were on board the vessel when it was stopped by the agents?

A. Five people; two women and three men.

Q. And, of course, Mr. Faller was among those aboard the Southern Comfort at that time, wasn't he?

A. He was.

Q. At any time after his arrest, did Mr. Faller admit to you that he was aware that there was cocaine on board the vessel?

A. No, sir.

Q. In fact, he has continuously denied it, hasn't he?

A. As have all of the other defendant's, yes.

Q. And, there was a search conducted on board the vessel after its seizure to locate cocaine, wasn't there?

A. Yes, there was.

Q. And, you and your agents knew that there was cocaine on board before the search, isn't that correct?

A. That's correct.

Q. And, you received that information from an informant in Cancun, Mexico, correct?

A. Correct.

Q. You wouldn't want to name that informant, would you?

A. No, I would not.

Q. I thought not. Did this informant provide any names to you of any of the defendants on trial here today?

A. Yes, those of Mr. Helfrick, and Mr. Myers.

Note: There were nine defendants all together, Myers and Helfrick were the alleged kingpins of the operation, and were on board the vessel when the photos were taken in Cancun but not when the boat was stopped near Sarasota, Florida.

Q. But not Mr. Faller?

A. No, sir.

Q. Knowing that the cocaine was on board

the vessel, were you and the other agents able to locate it right away?

A. No, sir.

Q. How long did it take for you to find the cocaine?

A. Quite some time.

Q. In fact, Agent Stauffer, it took just over seven hours, did it not?

A. That's correct.

Q. And, how many agents conducted the search?

A. Between five and seven, at various times.

Q. Between five and seven. Well, using six as the average, it then took over forty-two man hours to locate the cocaine, isn't that correct?

A. I suppose.

Q. And, your team even used drills to puncture holes in the bulkheads in an attempt to locate the cocaine, isn't that so?

A. That's correct.

Q. You couldn't smell it or anything, could you?

A. No, sir, it gave no odor. It was refrigerated and wrapped in plastic.

Q. But, other substances, marijuana, for example, would have given off an odor if 1100 pounds of it were on board, correct?

A. Probably, this was not marijuana, it was 1100 pounds of cocaine.

Q. Exactly, and it didn't give off any odor. So, it is reasonable to assume that people could be on board the vessel on a trip across the Gulf of Mexico without even knowing that the cocaine was on board, isn't it?

A. Not your client.

Q. But, why not?

A. Because, your client was on board when the cocaine was loaded.

Q. Well, you don't actually know that. I mean, your surveillance team didn't actually photograph the boat as it was being loaded, did they?

A. We didn't photograph it because it was

loaded at night, and we didn't want to use flash cameras, for obvious reasons. But, we did see the boat being loaded, and your client was there.

Q. Don't you have equipment that can photograph in the dark?

A. Yes, sir, infrared equipment, but we didn't have access to it at that time.

Q. You were on the surveillance team, correct?

A. Correct.

Q. And you took this photo, didn't you? (referring to Govt. exhibit 35-D)

A. That's correct.

Q. And, you also saw the cocaine being loaded, didn't you?

A. Yes, that's correct.

Q. And, my client was one of those who brought the duffel bags on board, isn't that what you said?

A. That's correct.

Q. And, when you observed this you were the same distance away as when the photos were taken, correct?

A. Correct.

Q. And we established that distance to be about 70 yards, or a little over 200 feet away, correct?

A. Correct.

Q. Were you using binoculars?

A. Yes.

Q. And you saw the same people then as when you took the photographs?

A. Yes.

Q. Including Mr. Faller?

A. Including Mr. Faller.

Q. You're sure that the people you saw loading the duffel bags are the same people in the photograph?

A. I am.

Q. It would be nice if we had a photo. That way we could be sure, couldn't we?

Note: The defense attorney is forcing the witness into a commitment, not that the defendant was one of the people who loaded the bags, but that the person he saw loading the bags was one of the people in the photo.

A. I am sure.

Q. You're saying that we do have a photo, then, since those people are the same?

A. I didn't say that, but that is true.

Q. And, you're absolutely sure that the Mr. Faller in the photo is the same man you say you saw loading the boat?

A. I am.

Q. No mistake?

A. No mistake.

Q. Stake your investigation on it?

Note: The attorney is baiting the agent, trying to tie the photo into the rest of the investigation. This should have raised a red flag for the agent, but he was certain of his work, and had no fear, believing that the attorney was on a fishing expedition.

A. Yes.

Q. Agent Stauffer, what would you say if I told you that the man in the photo, the one you identified as Mr. Faller, isn't really Mr. Faller at all?

A. I'd say you were wrong.

Q. It is pretty ridiculous. After all, we know that Mr. Faller was on board the Southern Comfort when it was stopped, don't we?

A. Yes, we do.

Q. And, we know that the other two men found on board were also in the photo, don't we?

A. Yes, we do.

Q. Therefore, this must be Mr. Faller in the photo, correct?

A. That is Mr. Faller.

Q. Right, but if it weren't Mr. Faller in the photo, would you then concede that Mr. Faller was not one of the men who loaded the bags?

A. That's a ridiculous question, because Mr. Faller is in the photograph.

Q. I know, but if the person you saw loading the bags was the same person in the pho-

tograph, and if that person was someone other than Mr. Faller, would it be fair to say that Mr. Faller was not the person you saw loading the bags?

A. If that were the case, yes.

Q. Thank you. Would it also be fair to say, then, that if that person was not Mr. Faller, that Mr. Faller, who was on the boat when it was stopped, might not have known about the cocaine?

By the prosecutor: Objection, your Honor. All of counsel's statements are predicated on the supposition that the man in the photograph is not Mr. Faller, and all of the testimony and evidence show that it was.

By the court: Overruled, you may answer the question.

A. Yes, if that were not Mr. Faller in the photo, but it is.

Q. Right. Thank you. Agent Stauffer, I took the liberty of blowing up a portion of Exhibit 35-D, and I now ask that it be marked as Defendant Faller's Exhibit 1. (The exhibit was marked.)

Q. Please look at this photo closely. Then please compare it to Exhibit 35-D, and tell me if you agree that Defendant Faller's exhibit 1 is a blown up portion of 35-D.

A. Yes, your exhibit is part of 35-D

Q. Please look at my exhibit one, and tell me if you know who that person is.

Q. That's not Mr. Faller, is it Agent Stauffer?

A. No, it doesn't appear to be.

Q. And, you agree that the blow up is of the person in Exhibit 35-D who you have identified as Mr. Faller?

A. Yes, I do.

Q. So, that is not Mr. Faller in your photograph, is it, Agent Stauffer?

A. No, sir, I guess it isn't.

Q. You guess it isn't? Didn't you say earlier that you would be willing to stake your investigation on that being Mr. Faller?

By the prosecutor: Objection, your Honor, argumentative.

By the Court: Sustained. You made your point, counselor. Please move on.

Q. Thank you, your Honor, I have no further questions.

Note: As you saw, Agent Stauffer was drawn into commitments about the evidence which he really didn't have to make. He did not want it to appear that he had conducted a questionable investigation, but in trying to protect his work, he went too far.

Even though the prosecutor did less than a sterling job of trying the case, much of what resulted was caused by this blunder, and what resulted was that all of the defendant's were acquitted.

When you don't know where the defense attorney is going, be careful. He usually will know where he wants to go, and you will probably not want to go there. Without qualifying his answers to the questions about how sure he was that the photo was of defendant Faller, he might have hedged his bet a little by providing an answer similar to this:

A. Sir, I took the photos, and I believed at the time that they were of the defendant. We were closer to the defendant on several occasions, close enough that I can identify him now as being one of the men on board that vessel at various times during those three days.

6.08 Specific Topics

A. Identification Testimony

If the officer is identifying the defendant from personal observation as the person who committed the crime, or as the person that he pursued following the crime, or if the officer is testifying regarding identification procedures conducted by him during the course of the investigation, such as an in-person lineup or a photo identification, you may expect the defense attorney to attack the basis of the identification. Here we will deal with them one at a time:

1. Line-up or Photopack Identification

If, during the course of the investigation, the testifying officer produced the defendant or a photograph of the defendant for identification purposes, the defense attorney may be expected to attack the procedure used by the officer as unfair or prejudicial to the defendant. Through his questioning, the attorney will attempt to leave the impression with the jury that the procedure followed by the officer was suggestive.

In his cross-examination of the lay witness who was asked to view the lineup, the defense attorney will have made an attempt to do damage to the procedure followed by the police officer, and, at that point, there is very little that the police officer can do about it.

However, a juror will be more sympathetic to a lay witness's testimony than to that of a professional law enforcement officer and will be more receptive to the prosecutor's argument during closing that the lay witness was confused by the tactics of the defense attorney, and that the police officer who conducted the lineup, and who is a professional, more familiar with the procedures to be followed, is the best witness regarding the procedures followed in that case.

Where the viewing was a formal, *in-person* lineup, the defense attorney may, on cross-examination, demand a photograph of the lineup that was shown to the witness.

If the identification was made from a *photopack*, the defense attorney will demand to see the photopack shown to the witness who made the identification. He will use these photographs to point out to you the differences between the individuals in the lineup, and by exaggerating features, will try to demonstrate that the lineup was unfair and that the persons in the lineup were not of the same height, weight, age, or general appearance, and did not have one or more of the characteristics mentioned by the initial witnesses following the commission of the crime.

In response to these questions, the police officer should avoid interpreting what the photographs show. The matter of whether or not the lineup was fair is essentially a legal matter to be taken up by the court and the attorneys during pre-trial motions or, if raised during the trial itself, a matter to be handled by the prosecution, either during sidebar argument or during closing argument. The officer should answer questions regarding what is seen on the photograph, such as questions of height or description of clothing or other physical peculiarities (i.e., scars, tattoos, or mustaches) which are visibly apparent from viewing the photograph. The officer should stay away from answering any questions which call for speculation, and which were not noted by the police officer at the time of the lineup, such as the weight or age of the subject in the lineup.

2. Personal Observations

If the officer is testifying that, from his own observations, and can identify the defendant as the person who is the subject of this testimony, the officer may expect to be questioned about the conditions under which he saw that person. The officer may expect to be questioned on matters such as the distance or lighting; the speed with which the event occurred; whether or not the officer had an unobstructed view; the officer's state of mind at the time of the observation; and whether or not the officer had any personal interest in

the case or whether he had any reason to lie about the defendant being the person he saw. If any of the conditions under which the observation was made formed the basis of the identification, the defense attorney will attempt to appeal to the officer's sense of fair play, and mostly by patronizing him, will attempt to entice the officer into testifying that, though he is confident that the person he saw was the defendant, he cannot be absolutely sure beyond all doubt.

One question that defense attorneys are fond of using is, in some form or another, this one:

Q. I understand, officer, that you are identifying the defendant as the person you think you saw on that day, but you couldn't actually swear to that, could you, sir?

Note: The officer should never play into a defense attorney's plan to later misinterpret in his closing statement to the jury the officer's answer to that question. Often the police officer, desiring to be absolutely fair in his testimony, will admit that there is a very slight and remote possibility that the person he saw may not be the defendant, when actually the officer is certain that the person he saw was the defendant. Experienced officers are aware that there is almost nothing about which there cannot be some doubt, but, when applying that fact to their testimony, are often misunderstood by the jury. When asked if the officer could swear to his identification of the defendant, his reply should be:

A. Sir, I have indeed already taken an oath to tell the truth and so, I am swearing that I am quite certain that the person I saw on August 25th at the warehouse was the defendant.

Note: Though it may seem so, this situation is not the same as that presented in Situation 6-40. In this case, the officer is testifying about a person he saw in person and later recognized as the defendant, rather than making the identification from a photograph.

B. Distance and Speed

1. Distance

As was discussed in an earlier chapter, every *distance* which may become important in the trial of a case should have been measured by the investigator. If the investigator measured those distances, he should be prepared to state the distance exactly. Otherwise, if asked, the officer should estimate the distance as best he can, always remembering that the defense attorney will attempt to change the distance, making it longer or shorter than it actually was, depending on which best suits his client's interests.

Situation 6-44: Officer measured the distance. In the trial of a murder case, the gun which caused the death of the victim was lying a distance from the body. The victim's body was found outside on his property in the country. His fingerprints were on the gun, and a paraffin test performed on the victim's hands was positive. The gun, a shotgun, was found some distance from the body, and on the other side of a wooden rail fence. For other reasons, the police determined that the scene was set-up and that the defendant had killed the victim and tried to make the crime look like a suicide. The defense theory was that the victim had committed suicide, and that the defendant wasn't even at the scene at the time. An expert had already testified that if the victim had shot himself in the head using his right hand, and that if he had been standing where the evidence indicates he was when the shot was fired, the gun could not have been more than seven feet from the body, and probably

would not have traveled over the four-foot high fence. He did admit on cross-examination that it was possible, however, that the gun might have gone over the fence, since the victim was only approximately three and a half feet from the fence when he was shot. Questions by the defense attorney:

Q. Officer, your testimony, as I remember it, was that the first thing that caused you to question the fact that this was a suicide was that the gun was too far away from the body to have traveled over the fence and land that distance away from the victim's body, correct?

A. You're correct about my theory; however, your statement stating that the fact was that this was a suicide is incorrect.

Q. Well, let me ask you this. Did you measure exactly how far from the body the gun was when it was found?

A. In fact, I did, sir. The distance was thirteen feet, seven inches from the body.

Q. Why did you not state that during your direct-examination?

A. I wasn't asked until now.

Note: Here, the officer and the prosecutor took a chance by baiting the defense attorney. The prosecutor expected that the officer would be asked that question. However, if he had not, and there was no way to ask it on re-direct, the prosecutor would have been in a bind. The question should have been asked by the prosecutor on direct-examination. The point here, however, is that since the officer measured the exact distance, there was serious damage done to the defendant's theory.

Note: Had the officer not measured the exact distance, the matter could have become a serious problem for the prosecution, and the questions would probably have gone something like this:

Q. Let me ask you this, did you measure exactly how far from the body the gun was when it was found.

A. It was more than seven feet.

Q. I'm sorry, I didn't make myself clear. I thought I asked if you had measured the exact distance from the body to the gun.

A. No, I did not measure the exact distance, but it was more than seven feet.

Q. Well, how can you be sure if you didn't measure it?

A. I just know it was.

Q. I see, you just know it was, but you aren't able to prove it was, is that about it?

Note: Under the circumstances, there would have been no answer to the question which would have satisfied the jury, and the defense attorney would have had no need to proceed with questioning on that point.

2. *Speed*

Estimates regarding the *speed* with which an event occurred can be dangerous if there is nothing against which the witness can make such an estimate. If the witness did not time the event, it is best to simply generalize, or if the witness is providing only a rough estimate or guess, it should be made clear in the answer to the questions that the information is based on an estimate.

Examples:

A. It happened quickly.

A. I wasn't keeping track, but it seemed like a considerable length of time.

A. I can only give an estimate, but I would say the car was traveling somewhere around 65 miles per hour.

C. Confessions

Any time an inculpatory statement is made by a suspect, countless situations and opportunities arise for cross-examination. This is not to say that the officer shouldn't make an attempt to obtain an admission of guilt; naturally, a confession is one of the most convincing pieces of evidence which can be presented to a jury. It is important, however, to illustrate the importance of handling such a situation properly.

Some of the areas which are traditionally explored by the defense attorney on cross-examination are:

1. The conditions under which the confession was taken;
2. Whether or not the confession was written or made orally;
3. Whether or not the confession was taped;
4. The length of time that passed between the time of the arrest and time of the taking of the statement;
5. The time of day during which the statement was taken;
6. The defendant's physical condition at the time of the statement;
7. Whether or not there were any promises or threats made to the defendant in order to obtain a statement; and
8. Whether or not there was any ambiguity in the text of the defendant's statements.

Because a defendant's confession is such overwhelming evidence of his guilt, any defendant going to trial in the face of a confession must make an attempt to discredit his statement or deny making the statement altogether. Obviously, in this situation, taped or written confessions are the most difficult for the defense attorney to deal with on cross-examination, or otherwise explain to the jury during his closing argument. Even so, you may expect the defense attorney to hit hard on the areas concerning the defendant's physical condition at the time of the statement and whether or not any promises of immunity or other favors may have been made in order to entice the defendant to make the statement.

Situation 6-45: Fairness in obtaining a confession. Though there are others, the two most common attacks upon the fairness of the manner of the collection of evidence, other than constitutional questions, usually raised in pre-trial motions, are entrapment and the use of unfair persuasion during an interrogation.

In this example, the detective who obtained a confession from the defendant is questioned about his tactics during the interrogation. The defense attorney wants to leave the impression that the officer put words into the defendant's mouth, and coerced the defendant into making some admissions by frightening him on one hand and, on the other, promising lenient treatment in return for the admissions. The defendant is 22 years of age and slightly retarded. He is on trial for a non-violent child molestation.

Questions by the defense attorney:

Q. Detective Bell, did you know that the defendant was retarded?

A. I do now.

Q. Did you know that at the time of the arrest?

A. No, sir, it wasn't apparent to me that he was.

Q. Did it become apparent to you at any time during the interrogation?

Note: The use of the word interrogation conjures up visions of pressure and force in the minds of a jury, especially in the case of a person who may be retarded, even slightly, and while, for obvious reasons, the term may be acceptable with reference to a violent or career criminal, it's best to stay away from that term when referring to someone such as this defendant. While the defense attorney will prefer the word interrogation, you should use the word, interview.

A. At no time during my interview of the defendant did he appear other than of average intelligence.

Q. When did you learn of his condition?

Note: There isn't much you can do about it, but you should be aware that defense attorneys like to use words like "condition" when referring to some fact about their client. The use of the term lends the impression that, if the defendant committed the act, it was the result of his "condition," and not a depraved heart. In the case of an interrogation issue, it will be used by the defense to paint a picture of the defendant as one who is easily frightened and who is easily convinced to say whatever is suggested to him to say.

A. I learned that the defendant's intelligence level was slightly lower than average when I was shown, by the district attorney, a medical report obtained by you from Dr. Miller.

Q. Is it your testimony that the defendant displayed no signs that he was retarded?

A. I saw no such signs.

Q. Is it true that at one point during your interrogation, my client began to cry?

A. Yes, at one point he did.

Q. In fact, your report suggests that he had episodes of crying several times during the interrogation, isn't that correct?

A. That's correct?

Q. And, he appeared frightened, isn't that correct?

A. I wouldn't say frightened, maybe a little nervous, which under the circumstances is pretty normal.

Q. Looking at your comments about what my client said to you, it's clear that he was confused about the facts of the events about which you were interrogating him.

A. I'm sorry, is that a question?

Q. Yes, was he confused?

A. I'm not sure how you mean. He was well oriented in time and place. He knew why he was being questioned, he was offered an opportunity to call a lawyer and refused, and he acknowledged that he could stop the questioning at any time. He was confused about some of the details of the crime he committed, which in my experience is not unusual. Is that what you were asking?

Note: The officer is obviously picking something up from the tone or manner of the defense attorney's speech that leads him to believe that the attorney is becoming frustrated because he wasn't getting the answers he had hoped for. Yet, while it is apparent that he is trying to stick it to the attorney, he remains respectful. The attorney moves on to another area.

Q. How long was the interrogation? How long did it last?

A. We spoke for an hour and ten minutes total.

Q. And during much of that time, he was denying his involvement in this crime, isn't that true?

A. As I said, we spoke for about an hour and ten minutes. During that time the defendant told me what he had done. At times when what he said was inconsistent with something else he said earlier, I would ask him questions about it, and at times he would deny that he made the earlier statement. This defendant was a suspect at the time, and it was my job to inquire of him about the matter. He told me what he wanted to tell me; I did not choose his words.

Note: At this point many defense attorneys will begin to become frustrated. The witness is holding his ground against the accusations of the attorney. Often, when this happens, the attorney will try a more forceful and accusatory style in the hope that the officer will lose his poise and make a mistake. He must successfully attack the confession if he is to have any chance of getting his client out of the trouble he's in. Therefore, while it is risky to move into direct confrontation with the police officer, at this point, he has nothing to lose.

Q. Isn't it true, Mr. Bell, that you told my client during the interrogation that, with the evidence you had, you had him locked, and that he may as well tell you that he did it?

Note: One suspect interview technique employed by experienced police officers is to convince the suspect that they are confident of his guilt. One way to do this is to point out to the suspect evidence that points to him, and no other, as the person who committed the act. This technique, though it may be successful in practice, is dangerous in its style because in court it suggests intimidation by the interviewer.

A. I didn't use those words, but I did share some of the facts of the investigation with your client, since those facts were the reason for his arrest, and asked him about them.

Q. Didn't you tell him that you knew he did it and that his denials were useless?

A. I was and am convinced of the defendant's guilt and I informed him during the interview that the strength of the evidence was the reason for his arrest. I did not browbeat the defendant, as you are suggesting.

Note: The last part of this response can be dangerous since it could be interpreted as being somewhat defensive. The manner of the question, however, along with its repetitiousness clearly make it accusatory, and so, in this situation, the response is appropriate.

Q. Did you not tell the defendant that if he admitted to you that he committed this crime, you would intercede on his behalf with the court and see that he got help?

Note: The detective did suggest to the defendant that if he needed medical or psychological help because of the nature of the crime (child molestation), it would be provided, and he did assure him that he would be safe, but since the question suggests that the assistance was predicated on the defendant's admission, the appropriate answer is:

A. No, sir.

Note: The detective has kept calm and has demonstrated to the jury that the manner in which the interview was conducted was fair and not suggestive or intimidating.

If the defendant made an oral statement but refused to sign a written statement, and the oral statement was not taped, expect that the defense attorney will make a point of asking you why the defendant was not asked to give a written statement, or, if he was asked, the reasons the defendant gave for not doing so.

It is not uncommon for a defendant to make an oral statement while refusing to give one in writing. However, most often when this is the case, the defendant is willing to give his signature on a piece of paper which states that, while he was not willing to give a written statement, that he has voluntarily given an oral statement.

Even if this statement, signed by the defendant, does not restate a single matter touched by him in his oral statement, it is at least confirmation that he made an oral statement to the police officer, and explains why there is no written or taped statement. This should be done in every case where the suspect would not give a taped or written statement.

You may be assured, in every case involving a confession, especially when the confession is the strongest piece of evidence presented by the prosecution, that the defense attorney will pursue any line of questioning that bears on the accuracy and voluntariness of the statement.

Any statement given by a defendant requires a waiver of the defendant's right to remain silent. Any such waiver by the defendant must be voluntary and must be "intelligently" made, meaning that the defendant must have fully understood his rights and the effect of giving up those rights.

Further, using his cross-examination, the defense attorney will go over, line by line, the statement made by his client, seeking to establish that it is not accurate, or that it does not square with the known facts of the case, or that the words in the statement were those of the officer and not those of the defendant. If a statement was oral and not written, and if more than one police officer was witness to the statement, you may be assured that the defense attorney will attempt to show inconsistencies in the versions of the statement made by the defendant given in testimony by each of the officers who were present at the time the statement was made. In any situation of this type, where the statement was not recorded or written, there are bound to be inconsistencies in the retelling of the statement by each of the witnesses to it. It is important, however, that the inconsistencies that do exist are insignificant and do not go to the thrust of the incriminatory portions of the statement. Comparing notes prior to trial with the other officers who were present at the time the statement was made should prevent any disastrous inconsistencies in testimony. This is not to suggest, however, that the officer should allow the recollections of the other officers to change his own honest recollection. If there are significant differences in the same facts, try to resolve them, if that is possible.

If the differences in your recollections cannot be reconciled, then whatever problems presented by that will have to be overcome by the other evidence in the case and by the prosecutor's handling of the matter in his closing arguments.

D. DUI Cases

1. The Crime

Evidence, or the lack of evidence, will determine the outcome of every case! DUI cases are no exception. Often, officers and prosecutors both tend to treat DUI cases in a less serious way than other "more serious" cases. Without regard to your personal feelings about the increasing penalties, and without regard to the agenda of MADD, those who drive motor vehicles while under the influence of alcoholic beverages present a real danger to the welfare of the average citizen, more than burglars, and more than many other types of criminals we consider to be more serious.

I believe the relaxed attitude about DUI is the result of two facts. First, two of the three acts required to satisfy the elements of the crime are legal. Drinking alcohol is legal for those at or over the legal age, and driving a motor vehicle is legal for those holding a valid license. Only when the two are combined and the driver exhibits an inability to safely operate the vehicle, or when the driver's blood alcohol content exceeds the state limit, is the crime of DUI committed. The second fact is that many of the people who commit this crime are not really considered criminals. Anybody can be guilty of DUI without an intent to commit a crime, especially now that the limit is so low in many jurisdictions that many drivers are on the road believing they are not over the limit. This attitude can be dangerous to the success of DUI prosecutions. It results in the officer expecting the jury to rely on his opinion of the defendant's condition, rather than collecting sufficient evidence, most of which will be available, to insure the jury's satisfaction with the strength of the case.

2. Preparation

In many jurisdictions, the officer is forced to present the evidence at a preliminary hearing without the assistance of a prosecutor. Most DUI cases are fairly routine and most experienced officers have no problem with handling the hearing. However, when there are any unusual circumstances with which the officer is not familiar, he should at least speak to a prosecutor about what problems those circumstances may present. The officer should never go into a vehicular homicide DUI case without a prosecutor. Even the most experienced police officer may not be prepared for cross-examination in such a case. Vehicular homicide will be discussed in more detail later in this chapter.

During the confrontation and arrest of the defendant, and in the minutes or hours following the arrest, the officer is in a position to win or lose the case. What efforts he makes to secure all of the available evidence will often determine whether the case goes to trial or ends up in the defendant taking a plea, and will determine the extent, and effect, of the defense attorney's cross-examination on the jury.

Naturally, the best case will include evidence of the defendant's blood alcohol content (blood or urine tests, or breath-o-lizer results); a video recording of the defendant's driving; a video recording of the defendant's attempt to perform the field sobriety tests, and of his general condition; an audio recording of his manner of speech; detailed information regarding the defendant's movements and alcohol consumption (what, when, where, how much); what, when, and how much the defendant had to eat while he was drinking; and when he last slept, and for how long.

There are times when not all of the evidence will be available. The defendant may not submit to a test of his alcohol content, he may not be willing to perform the field sobriety tests, and he may not be willing to provide any information about his movements or activities on the day of his arrest. Even when the defendant refuses to cooperate by performing field sobriety tests or providing a voice recording, he often is willing to sign a form confirming his refusal. And, if your car is equipped with a video camera, and almost every department is able to afford this, you will have evidence of his driving to show the jury, and if there is videotape equipment at the department station, you will be able to show the jury the defendant's general condition regarding his balance and demeanor.

Juries are no longer always willing to accept the word of the officer regarding the intoxicated condition of the defendant unless he is able to show that every attempt to secure evidence was rebuffed by the defendant.

Situation 6-46: DUI cross-examination.
Questions by the defense attorney:

Q. Officer, what time did you stop my client's car?

A. One thirty-five in the morning.

Q. And, why did you stop him?

A. He was weaving from lane to lane and off onto the right berm. He had also moved into the oncoming lane on several occasions.

Q. Did he hit another car or any other object?

A. Not while I was following him.

Q. And for how long did you follow him?

A. I'm not sure, it was quite a distance.

Q. Well, in terms of from where to where?

A. From the blinking light at Rt. 98 and Harmonsburg Road to the area of the Norrisville Road.

Q. If I told you that I measured that distance and found it to be 6.3 miles long, would

you have a problem with that?

A. If you say so.

Q. That road is not the best road, is it officer?

A. I wouldn't say that.

Q. Well, it's bumpy in places, and the road sort of waffles in places, and the berm is sort of chewed up, isn't it, officer?

Note: The defense attorney is trying to make it appear that the road is responsible for the officer's observations of the defendant's erratic driving. Putting things back into perspective will defeat this tactic.

A. I can see that for someone under the influence, it might be difficult to traverse that road, but I've never had any problems with it, and, unlike your client, I wasn't having any trouble with it that night.

Q. Does your department have any video equipped cars, officer?

A. Yes, we have two of them.

Q. But, you weren't driving one of them that night, were you?

A. No, I wasn't.

Q. Were any of your officers using either of the video equipped cars that night?

A. No.

Q. Do you know why that is, officer?

A. Yes, neither of the video units is working properly.

Q. And, how long has that been that they haven't been working?

A. I'm not sure.

Q. If I told you that they've never been used in a DUI arrest in this county, would that surprise you?

A. I wouldn't know if they've been used or not.

Q. Well, you've never used it, have you?

A. No.

Q. And how long have you been a police officer with this department?

A. Nine years.

Q. And, you testified on direct that you've make hundreds of DUI arrests, isn't that correct?

A. That's correct.

Q. And during that whole time, the video equipment has never been working, has it?

A. Not that I know of.

Q. However, if it had been working, and if you had it in your car, then, you could have made a recording of the defendant's driving and brought it in to show this jury how he was driving erratically, correct?

A. Correct.

Q. And if you had that equipment in your car, you could have made a recording of the defendant's performance during the field sobriety tests, correct?

A. I suppose.

Q. Is there any video equipment at the department, officer?

A. Yes, there is.

Q. And, is it available to the officers for taping DUI suspects?

A. I suppose.

Q. And, I heard you testify that you took the defendant back to the station after you left the hospital. After you say he refused the blood alcohol test, isn't that correct?

A. That's correct.

Q. The same station where the video equipment is located?

A. There is only one station, sir.

Note: The officer knows where this is going and he's becoming a little defensive. That's a mistake, and by so doing, the officer is playing into the defense attorney's hands. The officer should have simply said "yes" to that question.

Q. And was the equipment at the department working that night?

A. I don't know.

Q. But, you hadn't heard that it wasn't working, did you?

A. No.

Q. And still, you didn't use the tape, did you?

A. No.

Q. Was there a reason for that?

A. No special reason.

Q. You just didn't feel like doing it that night, is that correct?

By the prosecutor: Objection.

By the court: Sustained.

Note: Because of the officer's failure to use the video and the lack of a good reason why he did not, the prosecutor was in a position of having to come to the officer's rescue and object. Still, the attorney for the defendant made his point.

Q. In any case, had you used the video, you could have brought that video into the courtroom and shown it to the jury so that they could have seen for themselves, and determined for themselves what the defendant's condition was regarding sobriety, isn't that correct?

A. Correct.

Q. And, then, the jury wouldn't have to take your word for this, there might have been some evidence to backup your testimony, isn't that correct?

By the prosecutor: Objection, argumentative.

By the court: Sustained.

Q. When you asked my client to perform the field sobriety tests, he told you about his leg operation, didn't he?

A. He mentioned something about his leg. I don't think he said anything about an operation.

Q. But, he tried to do that test, didn't he?

A. Well, I asked him which leg was bothering him, and he said, I don't remember which one it was now, but whichever it was, I asked him to do the one leg stand on the other one.

Q. And he didn't do well, did he?

Note: The defendant's attorney is trying to make it seem that the defendant's bad leg was the cause of his poor performance during the test. The officer should add any facts that point away from the injury as the cause for his failure to perform adequately.

A. Well, when I asked him if he could try, he did. When he was doing it, he was on his good leg, and he was swaying, and losing his balance, not something the other leg would have affected.

Q. How do you know that, sir?

A. Because, I've done these tests hundreds of times, and the claim of a bad leg is not unusual. They all seem to be effected in the same way, they sway and lose their balance.

Note: The officer may have made a costly error here. By using the word "claim," the officer has invited the defense to provide proof of the injury and condition of the defendant's leg. If they do that, the officer will look unfair in the eyes of the jury.

Q. These tests that you give, the one-leg stand and the walk and turn, are both standardized tests, is that correct?

A. Yes.

Q. And, you learned to administer these tests while at the academy, is that correct?

A. Yes.

Q. And like you said, you've given these tests hundreds of times, correct?

A. Yes.

Q. And, do you always demonstrate as you did in this case before asking the defendant to do the tests?

A. Yes, I do.

Q. And you don't have any trouble doing them anymore, do you?

Note: The key words in this sentence are "any more." Pay attention to the question, and your chances of doing well increase significantly.

A. I never have had trouble with doing the tests.

Q. But, you yourself have performed these tests hundreds of times, is that correct?

A. Yes.

Q. Have you ever heard the old saying, "practice makes perfect"?

A. I have.

Q. Would you agree that doing these tests hundreds of times has made you better at them than when you first started?

A. I wouldn't say so.

Q. How old are you, officer?

A. Thirty-one.

Q. And my client, do you know how old he is?

A. His license said he was fifty-six years old.

Q. Would you agree that the performance of these tests depends upon balance?

Note: This question is designed to put the entire performance of the tests on balance, when there are other things that the officer is trained to look for during their performance. If the officer is alert, he will pick up on the attorney's intention and combat it.

A. Well, balance is only one of the factors which determine success or failure in these tests. We also look at the ability of the suspect to follow instructions. As I said earlier, your client began the test before I told him to, he took too many steps on the walk and turn, and he turned the wrong way also. His eyes were glassy and bloodshot and red. And, his speech was slurred and confused.

Q. But, balance is a big part of it, isn't it, sir?

A. Balance is a part of it, yes.

Q. And, would you agree that one person's ability to balance himself is different from that of another?

A. I would agree with that.

Q. And while some people are able to balance themselves well, others are not, regardless of their condition of sobriety, correct?

A. I would agree with that.

Q. And, you don't know the ability level of my client, do you?

A. No, I don't.

Q. And, would you agree that the older a person gets, the less he is able to balance himself?

A. I wouldn't know, but that sounds reasonable.

Q. Okay, now, when you testified on direct, you said that the defendant's speech was slurred, is that correct?

A. Yes, very.

Q. Right, very. You do have audio taping equipment at the station, don't you?

A. Yes, we do.

Q. And may I assume that is in operating condition?

A. I believe so.

Q. And it was available to you, as it is to all of the officers, isn't that correct?

A. Yes.

Q. Did you ask my client if you could record his voice?

A. No, I didn't.

Q. But, you could have, correct?

A. I suppose so.

Q. But, you didn't, did you?

A. I did not, no.

Q. Any reason why you didn't?

A. No reason, I just didn't do it.

Q. But, if you had, then you could have brought the tape in for the jury to see for themselves whether or not the defendant's speech was slurred, isn't that correct?

A. I suppose so, yes.

Q. Then, the jury wouldn't have to merely take your word for it, would they?

By the prosecutor: Objection, argumentative.

By the court: Sustained.

Q. Thank you, that's all I have for this witness.

Note: It's easy to see the damage which can be done to the case when evidence that was available wasn't collected. This defense attorney argued to the jury that it would be violating their oath to merely take the officer's word for his observations when there may have been so much evidence available. In this particular case, the jury acquitted the defendant.

3. DUI Cases Involving Accidents

a) Serious injuries suffered by the defendant.

When the defendant was involved in an accident and was injured to the extent that he required hospitalization, the officer, unless he witnessed the accident and the defendant's driving prior to the accident, will probably not be able to make any relevant observations of him. In such cases, if the defendant is admitted to the hospital, the hospital personnel will generally, as a matter of procedure, take a blood sample from the defendant upon his arrival at the hospital. The officer should go to the hospital and advise the person taking the blood that a warrant will be secured, and that the sample of blood should not be destroyed. Then, the officer should apply for a warrant as soon as possible, and seize the blood, or the results of any test which may have been taken of the defendant's blood alcohol content.

Later, when the defendant is able to be interviewed, the officer should ask the defendant to reconstruct for him his movements that night, including the names of people he was with and the places he went. Then, the officer should investigate to find any witnesses who might be able to give an opinion as to the defendant's condition, regarding sobriety, at any time at or near the time of the accident.

b) *When there are minor injuries to the defendant and he refuses or does not require medical treatment.*

In a situation where there was an automobile accident, and where the defendant was injured, but not seriously, you should always expect the defense attorney to claim that his client hit his head causing some degree of injury, and his inability to perform up to the level expected by the officer was a direct result of the injuries to the defendant and not to an intoxicated condition. This is one situation where the general rule that the police officer refrain from giving his opinion does not apply. In this situation, the police officer must rely upon his experience and when cross-examined on the various matters which led him to conclude that the defendant was intoxicated, to inform the jury, through his responses on cross-examination, that his experience observing people who were intoxicated led him to conclude, without hesitation and beyond any doubt, that the defendant was intoxicated.

In such cases, the officer should inquire of the defendant concerning his condition and possible injuries. Even when the officer has done that, however, he should be prepared to be asked on cross-examination, why, if he was convinced that the defendant was so intoxicated that he was unable to safely operate a motor vehicle, would he have taken the defendant's word for his own physical condition, realizing that an intoxicated condition could numb the pain or conversely, that a serious head injury could have rendered the defendant unable to confirm his injuries. Naturally, this should be done prior to any attempt at having the defendant perform any field sobriety tests.

If the decision is made to ask the defendant to perform the tests, the officer should inquire of the him whether or not he feels able to perform the test. If he says no, ask why he is unable to do it. Make a note of his response, and get details, if details are relevant.

If the officer is able to confirm the defendant's responses to his questions, this should be done. The officer may ask the suspect if their conversation could be recorded. Most of the time the defendant will have no objection to that. The officer may also write the responses down on a note pad, and ask the defendant to review the notes and sign his name at the end.

Situation 6-47: This case involves a drunk driving charge where there was an accident and the defendant suffered slight injuries. The defendant neither asked for, nor appeared to require, medical treatment. No photographs were taken of the automobiles. The defendant refused a blood or breath test, and there was no video taken of the defendant.
Questions by the defense attorney:

Q. Trooper Strong, when you arrived on the scene, what was the situation?
A. Other than the two vehicles involved in the accident, I was the first on the scene.
Q. And, what time was that?
A. Approximately 2:45 in the morning. (Note, the trooper avoids use of military time.)
Q. Were the cars still on the road?
A. Yes, it was apparent to me that the collision had occurred only minutes prior to my arrival
Q. Were you called to the scene?
A. No, I was on patrol in the area and just came up on it.
Q. What did you do when you saw it?
A. I stopped my patrol car, radioed my position, and immediately went to see if there were any injuries.
Q. Did it appear from the condition of the automobiles that there might be injuries?
Note: In any collision, no matter how slight, there is the possibility of injuries. Here, the defense attorney wants the trooper to testify that he was checking for injuries

because of the seriousness of the accident. If the trooper answers "yes," the jury will have an image of badly damaged automobiles with dripping gasoline and smoke rising from the engines. This would play into the defense attorney's hands since he will later attempt to create the impression that the defendant's apparent condition was the result of an injury and not an intoxicated condition.

A. No, sir. The damage to the vehicles was only minor, but checking for possible injuries is standard practice with any accident.

Q. On direct-examination, you gave testimony about your observations of the defendant and that your observations led to an opinion that the defendant was intoxicated, isn't that correct?

A. Yes, sir.

Q. And, it was on the basis of that conclusion that the defendant was arrested?

A. Yes.

Q. Did you ask my client if he would take a breath test?

A. I did.

Q. Before or after you placed him under arrest?

A. Before.

Note: The defense attorney wants to establish that the reason that the trooper wanted the breath test was to confirm for him that the defendant was intoxicated, and that, therefore, the trooper wasn't certain of the defendant's condition.

Q. And, did he agree to take the breath test?
A. No, he did not. He refused.
Q. Then, you placed him under arrest?
A. Shortly after that, yes, sir.

Note: Be careful not to answer in such a way as to allow the defense attorney an opportunity to suggest that you arrested him, not because of your belief in his client's intoxicated condition, but because of his

unwillingness to cooperate.

Q. I'd like to ask you about those observations if you don't mind. You said that there was an odor of alcohol on the defendant, is that correct?

A. No, sir, the odor was coming from the defendant's breath.

Q. And, you described the odor as moderate. What does that mean?

Note: The term moderate is an ambiguous one and the defense attorney is counting on the trooper's inability to adequately define it. The trooper should not get wrapped up in semantics but should use it as an opportunity to otherwise describe the defendant's condition.

A. It means that the odor is consistent with someone who had more than just a couple of drinks.

Note: That response will have hurt the defendant. The defense attorney may choose to abandon this point and move on, or he may choose to question more intensely on it, challenging the trooper's statement with questions such as "how many drinks does it take from the odor to go from slight to moderate?" If he does ask such a question, keep your poise and the jury will see him as the wounded party, not you.

Q. But, you didn't conclude then, that the defendant was intoxicated on that basis, did you?

A. Not by that fact alone, no, sir.

Q. And you've described his gate as unsteady?

A. Yes, sir.

Q. Unsteady, how?

A. He was unable to walk a straight line.

Q. He didn't fall over, then, he was just unsteady when he walked?

A. That's correct.

Q. And, I heard you say that his speech was slurred, correct?

A. Yes, it was.

Q. Could you understand what he was saying?

A. Part of it.

Q. Was his speech disjointed? In other words, did his sentences end before they were finished, or did he change subjects in the middle of a sentence?

A. Yes, sir, his speech was disjointed.

Q. How about his eyes? You didn't say anything about them. What were they like?

A. Sir, I believe I testified that his eyes were glassy and red.

Q. I'm not sure what you mean when you say glassy. Did they have a look of pain?

A. No, sir.

Q. What, then?

A. There was little or no movement in them, and he seemed to be looking past me. They just didn't seem to be focusing on anything.

Q. As though he was dazed?

Note: The word "dazed" is defined by the dictionary as "Stunned, as with a heavy blow or shock," and is usually used when referring to a physical injury. The defense attorney will use this or other terms to put the witness in the position of agreeing that the defendant's condition was caused by an injury.

A. I wouldn't say dazed.

Q. Why not?

A. Because, being dazed involves more that a certain look in the eye. I associate it with someone who is wandering around like he's lost. They also usually complain of a head injury. Your client didn't act that way, never complained of a head injury, and gave no sign that he had suffered one.

Q. Disoriented, then?

A. No, sir, intoxicated.

Q. Your opinion?

A. Yes, sir, my opinion.

Q. There was an injury to the head though, wasn't there?

A. There was a small bruise.

Q. So, he was injured, then?

A. Well, he had a bruise. I don't know that he got it from the accident, and I don't even know that it was recent. When I asked him if he had any injuries, he said no, and when I asked him about the bruise, he said he didn't remember where he got it.

Q. Isn't that consistent with an injury, not remembering how the wound was received?

A. You'd have to ask a doctor about that, sir.

Q. What would you say if I told you that the types of responses you observed by the defendant: slurred speech, unsteady gate, glassy eyes, and a bruise on the head, were all medically consistent with a head injury?

A. Sir, I have been a state trooper for over ten years. I have seen many people who suffered head, and other injuries as the result of all kinds of things, and I've seen how they reacted to them. I have also seen a lot of people who were intoxicated, and how they reacted. Your client was intoxicated.

Note: Great answer! The trooper came back to the main issue in the case; the defendant's intoxicated condition. He left the defense attorney no place to go.

4. Intoxication and Incident Reports

Written DUI reports prepared by the officer will play an important part in his testimony on cross-examination.

Most reports note the various observations made by the officer concerning the defendant's condition. Often, the terms used to describe the various observations do not justify the officer's final conclusion as to the degree of the defendant's intoxication. For example, when the officer describes in his report the odor of alcohol on the defendant's breath as being moderate, and his balance simply unsteady, and his eyes glassy, and his speech slurred, those descriptions are not necessarily consistent with the police officer's testimony concluding that the defendant was "falling down drunk." One of the reasons for this problem is that the reports very seldom offer opportunity or space for the police officer to do much more than put a one word description of the condition which he observed. It is, therefore, incumbent upon the police officer to be more specific in his description of the various aspects of the defendant's condition.

5. Sympathetic Juries

It is not uncommon, in DUI cases, where there has been no automobile accident or injuries to other people, for the jury to sympathize with the defendant. The defense attorney knows that the jury, in many cases, will look for anything in the evidence or testimony of the police officer which might allow them to conclude that even though the defendant may have been drinking while he was driving, he was not in such a state as to have been unable to safely operate a motor vehicle. That is why the evidence gathering of a DUI investigation is so important, and that is why anytime a police officer has video taping equipment at his disposal, he should use it. If he does, the ultimate conclusion regarding the defendant's intoxication will be inescapable, even to the jury.

6.09 General Recommendations

The following is a list of "do's" and "don'ts" regarding testifying on cross-examination. Some have been covered earlier in specific topics under this subject, and some will apply generally to the officer's conduct on the witness stand.

A. Do's

1. Listen carefully to each question asked and answer only if you heard and understood the question, and if you know the answer. If you are not clear as to the meaning of the question asked, ask for clarification, or for the meaning of the word or words that you do not understand. If you do not know the answer to the question, say so.
2. Know the elements of the crime about which you are testifying.
3. Anticipate and understand the defense and prosecution theories of the case.
4. Always appear confident, but never cocky, both in your demeanor and in your responses. Preparation before trial will help.
5. Always be polite, but never informal with the court or the attorneys.
6. Speak clearly and loudly enough to be heard by all of the jurors.
7. Be clear and concise in your responses.
8. If you have an upcoming trial and you know the attorney who will be representing the defendant in your case, but you are unfamiliar with his style and tactics, it is a good idea, when possible, to go and watch this defense attorney in another case prior to yours, especially in situations where he would be cross-examining a police officer.
9. Take your time when answering each question. You should pause long enough before answering each question to organize your response. You should never allow the defense attorney's pace to quicken or shorten your responses.
10. Always correct the defense attorney's misuse of any word or phrase referring to your investigation, personal feelings or philosophy, observations, actions, conclusions, or prior statements or testimony.

11. Stay alert. Keep your concentration on the job at hand. Do not allow yourself to be lulled into a feeling of security.
12. Be frank, modest, and natural.
13. Keep control of your emotions.
14. Be fair. Be accurate in your description and recitation of the facts, but be firm and do not allow the defense attorney to put words in your mouth.
15. Retain your poise. Don't give in to nervousness. Look squarely at the jury, judge and lawyers, and tell the facts as you know them to be. Knowing the facts of your case thoroughly is the best protection against nervousness.
16. Organize your report so that when you are on the stand. you will have immediate access to those sections which you anticipate will contain information about which you will be asked.

B. Don'ts

1. Don't argue with the defense attorney. That does not mean that you should accept his version of the facts or his interpretation of your testimony. Be firm in your resolve, but do not become involved with the defense attorney in an argument over the meaning or interpretation of facts or testimony.
2. Never refer to the defendant by his or her first name. Refer to the person by their last name by using the proper title, or simply refer to him or her as the defendant.
3. Never look at the prosecutor when answering questions of the defense attorney on cross-examination. The jury will think that you are looking for an answer or for help.
4. Don't volunteer information. Answer the question asked as directly as possible, and stop.
5. Do not appear to be shaken if something

goes wrong. If you treat the matter as if it were not of earth shaking importance, the chances are the jury will also.
6. Don't show hostility toward the defendant or the defense attorney.
7. Do not speculate or guess.
8. Do not give opinions that you are not qualified to give.
9. Do not inject humor into your testimony. It is appropriate to respond in an appropriate manner when something humorous is raised or occurs in the courtroom. However, do not allow the defense attorney to turn the procedure into a laughing matter or a farce.
10. Do not allow the defense attorney to change your demeanor.
11. Do not engage in conversation with the defendant, the defense witnesses, or the defense attorneys during any of the breaks in the trial. This tactic is sometimes used by the defense attorney who may then, on cross-examination later, refer to things that were said during those conversations, or just bring up the fact that the conversation between you and he was had in such a way as to make it appear that you are friendly with the defendant or his witnesses.
12. Do not allow the defense attorney to turn the cross-examination into a study of what you failed to do, rather than what you did. Remain positive and confident in the work you did.
13. Don't be drawn into specific responses to general questions. If the defense attorney wants a specific response, force him to ask a specific question.
14. Don't admit to mistakes that you did not make. Usually, the defense has to chip away at small things (errors, inconsistencies) to weaken the overall conclusions which are inescapable, given the prosecution's evidence. If the defense attorney can even slightly weaken enough of the

evidence, he might be able to shake the jury's confidence in the prosecution's credibility. That's all the defendant has to do. Remember, the defendant does not have to prove his innocence, he only has to create a doubt as to his guilt.

6.10 Conclusions

There are several key phrases that come out of, and recur during, a study of the proper way to testify on cross-examination. They can be summarized by saying that the officer should prepare well before taking the stand; he should be polite, clear, and firm in his responses to the questions; he should be fair, yet unyielding in his recitation of the facts of the case; and he should display a confident attitude and expres himself in a clear and concise manner. If the officer is able to do those things, he will maintain control of the situation and will make effective cross-examination by the defense attorney very difficult.

Appendix

SAMPLE DEA REPORT FORM

REPORT OF INVESTIGATION			Page 1 of 2
1. Program Code	2. Cross Related files File	3. File No. 99-1240	4. G-DEA Identification
5. By: S/A Jacob Ernest At: Miami, Florida		6. File Title KEEFER, Andrew	
7. __Closed __Requested Action Completed __Action Requested By:		8. Date Prepared September 8, 1999	
9. Other Officers: Tom Tyre, Art Scott, Organized Crime Div., Ft. Lauderdale, PD			
10. Report Re: Interview with David E. CARLTON			

DETAILS

1. On 9/1/99, S/A Jacob Ernest, OCB Officers Tyre and Scott met in Ft. Lauderdale, Florida with David E. CARLTON, 505 NW 8th Street, Dania, Florida, in reference to the smuggling of cocaine by Andrew KEEFER, et al.

2. Intelligence information developed subsequent to the seizure of 727 lbs. of cocaine *indicates* that CARLTON may have been the pilot utilized by the organization to make the air drop of cocaine off the coast of Cancun, Mexico.

3. CARLTON is currently on State probation stemming from narcotics related charges filed against him in 1997 by the City of Ft. Lauderdale, Florida.

4. On 9/1/99, S/A Jacob Ernest interviewed CARLTON in Ft. Lauderdale, Florida relative to his involvement with the smuggling organization. CARLTON *stated* that he had been hired by Jack TARKEE, 290 Playa Pkwy., Coral Gables, Florida, to fly him from Ft. Lauderdale, Florida and Freeport, Bahamas to Caucun, Mexico. CARLTON stated that TARKEE supplies the airplane, N-6468C/Cessna 404 Titan, and paid CARLTON $350.00 a week for his services.

5. CARLTON stated that during the month of July, 1999, he flew TARKEE from Freeport, Bahamas to Cancun, Mexico approximately 4 times. CARLTON also stated that he flew TARKEE and a Latin male, PACO (LNU), from Cancun, Mexico to Chetumal, Mexico on approximately 3 or 4 occasions during this period. CARLTON also stated that while in Cancun, he stayed at the Plaza Blanca and Case Maya Hotels at TARKEE'S expense. CARLTON stated that on one return flight from Cancun, he brought back a passenger, Joan CULK, who was having some dental problems.

11. Distribution
      Region
      District
      Other
	12. Signature - Agent	13. Date

	14. Approved - Name and Title	15. Date

1. Paragraphs numbered.
2. Proper use of the work "indicates".
3. Proper use of the work "stated".

REPORT OF INVESTIGATION			
(Continuation)		1. File No.	2. G-DEA Identification
4. Page 2 of 2		99-1240	
5. Program Code		3. File Title KEEFER, Andrew	
		6. Date Prepared September 8, 1999	

6. CARLTON stated that on 8/7/99 he flew TARKEE and Raymond SKEW from Ft. Lauderdale to Ft. Myers, Florida via N-5986C. The purpose of the trip, *according to CARLTON*, was to fly mechanics from Ft. Myers to Cancun, Mexico to repair a boat at the Plaza Blanca Marina. CARLTON stated that SKEW and TARKEE stayed in Ft. Myers, Florida about one hour and then he flew them to Cancun, Mexico. While in Cancun, Mexico, TARKEE and CARLTON stayed at the Case Maya Hotel, Cancun, Mexico, Room 1519, where they remained until 8/9/99. On 8/9/99, CARLTON stated he flew TARKEE, PACO, SKEW and Mark McKENSIE from Cancun, Mexico to Freeport, Bahamas where he cleared Bahamian Customs under the fictitious name of Joel ORLENGER. CARLTON stated the reason for his use of the fictitious name was due to the fact that he had been arrested in the Bahamas on a marijuana possession charge previously and he wanted to avoid any problems with Bahamian customs officials.

7. On 8/9/99 at approximately 4:15 P.M., CARLTON departed Freeport, Bahamas with PACO, arriving in West Palm Beach, Florida at approximately 6:00 P.M.

8. CARLTON stated that since 8/9/99, he has been contacted by a white make known as TOM (LNU), who stated that there had been some trouble with the boat and that Joan CULK was in jail. CARLTON stated that he has not been contacted by TARKEE since that time.

INDEXING SECTION

1. KEEFER, Andrew - NADDIS 1204364
2. CULK, Joan - NADDIS 9071511
3. TARKEE, Jack - NADDIS 5874460
4. SKEW, Raymond - 3356024
5. McKENSIE, Mark - NADDIS negative
6. CARLTON, David E. a/k/a Joel ORLENGER - NADDIS 2043488

---

4. Proper notation as to source of information

INDEX

EFFECTIVE RESPONSE TO SCHOOL VIOLENCE

Published 2001, 266 pages
Tony L. Jones
$61.95, hard, ISBN 0-398-07188-8
$39.95, paper, ISBN 0-398-07189-6

DOMESTIC TERRORISM AND INCIDENT MANAGEMENT
Issues and Tactics
To Be Published 2001, 284 pages
Mike Vohryzek-Bolden, Gayle Olson-Raymer & Jeffrey O. Whamond
hard, ISBN 0-398-07225-6
paper, ISBN 0-398-07226-4

THE SOURCES OF VIOLENCE IN AMERICA AND THEIR CONSEQUENCES FOR LAW ENFORCEMENT

Published 2001, 282 pages
C. Kenneth Meyer, Gregory G. Brunk, & Laura Ann Wilson
$62.95, cloth, ISBN 0-398-07150-0
$39.95, paper, ISBN 0-398-07151-9 (displayed)

PATROL FIELD PROBLEMS AND SOLUTIONS
847 Field Situations (2nd Ed.)

To be published 2001, 242 pages
Harry W More
$59.95, cloth, ISBN 0-398-07204-3
$39.95, paper, ISBN 0-398-07205-1

EVALUATING DYSFUNCTIONAL POLICE PERFORMANCE
A Zero-Based Approach

To be published 2001, 184 pages
D. J. Van Meter
$47.95, hard, ISBN 0-398-07187-X
$31.95, paper, ISBN 0-398-07220-5

THE DILEMMA OF THE SEXUAL OFFENDER

To be published 2001, 244 pages
George B. Palermo & Mary Ann Farkas
$49.95, hard, ISBN 0-398-07199-3
$33.95, paper, ISBN 0-398-07200-0

SEX CRIMES, PREDATORS, PERPETRATORS, PROSTITUTES, AND VICTIMS
An Examination of Sexual Criminality and Victimization

Published 2000, 298 pages
R. Barri Flowers
$61.95, hard, ISBN 0-398-07126-8
$41.95, paper, ISBN 0-398-07127-6

CHARLES C THOMAS • PUBLISHER, LTD.
P.O. Box 19265, Springfield, IL 62794-9265
Call 1-800-258-8980 or 1-217-789-8980
or Fax 1-217-789-9130
Complete catalog available at www.ccthomas.com •
books@ccthomas.com

Books sent on approval • Shipping charges: $5.95 U.S. / Outside U.S., actual shipping fees will be charged • Prices subject to change without notice

LAW ENFORCEMENT FUNERAL MANUAL
A Practical Guide for Law Enforcement Agencies When Faced With the Death of a Member of Their Department

Published 2001, 96 pages
William P. Sanders
$21.95, (spiral) paper, ISBN 0-398-07166-7

MANAGING CRISES
Threats, Dilemmas, Opportunities

To be published 2001, 424 pages
Uriel Rosenthal, R. Arjen Boin & Louise K. Comfort
hard, ISBN 0-398-07223-X
paper, ISBN 0-398-07224-8

SPIRITUAL AND RELIGIOUS DIVERSITY IN PRISONS
Focusing on How Chaplaincy Assists in Prison Management

Published 2001, 218 pages
Josiah N. Opata
$52.95, hard, ISBN 0-398-07179-9
$34.95, paper, ISBN 0-398-07180-2

PRIVATE INVESTIGATION AND PROCESS SERVING
A Comprehensive Guide for Investigators, Process Servers, and Attorneys

To be published 2001, 352 pages
Raymond P. Siljander
$71.95, hard, ISBN 0-398-07194-2
$49.95, paper, ISBN 0-398-07217-5

MENTAL DISABILITY ISSUES IN THE CRIMINAL JUSTICE SYSTEM
What They Are, Who Evaluates Them, How and When

Published 2000, 156 pages
Harlow Huckabee
$39.95, hard, ISBN 0-398-07089-X
$24.95, paper, ISBN 0-398-07090-3

LOCKS, SAFES, AND SECURITY
An International Police Reference (2nd Ed.)

Published 2000, 1440 pages
Marc Weber Tobias
$199.95, cloth, ISBN 0-398-07079-2

THE POLICE OFFICER IN THE COURTROOM
How to Avoid the Pitfalls of Cross-Examination Through the Proper Preparation and Presentation of Investigative Reports, In-Court Testimony, and Evidence
To be published 2001, 206 pages
Don Lewis
hard, ISBN 0-398-07212-4
paper, ISBN 0-398-07213-2

CRIME AND ELDER ABUSE
An Integrated Perspective

Published 2000, 244 pages
Payne, Brian K.
$46.95, cloth, ISBN 0-398-07056-3
$33.95, paper, ISBN 0-398-07057-1

ENDURING, SURVIVING, AND THRIVING AS A LAW ENFORCEMENT EXECUTIVE

Published 2001, 192 pages
Thomas J. Jurkanin, Larry T. Hoover, Jerry L. Dowling & Janice Ahmad
$43.95, hard, ISBN 0-398-07116-0
$28.95, paper, ISBN 0-398-07117-9